SILENCE IS DEADLY

SILENCE IS DEADLY

JUDAISM
CONFRONTS
WIFEBEATING

NAOMI GRAETZ

JASON ARONSON INC.
NORTHVALE, NEW JERSEY
JERUSALEM

This book was set in 11 pt. Berkeley Book by FASTpages of Montebello, NY.

"Hosea" by Gene Crumley reprinted with permission from *Judaism* vol. 33, no. 3 (summer, 1984). Copyright © 1984 American Jewish Congress.
Various extracts reprinted from *Tanakh: The Holy Scriptures*. Copyright © 1985 Jewish Publications Society.

Please address all correspondence to:
Naomi Graetz
P.O. Box 193
Omer, Israel 84965

Library of Congress Cataloging-in-Publication Data

Graetz, Naomi, 1943–
    Silence is deadly: Judaism confronts wifebeating / by Naomi Graetz.
      p. cm.
    Includes bibliographical references and index.
    ISBN 0–7657–6013–4
    1. Wife abuse (Jewish law)   2. Married women—Legal status, laws,
etc. (Jewish law)   3. Jewish women—Abuse of.   4. Women in Judaism.
I. Title.
LAW <GENERAL Graetz 1998>
296.3'8—dc21   97–39350
                                                 CIP

Manufactured in the United States of America. Jason Aronson Inc. offers books and cassettes. For information and catalog write to Jason Aronson Inc., 230 Livingston Street, Northvale, NJ 07647.

"ולא נבוש לעולם ועד"

that we may never live in shame
from the Prayer Book

It is not an enemy who reviles me—I could bear that;
It is not my foe who vaunts himself against me—
I could hide from him;
But it is you, my equal,
my companion, my friend;
Sweet was our fellowship;
we walked together in God's house.
Psalms 55: 13–15
Jewish Publication Society

the One
who heals also
wounds

despite contrary claims that
one who wounds
could never heal
and one who heals
would never wound

nevertheless
"Hosea"
G. Crumley, *Judaism*

Contents

Preface

Ten years is a long time to be working on a book. I first became interested in the subject of battered women in Israel as an outgrowth of my research into women in the bible and *midrash*.[1] In December 1988, when I was on the national board of the Israel Women's Network (IWN), Ofira Levi, the director of Maslan (the Center for Women's Support—Negev in Beer-Sheva) approached me to raise money for a battered women's hotline and shelter. Although I had been an activist for women's rights in Israel and had been doing research on women's place in Judaism, I had never recognized the incidence of wifebeating to be a significant problem in the Jewish community. I had read about women whose husbands had beaten and killed them, but these were "women in the abstract"; they were very much "the other" to me—no one with whom I could identify or possibly know.

I invited the director of Maslan to speak to our local IWN board. I had a "click" moment during her presentation when I realized that wifebeating is not limited to the underclass; that "the other" was in our midst and could

---

1. *Midrash,* or *midrash aggadah,* is a literary genre, which is a process of exegesis, or interpretation. It uses biblical text as its starting point and seeks to reveal new meaning in the primary text. It can retell the biblical tale, can add dialogue and or description to the original text. In doing so it contributes new insights and/or perspectives to the original version. *Midrash* is a genre which was begun by the rabbis in antiquity. Its classical period was roughly between the years 400 and 1200 C.E. For a good introduction to *midrash,* see Barry W. Holtz, *Back to the Sources* (New York: Summit, 1984).

easily be me (or one of my friends). Apparently, I was not the only one to be so moved. Our group helped Maslan raise money, write grants, and organize their brochure. I represented Maslan in New York at a parlor meeting in Sally Gottesman's home for the New Israel Fund in January 1989. To prepare for my maiden talk on a subject I knew virtually nothing about, I read every book in our university library—at the time, I could find three. In contrast, today several Ben-Gurion University graduate students are writing theses about battered women. I used the files of the Women's Jewish Resource Center in New York, ironically, reading clippings from *The Jerusalem Post* there. This cram course was an eye-opener for me. I encountered the names of three activists, Ruth Rasnic, Thelma Halperin, and Marcia Freedman, whose *cause célèbre* was wifebeating in Israel and in the Jewish community at large.

Except for an article by Mimi Scarf, "Marriages Made in Heaven? Battered Jewish Wives,"[2] and a handful of clippings, there was nothing else available. During the ten years I have been engaged in this research, unfortunately, a new field has opened up. Wifebeating in the Jewish community is no longer a secret. The distinguished psychiatrist and rabbi, Abraham Twerski has written a book bravely acknowledging the problem of wifebeating in the Orthodox Jewish community.[3] Many articles are appearing in both professional journals and lay sources, and Jewish historians are arguing over the interpretation of primary texts regarding wifebeating. No respectable conference on Women and Judaism can avoid the problem of wifebeating.[4]

During the Gulf War, the problem of wifebeating came to the forefront in Israel. Husbands and wives (and their children) spent time together in sealed rooms. Too much family togetherness apparently exacerbated the normal tension of living in a war zone. The mass media began to ask the question, "why." Strangely enough, the media seemed totally unaware that there

---

2. Mimi Scarf, "Marriages Made in Heaven? Battered Jewish Wives," in *On Being a Jewish Feminist: A Reader*, ed. Susanna Heschel (New York: Schocken Books, 1983), pp. 51–64.

3. Abraham Twersky, *The Shame Born of Silence: Spouse Abuse in the Jewish Community* (Pittsburgh, PA: Mirkov Publications, 1996).

4. At the *International Conference on Feminism and Orthodoxy* (February 16–17, 1997) in New York City, "Domestic Violence" was one of the topics discussed. (Audio-tape available c/o Esther Farber, 3333 Henry Hudson Pkwy, Riverdale, NY 10463). There was also a day-long conference, "*Shalom Bayit*? The Inside Story of Abuse in the Jewish Home," sponsored by the CONNECT committee of Jewish Women International on April 7, 1997 at Brandeis University.

might be a connection between the teachings of Judaism and the fact that Jewish women were being battered.

Since 1989, I have learned what Jewish tradition has to say about wife-beating mainly through the world of responsa literature. Fortunately, during this time period, the *Bar-Ilan Responsa Project* came into being, first via modem, and eventually via CD-ROM.[5] This has greatly facilitated tracking down all the pertinent *responsa*. In addition, Howard Adelman, Avraham Grossman, and Mordecai Frishtik have now published exploratory works on wifebeating in Jewish sources.[6] Electronic mail has opened up another world, with testimonies by women who themselves have been beaten by their adult male partners or by those who know such women. On "Mail-Jewish" there have been acrimonious discussions, in which I have participated, about wifebeating among Jews followed up by private communications. With the encouragement of all these people, I have persevered with my work on this book.

The topic of wifebeating is very difficult for me as a strongly identified religious Jewish woman. Although feminist issues have often appeared to conflict with my Judaism, a very solid traditional background has so far enabled me to hold my ground. In studying Jewish texts, I find that I am not alone—there are antecedents of my arguing with the way tradition is perceived.[7]

I am, first of all, the product of modern Orthodoxy: thirteen years of Ramaz Day School, New York City, and thirteen years of Massad Hebrew-speaking summer camps. This was followed by six years at the Jewish Theo-

---

5. Many of the primary sources referred to in this book were originally found through use of the *Bar-Ilan Responsa Project: The Database for Jewish Studies*. This unique collection, all in one CD-ROM, includes the complete Bible, *midrash aggadah* and *midrash halakha*, the Babylonian Talmud and Jerusalem Talmud, and commentators on the Talmud. It includes more than 1,000 years of responsa from rabbis, starting with the Geonic period until contemporary times, and is constantly being updated.

6. Howard Adelman, "Wife Beating in Jewish History," paper given at the *Association for Jewish Studies: Twenty-Fourth Annual Conference* (Boston, 1992); Mordechai Frishtik, "Physical and Sexual Violence by Husbands as a Reason for Imposing a Divorce in Jewish Law," *Jewish Law Annual 9* (1992): 145–169; Avraham Grossman, "Medieval Rabbinic Views on Wife Beating, 800–1300," *Jewish History 5* (1991): 53–62.

7. See my forthcoming article, Naomi Graetz, "Jerusalem the Widow," delivered at the *Western Jewish Studies Association Third Annual Conference* (April 6–8, 1997) at the University of Arizona, Tucson, which will appear in *Women in Jewish Life and Culture*, a special issue of *Shofar: An Interdisciplinary Journal of Jewish Studies* (Fall, 1998) edited by Esther Fuchs. See too Anson Laytner, *Arguing With God: A Jewish Tradition* (Northvale, NJ: Jason Aronson Inc., 1990).

logical Seminary (B.H.L. 1966 in Jewish History) and five years at Cejwin camps, while doing my B.A. and M.A. at City College of the City University of New York in English Literature. My husband and I came to live in Israel in 1967, and our three children were born and raised here.

I grew into feminism through Judaism. In the mid-1970s, I enviously followed from the distance of Israel the writings and doings of many of my Jewish feminist friends and former acquaintances. I began to read the Torah in our congregation, which lead to my writing *midrash*, and to the publication of *S/He Created Them: Feminist Retellings of Biblical Tales*.[8] This progressed to active politicking in the Masorti (Conservative) movement in Israel for the right of women to be ordained in Israel as rabbis—a fight we won. During all this, there was my very active involvement in the Israel Women's Network, from which I have taken a short break in order to remain focused on this book.

I would like to thank the Research Committee of the Humanities and Social Science Faculty of Ben-Gurion University of the Negev for awarding me a modest grant, which enabled me to engage the editing services of Catherine Logan, and to all the chairpersons of my department at BGU for understanding the value and importance of my engaging in interdisciplinary research.

The decision to devote an entire book to, what I then thought was, a limited topic is total serendipity. First of all, Hani Shalit offered to translate whatever I wrote into Hebrew if I would lecture to volunteers of Maslan who were being trained to staff a hot-line for battered women. This provided me with the first push to see what Jewish sources actually had to say on the topic. Second, I was in England on a lecture tour, organized by Tanya Novick of the Masorti Movement there, and gave a sermon on the weekly Torah portion of Numbers. Sitting in the audience was Alex Sklan, director of the Federation of Jewish Family Services, who, hearing me sermonize in the Edgeware Synagogue on the "metaphoric beating of Hosea's Wife," invited me to come back to do a workshop. If not for him and Judy Usiskin, who organized the event, there would be no book. During the Gulf War (January 1991) I did the workshop on "Battered Wives: A View From Jewish Tradition" in London for the Training Unit. In the process of over-preparing a resource pamphlet for this day-long workshop I realized how much material there was.

---

8. Naomi Graetz, *S/He Created Them: Feminist Retellings of Biblical Tales* (Chapel Hill, NC: Professional Press, 1993).

Third, I was very fortunate to have a semester as a Research Associate at the Five College Women's Studies Center at Mount Holyoke College in the Fall of 1992. There I met Howard Adelman, Director of the Program in Jewish Studies at Smith College, who shares my interest in the subject of rabbinic responses to wifebeating and who has been very supportive of my work. Rabbi David Golinkin's seminar was also useful to me in my approach to, and interpretation of, texts.[9]

I would like to thank my friends and colleagues for reading early and later versions of this manuscript, notably Ivan Marcus, Mayer Gruber, Connie Reisner, Reuven Lerner, Sylvia Horwitz, Nancy Rosen and the anonymous readers for the University of Nebraska Press for their comments. I would like to thank Lea Kacen of the Social Work School at Ben-Gurion University, who invites me to give a lecture to her students each semester, which gives me valuable feedback. I am indebted to the Rabbinical Assembly Convention Committees of 1995 and 1996, for giving me a forum in which to share my ideas and obtain useful criticism and comments. I would like to particularly thank Joel Meyers, Executive Director of the R.A., who in 1992 made it possible for me to send out a questionnaire to Conservative rabbis.

I am grateful for the support and understanding of my immediate family: My sister, Menorah Rotenberg, is always there for me. She is a constructive critic and shares my enthusiasm for Jewish texts. My mother, Charlotte Lebovics, is my principal cheerleader and I hope she continues to live a long and qualitative life.

My three children, Ariella (and her husband Menash), Tzvi, and Avigail (grown-ups now), have for years been patiently awaiting the day when they could see this manuscript—my fourth "child"—take on its final form, grow up, and leave the "nest" along with them. Now that I am the grandmother of Itamar Yehezkel, it is time for this book to take flight.

If one is fortunate, there is a significant person in one's life—one whose life-goals are similar; one with whom learning and support are mutual activities—a person who is respectful of one's life work—encouraging, yet not intrusive of the privacy and identity of the other. I have been blessed in that my life partner, Rabbi Michael Graetz, and I are engaged in such a relation-

---

9. Golinkin's seminar "Introduction to *Poskim*" [rabbinical religious authorities—arbiters] for rabbinical students at the *Beit Hamidrash* in Jerusalem in the Spring of 1991 included the topic of "Wifebeating."

ship. Without him, I doubt if the publication of this book would have come to fruition. For this, among other reasons, I dedicate my book to him.

Naomi Graetz
Omer, Israel

Introduction

Elliot N. Dorff*

In some ways, it would seem absolutely obvious that Judaism would not allow individuals to beat others, especially a family member. After all, the opening chapters of the Torah tell us that we are all created in the image of God.[1] That fundamental tenet would seem to require that, as a very minimum, we do not physically abuse others. The classical Rabbis of the Jewish tradition, those whose opinions appear in the Mishnah, the Talmud, and the *midrash*, certainly understood that to be the case, for rabbinic law assumes that we do not have the right to strike others and thus specifies five sorts of compensation for personal injuries. Specifically, assailants must pay their victims for their lost capital value, their time lost from work, their pain and suffering, their medical expenses, and the embarrassment they suffered.[2]

Courts may impose lashes for trespasses of law, but due care had to be taken in the process to preserve the dignity of God and God's human creature. Indeed, the Rabbis took the notion of the integrity of the individual so far as

---

* Elliot N. Dorff is Rector and Professor of Philosophy at the University of Judaism in Los Angeles. He is the Vice-Chair of the Conservative Movement's Committee on Jewish Law and Standards and author of its rabbinic ruling on family violence.

1. *Genesis* 1:26–27; 5:1; 9:6.
2. *M. Bava Kamma* 8:1, and the Talmud thereon.

to say that those who slander others (let alone cause them physical injury) are as though they had denied the existence of God.[3] Conversely, Rabbi Eliezer said, "Let your fellow's honor be as dear to you as your own."[4] Given these underlying principles, one would expect that any family violence that occurred within the Jewish community would be based on misinformation about the Jewish tradition, neglect of it, or simply the foibles of individuals.

Jews expect their tradition to give them guidance beyond the demands of civil law, for they aspire to holiness. Given that expectation, Jewish law certainly cannot be interpreted to allow Jews to be less moral than what civil law requires. Jews must also avoid family violence, then, because they are bound by civil law under the talmudic dictum, "The law of the land is the law" and/or to avoid desecrating the name of God and of Judaism in the eyes of non-Jews and other Jews.[5] Since civil law in most areas of the Western world now prohibits most forms of family violence, Jews must eschew it for those concerns in addition to the grounds afforded by the Jewish tradition itself.

When we probe classical Jewish texts, however, we find that some permit forms of family violence, and some actually encourage it. It is therefore critical

---

3. *J. Pe'ah* 1:1.

4. *M. Avot* 2:15.

5. While it is possible to argue that Jews must avoid family violence because we are bound by civil law under the dictum, "the law of the land is the law" (*dina de'malkhuta dina*: *B. Nedarim* 28a; *B. Gittin* 10b; *B. Bava Kamma* 113a; *B. Bava Batra* 54b–55a), that dictum was usually restricted to commercial matters. Even during the Middle Ages, though, Jews were forced by the governments under which they lived to abide by their laws, and rabbis generally saw that as a Jewish obligation as well as a civil one—at least to protect the Jewish community from expulsion or governmental interference. Certainly, when Jews began living as full citizens under governments shaped by the philosophy of the Enlightenment, they saw themselves both legally and morally bound to abide by the government's laws, and that view continues to this day. The operative principle, then, is not so much "the law of the land is the law" as it is (1) the need to avoid the *hillul hashem* [desecration of God's name] involved in Jews breaking just civil law and (2) the requirement in Jewish law that Jews see themselves bound by moral standards beyond those of other nations.

For a discussion of the scope and rationales of "the law of the land is the law," see Elliot N. Dorff and Arthur Rosett, *A Living Tree: The Roots and Growth of Jewish Law* (Albany, NY: State University Press of New York, 1988), pp. 515–522. For a discussion of sanctification of God's name (and avoiding desecration of God's name) and holiness as reasons to obey Jewish law, see Elliot N. Dorff, *Mitzvah Means Commandment* (New York: United Synagogue of America, 1989), pp. 113–134. For the demand that Jews be at least as moral as non-Jews, see, for example, David Novak, *The Image of the Non-Jew in Judaism* (New York: Edwin Mellon, 1983), pp. 90–93; and "*Kiddush Ha-Shem,*" *Encyclopedia Judaica*, vol. 10 (Jerusalem: Keter, 1971), pp. 979–980.

to declare at the very outset that all Jewish sources must be understood and interpreted within their historical context, especially when those sources are to be used to make judgments appropriate to our own time. The Jewish tradition, after all, has spanned many centuries. During that time, it has not remained the same. Sometimes its development has been an internal unfolding of its inherent commitments in thought and practice, and sometimes the example of other peoples among whom Jews have lived have produced changes within Judaism. Moreover, not all of the tradition is of an everlasting and compelling quality, and so generations of Jews have reinterpreted some parts of the tradition, all but ignored some, added other elements, and have even taken steps to make some portions of the tradition effectively inoperative. These changes have sometimes occurred through conscious, judicial decisions, and sometimes through the changing customs of the people Israel in many times and climes. This historical understanding of the Jewish tradition, characteristic of much of modern Judaism, is critical for identifying its contemporary message on any subject, especially those like family violence, where social conditions and norms have changed over time.

Jews look to their tradition for enlightenment and guidance, and they often find it in a simple, straightforward way. Sometimes, however, traditional sources say things that contemporary Jews find obsolete or even offensive. When that occurs, modern Jews have not only the right, but the duty to exercise judgment. They must determine whether a given mode of thinking or acting recorded in traditional texts or common in popular practice is an historical remnant that must be altered because contemporary circumstances or moral sensitivities have changed, or whether the tradition as it stands is instead a proper indictment of modern thought or practice, and thus a challenge to reevaluate them. Thus, to be taught by the tradition, contemporary Jews must be aware of the twin duties they have as its heirs: they must learn it and preserve it and, at the same time, they must evaluate it and reinterpret it when necessary. Only then can it continue to speak with wisdom and power.

Family violence is not only an unpleasant memory from sources of the past; it afflicts contemporary Jewry as well. It has not been part of the Jewish community's self-image; Jewish leaders, in fact, are only now openly admitting that family violence occurs among Jews. Somehow, Jews often feel that Jews are supposed to be immune to such behavior—it is, Jewish sources have assured us, what non-Jews do, not how Jews behave. It is too early to know whether Jews engage in the various forms of family violence to the same degree as do other groups within the general population, but the Jewish community surely suffers from all modes of this malady.

Moreover, family violence occurs among the Orthodox at least as much as it does among Conservative, Reconstructionist, and Reform Jews. Devotion to tradition has not, unfortunately, prevented violent behavior within the family. Nobody, though, has the right to brag, for no part of the community is exempt.

Jewish communities throughout North America, Israel, and indeed the world are, to different degrees, finally acknowledging the problem and taking steps to deal with it. The Los Angeles Jewish Family Service, for example, sponsors a Family Violence Project, with three shelters for battered women and children and therapy groups for both batterers and their victims. On a different plane, the Conservative Movement's Committee on Jewish Law and Standards has approved a rabbinic ruling that I wrote condemning all spousal and child abuse, making that the official stance of the entire Conservative Movement.

In this area of family violence we must be careful to distinguish acceptable forms of physical contact from abuse. Affectionate or supportive forms of touching each other between spouses are certainly not included in the category of abuse; they are easily distinguished from objectionable behavior by their motive, the willingness of the partner to be touched in that way, and the absence of physical and emotional wounds inflicted by the touching.[6] Even a one-time slap in anger, while not pleasant or ideal, does not always constitute abuse. Beating a spouse, then, refers to repetitive blows delivered out of anger, a desire to control, or some other motive inimical to the welfare of the victim and which often—although not necessarily—inflict bleeding or an injury, even a temporary one.

In this book, Naomi Graetz has shown that wifebeating stems at least in part from the inherent inequality in a Jewish marriage, both metaphorically and legally. In her sections on the metaphoric inequality built into classical

---

6. A similar distinction applies to parents or parent-substitutes like teachers or camp counselors touching children in their care, although there the child's inability legally to consent to such touching complicates matters considerably. Even so, a proper treatment of that subject would require distinguishing child abuse from, for example, hugging a child to comfort him or her or even slapping a child on the shoulder as a mark of enthusiastic congratulations in a ball game. My rabbinic ruling, "Family Violence," adopted unanimously by the Conservative Movement's Committee on Jewish Law and Standards in October, 1995, attempts to formulate rules for drawing such distinctions. This introduction is based, in part, on that paper.

Jewish marriage (Chapters 2 and 3), she makes a case for the powerful impact of biblical metaphors of battering on women's lived experience. Biblical husbands, after all, are not forbidden from abusing their wives psychologically, socially, or even physically. Perhaps Graetz's unique contribution is her connecting the metaphoric aspects of the Jewish tradition to its laws, showing how the former directly and powerfully influences the latter (Chapter 4).

The bulk of Graetz's book deals with the halakhic aspects of wifebeating. She incisively shows that the Jewish tradition is not monolithic in its attitude toward women, that there are traces of misogyny along with a genuine care for women's welfare (Chapters 5 and 6).

There is an important legal institution underlying whatever permission exists in some sources for a husband to beat his wife—namely, that Jewish law assumes that the husband owns his wife. The Mishnah and Talmud went very far to protect the rights of the woman, but, after all is said and done, the very language for betrothal is that a man "acquires" (*koneh*) his wife. It is precisely this that Naomi Graetz suggests modern rabbis change, for it sets the underlying legal context that ultimately sanctions wifebeating. She analyzes the differing opinions toward wifebeating found in responsa literature by using the following typology: acceptance, rejection, denial and apologetics, and evasion.

In Chapter 7, she discusses acceptance—that is, those rabbis who know that some Jewish husbands beat their wives, but permit it. Such rabbis justify this practice either as a means for the husband to educate his wife in proper behavior, or as a way to obtain domestic harmony (*shalom bayit*). Rabbis who permit husbands to beat their wives when they fail to perform the duties required of them by law, or when they violate prohibitions in the law, include such luminaries as Rabbi Yehudai Gaon, Rabbi Shmuel ha-Nagid, Maimonides, and Israel Isserlein.

In Chapter 8, Graetz discusses the extent to which wifebeating is met with rabbinic rejection. The majority of rabbis have declared that wifebeating is unconditionally forbidden. This is the strain of rabbinic rulings most in keeping with our own contemporary point of view. The three medieval rabbis who were the most articulate exponents of this position were Rabbi Simhah B. Samuel of Speyer, Rabbi Meir b. Barukh of Rothenburg, and Rabbi Perez b. Elijah of Corbeil. They all condemn wifebeating in the strongest of terms. They see it as even more serious an offense than assaulting a stranger, for the husband takes on a specific obligation to honor his wife beyond the normal duties that we all have to respect the image of God embedded in every human being.

In Chapter 9, Graetz discusses the modern phenomenon of responding to wifebeating with denial and apologetics. There are rabbis who deny that Jewish husbands beat their wives, who consider it to be a "Gentile form of behavior," or who seek to defend the honor of the Jewish community by whitewashing the facts. This usually involves a heavy dose of denial. When the facts cannot be ignored, apologists seek to marginalize the phenomenon, stating that Jews who engage in wifebeating do so less frequently and less violently than non-Jewish batterers. Alternatively, apologists justify such behavior by maintaining that Jewish men who actually engage in it do so for a good reason and, in any case, do not really hurt their wives. Some in this group of rabbis displace the blame by shifting it to the surrounding culture. Graetz shows that, even while acknowledging some of the evidence of wifebeating, apologists often ignore other pieces of it that do not fit their thesis. She points to Rabbi Joseph Hertz, author of the most widely used Torah commentary in the 20th century, as one example of such apologists.

Graetz ends her discussion of responsa literature by discussing the phenomenon of evasiveness (Chapter 10). Evasion of responsibility by the rabbis is similar to a "wringing of the hands syndrome," in which rabbis recognize that wifebeating is wrong, but maintain that they are powerless to do anything about it. Such rabbis claim that the court cannot do more than tell the husband in strong language not to beat his wife. These rabbis are not willing to remedy the situation once and for all by forcing the husband to give his wife a valid Jewish divorce.

In sum, then, Naomi Graetz shows that the sources are not as unified in their stance against wifebeating as we might well have expected. She instead depicts a range of responses in the literature to the phenomenon of wifebeating, indicating all along some of the historical circumstances that undoubtedly influenced rabbis to respond to the phenomenon in a given way. In the end, though, social conditions cannot constitute an excuse for bad law: rabbis in times past, and in our day as well, must take the responsibility to formulate law that is worthy of the moral mission embedded in the Jewish tradition from its earliest roots. Rabbis interpreting the law, after all, are doing nothing less than articulating how they understand God's will.

With that theologically and morally deep understanding of the status and role of Jewish law, Graetz, in her conclusion, suggests enactment of legislation (a *takkanah*) that would change the very metaphor of Jewish marital law as an act of acquisition, and which would also change some of the provisions that have historically followed from that metaphor. At least as of this writing, I personally am not sure that that proposal is either wise or necessary. I can certainly say that, having read this book, I can no longer in good conscience think of Jewish marriage as the acquisition of the wife by the husband, even if we continue to use the terminology of purchase (*kinyan*). While previously I thought of that legal rubric as antiquated and even embarrassing but ultimately harmless, Graetz has shown me beyond any doubt that it is anything but harmless, that it can have, and indeed has had, severe effects on the very physical safety of women. Husbands in our day have no more right to discipline their wives than wives have to discipline their husbands. Indeed, those who want to retain the language of acquisition for marriage—and part of me still does, if only not to wrench Jewish marital law too severely—must understand that, in traditional Jewish law, when a husband "acquires" his wife, he thereby takes on a number of binding legal and moral obligations to her, and we, as serious Jews, understand wifebeating to be not only inconsistent with, but contrary to, those duties.

Moreover, in most cases where wifebeating occurs, the phenomenon cannot be corrected through therapy for the husband. Under those circumstances, we will do all in our power to help the woman free herself from the marriage. That includes counseling to help her make the decision to extricate herself from the abusive situation, referrals to Jewish Family Service or other such agencies that can facilitate that process and show her how to protect herself (and her children) from further harassment, guidance (if necessary) in obtaining legal help to dissolve the marriage in civil law, and then appropriate actions within Jewish law to dissolve the marriage by a formal Jewish writ of divorce (a *get*), if possible, or by an annulment of the marriage (*hafka'at kiddushin*), if necessary. A commitment to the life and health of the woman (and children) demands no less.

Naomi Graetz has written an important book. It should be on the shelf of every rabbi and, indeed, of every Jew prepared to confront this situation and remedy it. It will serve as a valuable resource for scholars in the fields of women's studies and Jewish studies, for social workers and those in other helping professions, and, truthfully, for anyone prepared to learn the nice, and not-so-nice, aspects of this situation in the history of the Jewish tradition and the methods by which it has purged, and continues to purge, a reprehensible practice from its midst.

Elliot N. Dorff
Rector and Professor of Philosophy
University of Judaism
Los Angeles, California

Wifebeating and Jewish Society

The existence of the battered wife in Jewish community life is difficult for Jews to face both psychologically and halakhically (i.e., according to Jewish law).[1] Is there something in Judaism that makes it permissible for a husband to beat his wife and get away with it?

How is wifebeating among Jews perceived by those in authority? When recognized, is it considered a new phenomenon, a product of modern times?[2] Or is there a willingness to see it as an ancient phenomenon—one that already existed in talmudic and medieval times?

---

1. The word *halakha*, derived from the root "h-l-kh" which means to follow a path. Jewish society was fashioned and ruled by *halakha*, which is a legal system with judicial and legislative functions, both of which are performed by rabbis whose authority is recognized by the Jewish community. *Halakha* is also a "religious" system which prescribes ethical behavior. The concept of *halakha* appears continuously in this work since my thesis is based on the literature and commentaries that have formed Jewish law. (See note 1 in Chapter Five.)

2. See Irving Greenberg, "Confronting Sexual Abuse in Jewish Families: Rabbis Can Help by Speaking Out," *Moment* (April 1990): 49.

Four myths have become integral parts of Jewish thinking: the myth of the happy Jewish family, the myth that Jewish males are not physically violent, the myth of the "sacramental" nature of marriage, and the myth of woman's role as merely helpmate (*ezer ke-negdo*).[3]

These myths have played a central role in forming the mindset of rabbis who created and applied Jewish law (*halakha*) to the life of the Jewish community. They are the "narrative" behind the *halakha* or *nomos*.[4] The reciprocal relationship between midrash/myth/narrative/metaphor and *halakha*/Jewish law/*nomos* is a central issue in this book (see Chapter Four).

The myth of the happy Jewish family and that Jewish men don't beat their wives is very entrenched, but despite the assertion that Jews are "better" than other people, family violence has been known throughout Jewish history and may be considered grounds for a Jewish divorce.[5] This being so, "why then have Jews been so reluctant to acknowledge its existence and to respond appropriately?"[6]

The idealization of marriage works psychologically to make light of wifebeating in the larger perspective of family and marriage matches that are seen as having been made by God. An underlying assumption is that, because the family is sacred, wifebeating should be "tolerated for a greater good."[7] The concept that "marriages are made in heaven" is found in an oft-quoted midrash that stresses God's matchmaking prowess. God "sits

---

3. *Genesis* 2:18. Aviva Cantor falls prey to accepting the second myth in *Jewish Women/Jewish Men: The Legacy of Patriarchy in Jewish Life* (San Francisco: Harper, 1994). See also my review of her book in *Bridges: A Journal for Jewish Feminists* 6:1 (1996):107–110.

4. Rachel Adler in "Feminist Folktales of Justice: Robert Cover as a Resource for the Renewal of Halakha," *Conservative Judaism* XLV:3 (1993): 41, writes that formal lawmaking is generated by a *nomos*, a universe of meanings, values and rules, embedded in stories. A *nomos* is not a body of data to master and adapt, but a world to inhabit." Robert Cover, discusses the categories "*nomos*" and "narrative" in his seminal paper, "The Supreme Court, 1982 Term-Foreword: *Nomos* and Narrative," *Harvard Law Review* 97:1 (1983). See also *Conservative Judaism* XLV:3 (1993): 4–55.

5. Mordechai Frishtik, "Violence Against Women in Judaism," *Journal of Psychology and Judaism* 14:3 (1990): 131–153.

6. Ellen Goldsmith, "Violence in the Jewish Family," *Reform Judaism* 12:2 (1983–84): 21.

7. "In Jewish society the family is viewed as a sacred institution with intrafamilial love and support believed to be the norm." Mimi Scarf, "Marriages Made in Heaven?" in *On Being a Jewish Feminist: A Reader*, ed. Susannah Heschel (New York: Schocken Books, 1983), pp. 55–56.

and makes matches...assigning this man to that woman, and this woman to that man."[8]

Dresner mentions how the home was a "sanctuary-in-miniature."[9] Examples abound that support this view. According to the tractate Yevamot of the Babylonian Talmud, "a man without a wife is not a man,"[10] and "whoever is not married is without joy, blessing, or good, (and some add) without Torah or peace."[11] The centrality of marriage means that the concept of divorce is repugnant to the rabbis. It is said that the Temple altar sheds tears for a couple who gets divorced.[12]

The stereotypical and often mythic view of the Jewish male is that he respects (even honors) his mother and father; he doesn't drink (except the kiddush wine); he loves and provides generously for his children. He certainly does not beat his wife. In Israel Zangwill's words, "Here and there the voice of a beaten woman rose on the air. But no Son of the Covenant was among the revelers or the wifebeaters."[13]

---

8. *Bereshit Rabbah* 68:4; see also *Numbers Rabbah* 3:4; *Leviticus Rabbah* 8:1; in the Talmud, in B. Sotah 3a.

A Roman lady asked R. Jose bar Halafta, "Everyone agrees that God created the world in six days. From the sixth day on what has He been doing?". . . . R. Berakhyah said . . . He said to her that He arranges matches in His world. . . . She said she could make a thousand matches in one day. . . . She brought a thousand male and a thousand female slaves and paired them off. . . . At night time, they started to fight. . . . She told R. Jose of the incident and he said that for God, the matter of marriage is as significant as the splitting of the Red Sea, for as Scripture states, "God settles the solitary in a home" (*Psalms* 68:7) (*Bamidbar Rabbah* 3:4).

9. Samuel Dresner considers the "institution of marriage and the consequent features of the family—home, permanence, fidelity, and mutuality—[to be] the national treasure of the Jewish people, the bulwark and irreplaceable center of their society, and which Judaism surrounds with all manner of support and protection." This quote is from Samuel Dresner, "Homosexuality and the Order of Creation," *Judaism* (Summer 1991): 315.

10. B. Yevamot 63a; see also B. Kiddushin 29b for rabbinic disapproval of the unmarried.

11. B. Yevamot 62b.

12. B. Gittin 90b.

13. "The Ghetto welcomed the Sabbath Bride with proud song and humble feast. . . . All around, their neighbors sought distraction in the blazing public-houses, and their tipsy bellowings resounded through the streets and mingled with the Hebrew hymns. Here and there the voice of a beaten woman rose on the air. But *"no Son of the Covenant was among the revelers or the wife-beaters"*; the Jews remained a chosen race, a peculiar people, faulty enough, but redeemed at least from the grosser vices—a little human islet won from the waters of animalism by the genius of ancient engineers." (I. Zangwill, as quoted by J.H. Hertz, in the section "Deuteronomy—Additional Notes," in *The Pentateuch and Haftorahs*, 2nd ed. (London: Soncino Press, 1962), p. 935; emphasis added.)

One of the most important myths about the Jewish male is that he makes a better husband than the non-Jew. G.G. Coulton, writing in 1938 about the Jewish Ghetto, compares the "Frank's" crude behavior and his practice of beating his wife with Jewish refinement, civilization, and culture: ". . . while the 'Frank' was not ashamed to strike his womankind, and definite prescriptions for wifebeating stood in his Canon Law, Judaism did at least legislate against this."[14]

Katherine Rogers in her introduction to a history of misogyny writes:

> the Jews, whose culture was as patriarchal as the Greeks', showed little of their bitterness toward women and in fact generally exalted the good wife and mother. . . . One probable reason is that patriarchy was so securely established in Jewish culture before the writing of the Bible that men no longer felt an acute need to defend themselves against women or to justify their position, and were thus free to appreciate the pleasures of female society and family life.[15]

Rogers is correct in claiming that Jewish culture exalted good wives and mothers, but it is not true that Jewish men did not need to justify their stances, nor is it true that they had free time to spend with their families. The classic role model of the husband who spends years of studying in the academy is well known and honored among Jews. These men neglect their wives and children for long periods of time. While they are not always praised for this, it is considered an ideal to sacrifice family life for the sake of learning.

A classic example of this syndrome is found in the story of R. Rahumi[16]

---

14. *Medieval Panorama* (New York: Meridian Books, 1960), p. 358.

15. Katherine M. Rogers, *The Troublesome Helpmate: A History of Misogyny in Literature* (Seattle, WA: University of Washington Press, 1966), p. 41.

16. R. Rahumi who studied with Rabbah at Mahuza
would return once a year to his home
on the eve of Yom Kippur—one day alone
could he spare from his precious studies.
His wife anticipated his coming: "Now . . .
he is coming. . . . Now . . . he is coming."
He did not come. Her heart broke.
A teardrop left her eye.
He sat on the roof.
The roof opened up underneath him
He died (B. Ketubot 62b).

who only returned home once a year to visit his wife on Yom Kippur. The irony of his coming on Yom Kippur is not lost on the Jewish reader. It is one of the few holy days in which there can be no sexual intercourse between man and wife. The root of his name Rahumi (*rhm*) implies compassion—something which he obviously lacked. His punishment was connected to the irony of this combination of Yom Kippur and his being misnamed: On Yom Kippur when the skies open and God judges who will be saved, who will be punished, and so on, the roof (read sky) opened up, and for mistreating his wife by neglect, he died.[17]

In writing about the Jewish family, the feminist historian Paula Hyman was one of the first to address myths about Jewish mothers. In emphasizing that "the Jewish husband and father was no remote tyrant, his role as patriarch notwithstanding" she inadvertently helped to perpetuate another

---

17. Another similar story has to do with Rabbi Hananya.

Rabbi Hannania, the son of Hochini, and Rabbi Simon went to study Torah with Rabbi Akiba.

They stayed there thirteen years.
R. Simon sent letters to his home and kept in touch with his wife.
R. Hananya did not send letters to his home;
he did not keep in touch.
His wife sent for him, saying,
your daughter is grown up,
come help marry her off.

  R. Akiba, inspired by the holy spirit, said,

everyone who has a daughter of marriageable age
must marry her off.
What did Hananya do?
He went to the center of town
where the women drew their water.
He heard the voices of the water drawers saying,
daughter of Hochini, fill your bucket and go.
He followed her until she went into his house.
His wife saw him, and her soul left her body.
There are those who say her soul returned.
(*Genesis Rabbah* 75) (manuscript)

Although the context of this *midrash* is that one should knock on the door, even if it is your own home, we have evidence in this story of a husband who felt free to neglect his wife for a long period of time. The rabbis acknowledged the cruelty of this by berating the husbands for being too zealous about their studies.

myth.[18] It is possible to draw a frightening implication from Hyman's conclusions; namely, that when Jews gain independence and start promoting physical prowess as an ideal, they will express masculinity through the physical oppression of women.

Another factor that has contributed to minimizing wifebeating in Jewish society is the concept of marriage known as *Kiddushin*. The root of the word is *kaddosh*, which means to set apart as special, or holy. The Talmud[19] suggests that, through the act of *kiddushin*, the man prohibits the rest of the world from having "sexual access to the woman as if she were a sanctified object (i.e., set apart for a special purpose)."[20] In such acts of sanctification, a man sets aside (*me-kaddesh*) an object, *which is his possession*, for a sacred purpose.

Finally, wifebeating is minimized because some Jewish texts studied by the scholarly Jewish male portray women as lesser beings: stupid, talkative, lewd. Other texts imply that she is spiritually higher than the male, and therefore potentially capable of more than the man. Since Jewish learning took place in a sex-segregated setting isolated from the presence of women, very often the only things a man knew about women was learned second-hand

---

18. "How fortunate for both Jewish women and men that the 'macho mystique' was not a Jewish cultural value. Deprived of political independence and in most places of the right to bear arms, Jewish men denigrated physical prowess as a cultural ideal. Instead, they cultivated intellectual and spiritual pursuits. They expressed their masculinity in the synagogue and in the house of study, not on the battlefield and not through the physical oppression of their women.

This absence of the 'macho mystique' freed Jewish men from the sharpest differentiation of gender characteristics: the strong emotionally controlled, yet potentially violent male vs. the weak, emotional, and tender female. . . ." (Paula Hyman, "The Jewish Family: Looking for a Usable Past," in *On Being a Jewish Feminist: A Reader*, ed. Susannah Heschel (New York: Schocken Books, 1983), pp. 24–25.) This article was written in 1975 and appeared in the *Congress Monthly*. In her Afterword to *The Jewish Family*, Hyman writes that "At a time when wifebeating was acceptable in Christian Europe, rabbinical courts issued sharp denunciations of instances of wifebeating that were brought to their attention and compelled recalcitrant husbands to divorce their wives and provide for their support" (in *The Jewish Family: Myths and Reality*, ed. Steven M. Cohen and Paula Hyman (New York: Holmes and Meier, 1986). She cites Goitein and Agus in her footnotes. In contrast to these two early articles, see her article "The Modern Jewish Family: Image and Reality" in *The Jewish Family: Metaphor and Memory*, ed. David Kraemer (New York: Oxford University Press, 1989), with its vigorous study of apologetic writers in the late nineteenth-century, especially pp. 186–188.

19. B. Kiddushin 2b.

20. Harvey Goldberg, "Jewish Weddings in Tripolatania," *Jewish Life in Muslim Libya* (Chicago, IL: University of Chicago Press, 1990), p. 63.

from books. The dual message he received (spiritual being vs. lewd being) led him to both admire and look down on women.[21] There is a lot of misogyny in Jewish texts. Yet it is a long way from misogyny to wife-battering.

It has to be directly admitted that Jewish tradition contains many statements detrimental to women. In addition, "the idealized concept of the Jewish family, while not causing wifebeating, does prevent women from seeking help,"[22] since she may see her own behavior as the root of the problem. Because many Jewish women do not seek help, there is under-reporting of wifebeating among Jews. This serves to reinforce the myth that the problem does not exist. Moreover, Jewish tradition assumes that in some sense the husband has control over his wife, and Jewish law objectifies that control in legislation. In Jewish law, it is the man, not the woman, who initiates marriage and divorce.

WHAT IS WIFEBEATING?: TWO APPROACHES

The battering of women can be defined as a behavior pattern of abuse that can take many forms: physical, emotional, psychological, sexual, and economic. In the professional literature, the pattern is referred to as "spouse abuse" although

---

21. Nazism had a similar attitude toward both Jews and females. The Nazi felt threatened by the "softness" inherent in Jewish and feminine values and tried to eradicate them. Yet they often put women on a pedestal (*kuche, kinder, kirche*). Even today, Arab political cartoons often depict weakness in leaders by giving them breasts and showing them dressed as women. Anne Marie Oliver and Paul Steinberg in "Pornography as Political Weapon," *The Jerusalem Report* (2 May 1991): 33, write about salacious faxes that are being circulated in East Jerusalem as a form of political protest. There is a picture of King Fahd as a curvaceous belly dancer. For a very sensitive treatment of the nexus between chauvinism and Nazism, see Susan Griffin's *Pornography and Silence*, especially her chapter "The Sacrificial Lamb" (New York: Harper & Row, 1981), pp. 156-99. Most fascinating is Harvey Goldberg's "Itinerant Jewish Peddlers in Tripolitania," in *Jewish Life in Muslim Libya* (Chicago, IL: University of Chicago Press, 1990), in which he suggests that the Moslems liken Jews to women. "In both instances there is an insistence on the separation of social categories, a demand for submission, and, at the same time, the necessity of maintaining relationships. Men cannot do without women, and Muslims cannot do without Jews. The peddling Jew is transformed into a woman both metaphorically and metonymically" (p. 80). Further on, he writes that the marginality and social weakness of the Jew turned him into an actor enveloped in female symbolism (p. 81).

22. Scarf, "Marriages Made in Heaven?", p. 52.

the abuser is usually a man and his victim is usually a woman.[23] There are several approaches toward attempting to understand the causes of wifebeating.[24] In this section I will present the two main approaches.

In one view, battering can be considered a man's attempt to assert his dominance because he is afraid of a woman's softness, which threatens to emasculate him.[25] Violence is thus an expressive and impulsive act brought about by loss of control. In this view the man can absolve himself of responsibility. When viewed instrumentally, he is clearly responsible, although he tries to convince himself and others that he is not. Often the man pleads provocation. However, men who batter often do know what they are doing. Their violence is calculated and controllable. Goldner writes that violence is a strategy of intimidation in the service of male domination—a strategy that a man consciously "chooses."[26] The paradox of this is that the man "chooses" loss of control as a mode of interacting with his partner.

The other view says the root of the problem lies in society's condoning male violence, and battering is seen as a social crime whose roots lie in social conditioning stemming from the political and economic control that men historically have had over women. Women today, as in the past, are vulnerable to marital violence, to assaults by their husbands. Agents of society, such as the courts, medical and psychiatric institutions, police, schools, and the church have until recently tacitly regarded "domestic" violence as acceptable.[27]

---

23. See Murray A. Straus and Richard J. Gelles, "Societal Change and Change in Family Violence from 1975 to 1985 as Revealed by Two National Surveys," *Journal of Marriage and the Family* 48 (1986): 465–479, who pointed out that women also behave violently in marriage toward their husbands. The repercussions of their survey still reverberates. They are sensitive to the fact that their findings are often used to minimize male battering.

24. See Richard J. Gelles, "Violence in the Family: A Review of Research in the Seventies," *Journal of Marriage and the Family* 42 (1980): 873–885, for his review of terminology. In general, the term "family violence," which is also used, tends to prettify wifebeating.

25. See Virginia Goldner *et al.*, "Love and Violence: Gender Paradoxes in Volatile Attachments," *Family Process* 29:4 (1990): 348, and Dorothy Dinnerstein, *The Mermaid and the Minotaur: Sexual Arrangements and Human Malaise* (New York: Harper & Row, 1976), p. 161.

26. Goldner, "Love and Violence," p. 346.

27. See Sandra Horley, "A Shame and a Disgrace," *Social Work Today* 21 (June 1990): 16, and p. 1 in "An Overview of the Problem," in *Wife Abuse in the Medical Setting: An Introduction for Health Personnel*, No. 7, Monograph Series on Domestic Violence, April 1981, which is available from the National Clearinghouse on Domestic Violence, P.O. Box 2309, Rockville, MD 20852.

It seems that, in both views, battering is "learned behavior." The woman, too, is "taught" to stay in an abusive situation. She has been conditioned to see that keeping the house together is her responsibility, even if her life is threatened, and that leaving such a marriage means she has failed. She may also remain because she has observed that, both economically and physically, it is more secure to stay. The message that society gives her is to "grin and bear it" and try not to "burn the string beans."[28]

I will concentrate on the second approach, which views wifebeating as a social phenomenon, separated and maintained by the main institutions of society.

BATTERED WOMEN, PATRIARCHY AND JUDAISM

In order to understand the phenomenon of battering, one must relate to patriarchal societies that allow, and perhaps even encourage, the battering of wives.

A good working definition of patriarchy is offered by Kate Millett in her pioneering book, *Sexual Politics*, written in 1969. She writes that "patriarchal government [is] the institution whereby that half of the populace which is female is controlled by that half which is male. . . ." She adds that "the principles of patriarchy appear to be two-fold: male shall dominate female, elder male shall dominate younger."[29] She writes that patriarchy got its impetus or its source of authority from its discovery of the principle of paternity. Once discovered, males downgraded the female contribution to life and constructed a religion that was run by a male God and whose theology was essentially "male supremacist, and one of whose central functions [was] to uphold and validate the patriarchal structure."[30]

According to Millett, "patriarchy's chief institution is the family."[31] As an agent of society, the family's function is to see that its members adjust and conform. It also serves as an intermediary between the government and individual members of society. Thus each unit is governed by its family head (a

---

28. I would like to thank Sylvia Horwitz, an experienced social worker, for the "string bean" expression.
29. Kate Millett, *Sexual Politics* (London: Sphere Books, 1971), p. 25.
30. *Ibid.*, p. 28.
31. *Ibid.*, p. 33.

man) and "women tend to be ruled through the family alone and have little or no formal relation to the state."[32]

In this unit, the father has absolute power over his family. He is both the "begetter and the owner in a system in which kinship is property."[33] In this system the "property" often includes "non-persons without legal standing,"[34] such as women, children, and slaves. In traditional patriarchies, women did not have the rights to the profits of their own work. Even in modern patriarchies, women's "relationship to the economy is also typically vicarious or tangential."[35] In this system, as Millett describes it, men have control over every domain: science, the arts, the professions, industry, government, and the military. How do men run this system? Millett's answer: by use of force.

We tend to think of marital violence as a domestic affair and force in general "as the product of individual deviance, confined to pathological or exceptional behavior. . . ." However, Millett makes clear that, in order for patriarchal society to operate, it has to rely upon force "as an ever-present instrument of intimidation."[36] According to Kalmuss and Straus, violence is the "ultimate resource by husbands to keep wives in their place."[37] According to Straus, in societies in which there is a clear patriarchal social structure, such as we have just described, there is ample opportunity and justification for violence in the family.[38] A whole set of assumptions about women as "other" or alien justify force as a form of social control: women are of a lower order, their biological differences set them apart, make them inferior. In addition, women are often seen as the cause of all human suffering, as responsible for the fall from grace and disrupting the relationship with God. According to Millett, it is the myth of the Fall, the story of Adam's temptation by Eve, that "represents the most crucial argument of the patriarchal tradition in the West."[39]

---

32. *Idem*.

33. *Idem*.

34. *Ibid.*, p. 39.

35. *Ibid.*, p. 40.

36. *Ibid.*, p. 43.

37. Debra S. Kalmuss and Murray A. Straus, "Wife's Marital Dependency and Wife Abuse," *Journal of Marriage and the Family* (May 1982): 278.

38. Murray A. Straus, "Wifebeating: How Common and Why?" *Victimology* 2 (1977): 443–458.

39. Millet, *Sexual Politics,* p. 52.

When women are grouped together in patriarchal societies with children and slaves, there seems to be a consensus that they have to be educated and disciplined.[40] This serves the purpose of ensuring that they fit into, and resign themselves to, their inevitable role of nurturer and helpmate.

According to Carolyn G. Heilbrun,

> "Men can be men only if women are unambiguously women," Deborah Cameron has written. What does it mean to be unambiguously a woman? It means to put a man at the center of one's life and to allow to occur only what honors his prime position . . . one's own desires and quests are always secondary.[41]

Besides their having no intrinsic value, women are perceived as being weak. What is the origin of the view that labels women the weaker sex in physical, moral, and spiritual terms?

There are a number of theories that explain the beginnings of patriarchy. Many of these versions cite evidence that, prior to patriarchy, there was matriarchal rule and goddess worship. These theories assume that when men began to understand their role in paternity—as only the bearer of the seed—they began to regulate women's lives to assure themselves of

---

40. Wifebeating was legal in England until the latter part of the nineteenth century. See Terry Davidson, "Wifebeating: A Recurring Phenomenon Throughout History," in *Battered Women*, ed. Maria Roy (New York: Van Nostrand Reinhold, 1977), pp. 2–23; for example, in 1874, North Carolina repealed the husband's right to beat his wife; in 1886 in Pennsylvania, an anti-wifebeating bill was almost passed; in 1871, both Alabama and Massachusetts rescinded the ancient privilege of wifebeating. As late as 1971, a California wifebeating law was referred to which says that visible bruises and injuries must be present. In British Common Law, there was a section regulating wifebeating in which the infamous "rule of thumb" was referred to. The law stated that the rod used to legally beat one's wife should be no "thicker than his thumb" (p. 18).

The famous English jurist, Sir William Blackstone, saw nothing wrong with the wifebeating law. He wrote, "For, as [the husband] is to answer for her misbehavior, the law thought it reasonable to entrust him with this power of chastisement, in the same moderation that a man is allowed to correct his apprentices or children . . ." (Blackstone, *Commentaries on the Laws of England*, 1765, p. 444, as quoted by Davidson, p. 19).

41. Carolyn G. Heilbrun, *Writing a Woman's Life* (New York: Ballantine Books, 1988), pp. 20–21. She cites Deborah Cameron, *Feminism and Linguistic Theory* (London: Macmillan, 1985).

the legitimacy of *their* offspring.[42] Though this theory is logical, it is also highly speculative.

The Nexus Between Patriarchy and Judaism

I think it important to state at the outset that patriarchy was not invented by the Israelite religion. The creation story of Genesis 2–3, in which Eve is created from Adam's rib after Adam himself has been created, and in which Eve is eventually blamed for having tempted Adam to sin, seems to express patriarchy. However, in Genesis 1 there is an equally famous passage which is that God created man (kind) in his (our) image to rule over the earth. "God created man in His image, male and female He created them" (Gen. 1:27).[43] Clearly the Bible is not monolithic. There is an egalitarian tradition as well as a tradition that emphasizes man's prominence and justifies his rule over women.

Not only was patriarchy not invented by the Israelite religion, it was also not invented by the Jewish religion. Both Judith Plaskow and Susannah Heschel, whose sense of their Judaism is as strong as their feminist beliefs, caution Christian feminists not to blame Judaism for the introduction of patriarchy to Western civilization.[44] In their articles, they attempt to warn Christian feminists against falling into the trap of sloppy scholarship, anti-Semitism (under the guise of anti-patriarchalism), and of avoiding a confrontation with the darker side of their own religion. Unfortunately, examples abound of Christian feminists who have adopted a theology that claims that Christianity represents liberation for women, whereas Judaism represents oppression for women.[45] According to the Jewish historian Shaye

---

42. But see Adrien Janis Bledstein, "The Genesis of Humans: The Garden of Eden Revisited," in *Judaism,* no 26: 2 (1977): 197–198, who makes the point that, in the Bible, woman also has "seed" (Gen. 3:15; 24:60; 16:10).

43. See Phyllis A. Bird, "Male and Female He Created Them," *Harvard Theological Review* 74: 2 (1981): 129–159. See also Phyllis Trible, "Depatriarchalizing in Biblical Interpretation," *Journal of the American Academy of Religion* (March 1973): 30–48.

44. In "Blaming the Jews for the Birth of Patriarchy," in *Nice Jewish Girls: A Lesbian Anthology,* ed. Evelyn Beck (Watertown, MA: Persephone Press 1982), pp. 250–254, and "Anti-Judaism in Christian Feminist Theology," *Tikkun,* no 5: 3 (1990): 25–28, 95–97.

45. See for example, Marla Selvidge's comparison of Mark's liberation message with the oppressive message of the "androcentric" book of Leviticus about the restrictive purity laws concerning menstruation. "*Mark,* 5:25–34 and *Leviticus* 15:19–20," *Journal of Biblical Literature,* no 103:4 (1984): 623.

Cohen, this is an example of "the old Christian animosity toward Judaism [resurfacing] in a new form."[46] The fact is that *all* religions of Western society are rooted in patriarchalism, not just the Jewish one.

Some writers are fond of comparing treatment of Jewish women in the ancient world with the treatment of Greek, Roman, and Muslim women. This comparison shows a relatively better status of Jewish women. Thus, the claim is made that Jewish women were better treated because Jewish tradition was intent on looking after women's best interests. This claim seems to be misplaced. When we look at Jewish sources we see that much of what was said that is negative about patriarchy is unfortunately true of Jewish society, past and present.[47]

Thus, Judaism is patriarchal in spirit. As we will see, even though Jewish law is often protective of women, it discriminates against and patronizes them. This is both because patriarchalism is intrinsic to Judaism and because Judaism is influenced by other patriarchal systems. This is true in the case of wifebeating as well. On the other hand, because Judaism's approach to life is not monolithic, its attitudes toward wifebeating are neither consistent nor simplistic.

Nevertheless, the question arises, what are the unique features in Judaism, aside from "normal" patriarchalism, that could be viewed as contributing to male chauvinism and could work tacitly and/or overtly to allow men to batter their wives? We will look for the answer to this in the norms of *halakha* and in the metaphors of Jewish society as revealed in the narratives (*nomos*) of sacred Jewish texts; namely, the Bible and *aggadah*.

---

46. Shaye Cohen, "The Modern Study of Ancient Judaism," in *The State of Jewish Studies,* ed. Shaye Cohen and Edward L. Greenstein (Detroit: Wayne State University Press, 1990), p. 57. See also Susannah Heschel, "Configurations of Patriarch, Judaism, and Nazism in German Feminist Thought," in *Gender and Judaism,* ed. T.M. Rudavsky (New York: New York University Press, 1995), p. 146, who writes that German feminists consider "negative depictions of Judaism" to be "accepted as legitimate evaluations of it, rather than as part of a systemic misrepresentation endemic to Occidental culture."

47. Writing this book as a woman who identifies both as a feminist Jew and as a Jewish feminist is a difficult experience for me; consequently, I both "bash" the sources and apologize for them. In a later chapter, I criticize those who indulge in apologetics and I knowingly run the risk of being accused of the same in this section.

2

Metaphoric Battering: The Groundwork for Domestic Violence in Patriarchal Society

In this chapter, we will discuss texts that, taken together, show the groundwork for the battering of women in the Jewish tradition. The texts we will study in the Bible and the *midrash* do not talk about *actual* battering of women; however, they do create a metaphor for viewing women as objects of violence. I hope to show by my reading of these texts that the values that are implicit in them can lead to a climate of social convention that tolerates *real* battering.

We will be looking at some seemingly unconnected episodes in the Bible and see how they are interpreted, commented on, and understood by *midrash*, which is a principal form of rabbinic literature consisting of pieces of creative expository writing based upon verses from the Bible. This independent literary creation serves to raise the reader's consciousness and help us rediscover the meaning and intent of the original metaphors.[1]

What connects stories such as Cain, Hagar, Lot's daughters, the Concubine at Gibeah, and the Sotah is an ambiance of explicit and implicit family

---

1. See Mayer Gruber, "The Midrash in Biblical Research," in *The Motherhood of God and Other Studies* (Atlanta, GA: Scholars Press, 1992), pp. 212–230.

violence.[2] These five stories will show that, in a patriarchal society, in which women have no power and little intrinsic value except as breeders, it is easy to perform violent acts against women.

THE BIBLE

In the Pentateuch, family violence is not unknown and the family is a very tough neighborhood to grow up in. The usual explanation of all this is that violence, like male dominance, is human nature—that it is wired into our genes.[3]

Family Violence

We will look first at the story of Cain and Abel. There are, of course, many interpretations of the first murder in history and the first act of violence depicted in the Bible. My reading of Cain's jealous act of slaughter, the result of sibling rivalry for the affection of God, is as follows: Cain slew Abel because God preferred animal sacrifice rather than grain offerings.

> . . . Cain brought an offering to the Lord from the fruit of the soil; and Abel . . . brought the choicest of the firstlings of his flock. The Lord paid heed to Abel and his offering, but to Cain and his offering He paid no heed. Cain was much distressed and his face fell. And the Lord said to Cain, "Why are you distressed, and why is your face fallen? Surely, if you do right, there is uplift. But if you do not do right, sin crouches at the door; Its urge is toward you, Yet you can be its master" (Gen. 4:3–7).

What is the meaning of animal sacrifice? The word *korban* (sacrifice) is rich in associations. *K-r-v* is the root of both closeness and relatives (*karov*) and warfare (*ke-rav*). By shedding blood, we are both demonstrating our power and admitting our weakness—for we, unlike God, die as

---

2. The laws of *sotah*, while *halakha*, have narrative or metaphoric nuances.

3. See popular science books such as Robert Ardey, *The Territorial Imperative* (New York: Athenaeum, 1966), and Desmond Morris, *The Naked Ape* (New York: McGraw-Hill, 1967).

well as live. It is possible to sacrifice grain which does not require killing, but it is less desirable.

Would there have been a first murder if God had not preferred an animal sacrifice? We can only guess why God prefers dead animals. God may have been testing Cain to see if his offering was genuine. However, Cain misread what he thought were God's instructions and clearly failed the test when he killed his brother when they were in the field. Because the instructions which God gave are unclear, God is somewhat responsible for the act. God is also not blameless in that he showed his preference too obviously. For whatever reason, "the choicest of the firstlings of Abel's flock" were preferable to the mere "fruit of the soil."

We should not view God uncritically, for it is God's stamp of approval for animal sacrifice and the spilling of animal blood that served as a [mis]guideline to Cain. Perhaps Cain's thought process was as follows: if his role model (God) preferred the killing of animals, he (Cain), would go one step further to gain God's approval, and make the ultimate sacrifice by killing a human being.

I argue that this first act of violence might have been avoided had God not "needed" sacrifices, and certainly not animal sacrifice. Had the deity not chosen to disturb the natural order—that is, had God been content to accept a grain offering rather than insisting on meat—had God not chosen one son (the youngest) over the other,[4] the first killing might have been avoided. Based on this interpretation, it can be concluded that aggressive behavior is not innate; it is learned. Cain learned from God that killing was a desirable act. Cain's social environment (and God) led him to believe that a violent act would be encouraged—that violence was an emulation of God.

As we know from the Bible, however, killing a person was not God's intention. Cain's act is an act of perverse obedience. One might argue that the Deity realized its partial responsibility for the misunderstanding and that was why God allowed Cain to live. Eventually God had to destroy the world he created and start all over after the Flood. This time God explicitly commanded Noah's children (i.e., all of humanity) not to kill: "Whosoever sheds

---

4. See Naomi Graetz, "In Search of Lost Paradise," *S/HE Created Them: Feminist Retellings of Biblical Stories* (Chapell Hill, NC: Professional Press, 1993), pp. 11–14; Jeremy Benstein, "Others, Brothers," *The Jerusalem Report* (17 October 1996): 36 suggests, as well, that animal liberation leads to human murder.

the blood of man, By man shall his blood be shed; For in His image did God make man" (Gen. 9:6).

Further on in Genesis there are other indications of family violence and abuse. There is the drunkenness of Noah, the casting out of the child Ishmael, the aborted child sacrifice of Isaac, and the elder abuse or manipulation of Isaac by Rebecca and Jacob. Later, there is a father's (Jacob) glaring silence in the face of his daughter's (Dinah) rape, silence which allowed her brothers (Simeon and Levi) to slaughter an entire town (Shechem) of innocent people in revenge—that at last provoked Jacob's response of outrage.[5]

Violence Against Women

There is an interesting precedent of a husband using his female children and wives to save his own skin. There are several cases in Genesis (chaps. 12, 20, 26) which demonstrate that women were intrinsically less important than men, that they were objects with trade value.

The story we will look at relates to Lot, Abraham's nephew, who, like his uncle, extends hospitality to two strangers in town, who are messengers from God. Lot's version of hospitality is, however, an inversion and travesty of the hospitality shown by Abraham to the three angels of God. These messengers arrive in Sodom with a message to him that the city is to be destroyed imminently. The townsmen surround the house saying they want to "know" these strangers: in contemporary usage, they propose homosexual rape of the new meat. As a good host, Lot could not tolerate such an act and went out to them saying:

> "I beg you, my friends, do not commit such a wrong. Look, I have two daughters who have not known a man. Let me bring them out to you, and you may do to them as you please; but do not do anything to these men, since they have come under the shelter of my roof" (Gen. 19:7–8).

Lot's understanding of the laws of hospitality means that rape of one's own daughters is preferable to the rape of his male guests. In his mind, as Bauman has said, "male gender and sexuality are so sacrosanct that female

---

5. See Naomi Graetz, "Dinah the Daughter," in *A Feminist Companion to Genesis*, ed. Athalya Brenner (Sheffield, UK: Sheffield Academic Press, 1993), pp. 306–317.

gender and sexuality are expendable, even when it is that of one's own daughters."[6]

Fortunately for the daughters, there is a *deus ex machina* at work in the form of the angels of God, who save them all by blinding the men outside.[7] The messengers force Lot to take his daughters and wife outside the city, urging them to flee for their lives. While Lot flees to Tzoar with his daughters, God destroys the towns of Sodom and Gomorra.

When Lot's wife looks back at the destruction and is turned into a pillar of salt, the daughters are left alone with their father. Thinking they are the only survivors left in the world, the daughters take it upon themselves to preserve the human race. They make their father drink wine and then each in turn has intercourse with him and gets impregnated with his seed. The story has a "happy ending," except for Lot's wife. The good people are saved, the wicked destroyed, and the human race is once again perpetuated, with the nations Moab and Ammon being the progeny.

Are the daughters culpable in their act of "seducing" their father? Is Lot an innocent victim? Is he being paid back by the daughters for his offer of them to the townsmen? Are there any hints of incest here? The *midrash* offers some interesting insights. One could read the story of Lot's daughters getting their father so drunk that they have to rape him as high comedy, but clearly the rabbis take a serious view.[8] Although King David is ultimately the progeny of Ruth the Moabite—the nation of Moab being the result of this incestuous coupling—the rabbis do not want to encourage incest.

The rabbis are very concerned with role models—as they should be. A role model misunderstood can end in tragedy, as we saw in the case of Cain and Abel. Although the story ends relatively well, incest is not to be sanctioned. R. Judan of Gallia, R. Samuel, and R. Tanhum recognize Lot's (every father's) incestuous longings. The three of them honestly face the desire for

6. Batya Bauman, "Women-identified Women in Male Identified Judaism," in *On Being a Jewish Feminist*, ed. Susannah Heschel (New York: Schocken, 1983), p. 90.

7. The entire story is the inverse of the adventures of Abraham. Lot's whole brand of hospitality is inferior to the kind Abraham offers. The rescue is a satirical parody of the story of the sacrifice of Isaac. In Isaac's case, he is rescued when his father, Abraham, "sees" the ram and doesn't slaughter Isaac. In this case, the daughters are rescued by the townsmen losing their sight.

8. Genesis Rabbah LI: 9. All quotations from the *midrash* are from *The Midrash*, 3rd ed, edited by H. Freedman and M. Simon (London: The Soncino Press, 1983), pp. 448–449.

one's "own flesh," and every father's need to guard himself against lusting after his daughters.

The last word, however, is R. Aha's. It is couched in misogyny and ultimately in the form of denial: "men were repelled by this reading, but women were attracted," implying that men are naturally repelled by longings for their daughters, whereas women are naturally attracted to their fathers. He blames the daughters for luring the fathers into an incestuous relationship, for it is daughters who are lustful. Rather than praise Lot's daughters for sacrificing themselves to preserve the race, as some midrashim do, R. Aha implies that their motivation is that "women were attracted" by the idea of intercourse with their fathers.[9]

An Ancient Femme Fatale

There are three other stories of matriarchs being treated as objects in Genesis—all three with a similar theme. The first episode occurs when Sarai (later to be called Sarah) and Abram (later to be called Abraham) travel in Egypt during a famine. Abram passes Sarai off as his sister to prevent himself from being killed.

> Please say that you are my sister, that it may go well with me because of you, and that I may remain alive thanks to you (Gen. 12:12).

Abraham does this again when he travels in the Negev area in Gerar (20:1–2). But this time he does not ask for permission. He does not say to Sarah "*Please* say that you are my sister," he just does it.

---

9. Sigmund Freud, in his "Introductory Lectures of Psychoanalysis" (1933), wrote: "Almost all of my women patients told me that they had been seduced by their father. I was driven to recognize in the end that these reports were untrue and so came to understand that the hysterical symptoms are derived from fantasies and not from real occurrences. . . . It was only later that I was able to recognize in this fantasy of being seduced by the father the expression of the typical Oedipus complex in women." As quoted by Judith Lewis Herman, *Father-Daughter Incest* (Cambridge, MA: Harvard University Press, 1981), p. 7. See also Otto Rank, *The Incest Theme in Language and Literature* (Baltimore: Johns Hopkins Press, 1975). See also Ilan Kutz, "Behind the Pillar of Salt," *The Jerusalem Report* (31 October 1996): 46, who points to Lot's family shifting the blame of incest from him to his daughters, as has been the case with incest throughout history.

> So King Abimelech king of Gerar had Sarah brought to him. But God came to Abimelech in a dream by night and said to him, "You are to die because of the woman that you have taken, for she is a married woman." Now Abimelech had not approached her. He said, "O Lord, will You slay people even though innocent? He himself said to me, 'She is my sister!' And she also said, 'He is my brother. . . .'" (Gen. 20:2–5)

The next morning, Abimelech summoned Abraham and angrily told him that he was wrong. Abraham justified his action by saying that since he thought there was "no fear of God in this place" that they would kill him because of Sarah. Abimelech gave a lot of gifts to Abraham and more important gave his wife back to him. To Sarah he said,

> "I herewith give your brother a thousand pieces of silver; this will serve you as vindication [kesut eynaim; literally a covering of the eyes, as compensation for shame perhaps] before all who are with you, and you are cleared before everyone." Abraham then prayed to God, and God healed Abimelech and his wife and his slave girls, so that they bore children; for the Lord had closed fast every womb of the house-hold of Abimelech because of Sarah, the wife of Abraham (Gen. 20:16–18).

Since this is the end of the chapter, people usually forget that the next two verses after this is "And God took note of [pakad][10] Sarah. . . . and Sarah conceived and bore a son to Abraham. . . ." (Gen. 21:1–2). Abraham's prayer resulted in God's intercession on behalf of Sarah as well.

What can we make of these two stories? The second story, although much longer, follows the pattern of the first. It is possible that this was not the first time that this couple had conned the local rulers. They got off because God was on their side. But Abimelech is more fearful of God than is Abraham. His anger is righteous. He is correct in not trusting Abraham in future dealings (Gen. 21:22–34). Presumably this is the last time that Abraham will do this, since Sarah gets pregnant. One senses too much protest about Abimelech's not approaching or even touching Sarah. There is real concern on the part of Abraham that Sarah was impregnated by Abimelech. Thus it is necessary to stress that she was untouched. This theme is reiterated when it is

---

10. Lifkod sometimes has the meaning of impregnate: see Genesis Rabbah (Vilna) 53 and Midrash Tanhuma (Warsaw) "Veyerah," 18. It is possible that the midrash implies that it is God (not Abimelech) who impregnated Sarah.

stated that God closed fast[11] everyone's wombs, because of Sarah, whose womb was now about to be opened by God. Would his paternity be one of those things that Abraham would doubt for the rest of his life? If so, could one speculate this as an explanation for Abraham's willingness to sacrifice his son? I have no answers to this except to point out the irony of an episode in which Sarah is treated as an object that results in the long-awaited heir.

The story with the same motif is repeated with Rebecca and Isaac in Genesis 26. In each of these three stories, the wife's beauty is a threat to the husband's safety and the husband is taught a moral lesson by the neighboring ruler. But despite the love that the husband has for his wife, he does not hesitate to use her to save himself when he is afraid. The two wives are clearly objects to their husbands. The way in which the wives are treated make them willing to abuse those under them or around them. If one is abused, then it is easy to abuse others. Thus Rebecca will abuse her aged husband and her first born son Esau, and Sarah in turn will abuse her handmaiden Hagar and son Ishmael.

Hagar: The Abused Handmaiden

Hagar the bondmaid [shifhah] and/or slave [amah], who qualifies as an abused (second) wife, is the last case we will look at in the Book of Genesis. According to Phyllis Trible, Hagar is "one of the first females in scripture to experience use, abuse, and rejection."[12] She is a triple-fold alien: from her country, in her status, and in her sex.[13] She is an Egyptian maidservant living in Canaan; she is "single, poor and bonded."[14] She is a powerless object.

> [Abram] cohabited with Hagar and [unlike Sarai], she conceived, . . .
> And Sarai said to Abram, "The wrong done me is your fault! I myself put my maid in your bosom; now that she sees that she is pregnant, I am lowered in her esteem. The Lord decide between you and me!" Abram

---

11. The Hebrew is *atzor atzar* (as tight as you can imagine).

12. Phyllis Trible, *Texts of Terror: Literary Feminist Readings of Biblical Narratives* (Philadelphia, PA: Fortress Press, 1984), p. 9.

13. Bruce Rosenstock, "Inner-Biblical Exegesis in the Book of the Covenant," *Conservative Judaism* (Spring 1992): 45, points out that the name Hagar may be a pun on *ger* [alien].

14. Trible, *Texts of Terror*, p. 10.

said to Sarai, "Your maid is in your hands. Deal with her as you think right" (Gen. 16:4–6).

Hagar is an object who is given by Sarai to Abraham. She plans to use Hagar as a breeder like the handmaidens in Margaret Atwood's science fiction novel, *The Handmaid's Tale* (1985).[15] However, like the heroine in Atwood's novel, the breeder rebels. She has her own personality and is able to see through Sarah. Sarah has given her to Abraham as a wife, not as a concubine. Consequently, Sarah's status in relation to herself has been diminished in Hagar's eyes; thus a threatened Sarah decides to discard this rebellious object. Sarah was tacitly allowed by Abraham to do with Hagar as she pleased. "Your maid is in your hands. Deal with her as you think right." Of course what is right for Sarah is not right for Hagar, for it is said that Sarah treated her harshly and Hagar ran away.

If we look at a *midrash* that interprets this passage, we can see how the physical and mental violence done to Hagar is spelled out.

> R. Abbah said: Sarah restrained her from cohabitation. R. Berekiah said: Sarah slapped her face with a slipper. R. Berekiah said in R. Abbah's name: Sarah bade her carry her water buckets and bath towels to the baths (Genesis Rabbah XLV:6).

The last comment implies that Hagar was not actually mistreated, *just* humiliated, by having to do slave type work.

When Hagar has her son Ishmael, Sarah is again incensed and this time tells Abraham to "cast out that slave-woman and her son . . ."(21:10). This time, as Trible points out, "Hagar has lost her name. . . . Moreover, the absence of dialogue continues to separate the females. Inequality, opposition, and distance breed violence."[16] Although the matter distressed Abraham greatly—not because of Hagar, but because it "concerned a son of his" (Gen. 21:11)—God tells him not to be

> . . . distressed over the boy or your slave; whatever Sarah tells you, do as she says. . . . As for the son of the slave-woman, I will make a nation of him, too, for he is your seed (Gen. 21:12–13).

---

15. Margaret Atwood, *The Handmaid's Tale* (Toronto, Canada: McClelland and Stewart, 1985).

16. Trible, *Texts of Terror*, p. 13.

Thus the "son" becomes a boy and "Hagar" becomes a slave. As Trible puts it, "if Abraham neglected Hagar, God belittles her."[17]

God identifies with the oppressor, not with the oppressed. God and Abraham are complicit in the decision to cast out the object, the slave-woman of no account. Abraham cares only about his seed, his son, not about the woman. It is Sarah who cares about being supplanted and who initiates the act. It would appear that the Bible sympathizes with Sarah's plight when it writes that it is a "loathsome" situation when "a slave girl supplants her mistress" (Proverbs 30:23).

By assigning blame to Sarah, we are missing the point. Sarah too is a victim. In this case, she is a victim of the ideology that dictates that happiness is only to be found in the maternal role. Thus the competition between Sarah and Hagar is "natural." One can view this competition between mothers, however, as Trible does, as an example of infighting among oppressed groups.[18] In this case, the oppressed are two women, one of whom is separated from the other by race[19] and class.

The attitude of the Bible toward Hagar is very sympathetic when she runs away from Sarai:

> An angel of the Lord found her by a spring of water . . . and said, "Hagar, slave of Sarai, where have you come from, and where are you going?" And she said, "I am running away from my mistress Sarai." And the angel of the Lord said to her, "Go back to your mistress, and submit to her harsh treatment." And the angel of the Lord said to her, "I will greatly increase your offspring . . ."(Gen. 16:7–10).

The angel clearly "cares" about her. She is a victim who is oppressed, no one will deny this. Yet she is given an unequivocal message to stay a victim. Go back to this oppressive situation. Stay rather than run away. Your reward will be a son who will be a strong warrior. She is the abused woman who runs away but doesn't know what to do with herself and thus returns to the abusive situation.

One can also read this text as follows: Because Hagar has not empowered herself by leaving, she is doomed to always be in the servant status. The

---

17. *Ibid.*, p. 22.
18. *Ibid.*, p. 31, Note 17.
19. Hagar, as an Egyptian, may have been black.

angel asks her where she is coming from and where she is going. She only knows where she is coming from. So she is told to go back and take more abuse, since she doesn't know how to use her freedom. Does this reading encourage Hagar to fight for her freedom or does it encourage her to remain in servant status? Ultimately the advice she is given is to stay where she is and to suffer for the sake of her future child. The message is that women have to accept abuse because their own lives have no intrinsic worth—their lives have worth only for the sake of others, in this case her son. This message is still being transmitted to women.

But the damage is not only to Hagar. Like battered women everywhere, the children suffer. We know that batterers often have abusive fathers who beat them and/or their mothers. Hints of this are seen in the blessing (or perhaps curse) given to Hagar by the divine messenger:

Behold, you are with child
And shall bear a son;
You shall call him Ishmael,
For the Lord has paid heed to your suffering.
He shall be a wild ass of a man;
His hand against everyone,
And everyone's hand against him;
He shall dwell alongside of all his kinsmen
(Gen. 16:11–12).

Ishmael witnesses that God has not "paid heed to [her] suffering" and that in fact she has been abused by all the people close to her. It is natural that he will grow up with a chip on his shoulder, perceiving that "everyone's hand [is] against him" and that "his hand [will be] against everyone." He, too, will become an oppressor when he gets the chance, even against the people of Israel. Trible sees the victimization of Hagar as prefiguring Israel's enslavement in Egypt. According to Trible, Hagar, unlike Israel,

experiences exodus without liberation, revelation without salvation, wilderness without covenant, wanderings without land, promise without fulfillment, and unmerited exile without return. This Egyptian slave woman is stricken, smitten by God, and afflicted for the transgressions of Israel.[20]

---

20. Trible, *Texts of Terror*, p. 28.

Following Trible's insights one step further, I would argue that Hagar the suffering slave-woman serves as the prototype for the metaphor of Israel as the suffering, mistreated wife of God. I will postpone this discussion of the prophet's use of the marriage metaphor until the next chapter. But before doing that, I want to leave Genesis and look at the case of another victim in the Bible.

Book of Judges

Judges 19 tells the story of another woman who is a victim of circumstances. It is the story of the unnamed concubine-wife (*pilegesh*) from the Judean town of Bethlehem, who deserted her Levite master-husband in Mt. Ephraim to go back to her father's home. The husband goes after her to "woo her and to win her back" (*daber al libah*) (Judges 19:3) and to restore the harmony prior to her leaving, since the *pilegesh* who has the status of wife cannot divorce her husband.[21]

The father of the *pilegesh* is delighted to have his son-in-law stay with him and offers him extensive, even exaggerated, hospitality which is reminiscent both in language and style of Lot's and Abraham's hospitality to the messengers of God. The Levite finally extricates himself (presumably with his wife) from his father-in-law's hospitality, starts traveling home, and, in sharp contrast to his father-in law's open house, finds himself on the street, homeless for the night in Gibeah which is in Benjaminite territory. An old man, who hails from the hill country of Ephraim, sees him sitting in the town square and asks him, "Where are you going, and where do you come from?" Trible points out in a footnote that this is the same question asked of Hagar (Gen. 16:8). His voluble answer, unlike Hagar who only knows she is fleeing her mistress Sarai, is that he is going home to Ephraim, having stopped on the way to Bethlehem on the way to his house and that "no man [*ein ish*] takes *me* into his house" (Judges 19:18). Considering the fact that this Levite had started his journey in order to speak to the heart of his *pilegesh* and convince her to return, he has, midway, forgotten all about her.

His countryman from Ephraim offers him shelter for the night in his house and they eat and drink merrily. While they are enjoying themselves,

---

21. *Ibid.*, p. 67. Trible points out that this is reminiscent of Shechem (Gen. 34:3) and Hosea (2:14[16]). I use her translation in this section.

they are interrupted by a group of worthless, no account townsmen, referred to as *bnei beliya'al*, who surround the house, pound (*mitdapkim*)[22] on the door, and ask for the Levite so that they can "know" [be intimate with] him.

In this Sodom there is no *deus ex machina*. In fact, this is a very ungodly community. As Niditch points out, this is a community in social disintegration.[23] On the microscopic level, the family is not in harmony. On the macroscopic level, Israelites are pitted against each other. In a community "where positive community-feelings should be found, they are not only lacking, but violated."[24] What rules of hospitality do exist, serve to protect only males. We have already seen that Abraham and Isaac used their wives to save themselves, so we should not be surprised that it happens again.

The host, who is faced with the same problem that Lot had, responds to the townsmen:

> Please, my friends [*ach-ay* = brothers], do not act so wrongly, since this man has entered my house [as my guest]. Don't do this nefarious [*nevala*] deed. Here is my virgin daughter and his concubine! I'll bring them out to you. Rape [*an-nu*] them, do to them what you want. But don't do this outrageous [*nevala*] thing to this man (Judges 19:23–24).

Thus the host offered his virgin daughter and the guest's concubine instead. There is a sense of male camaraderie here that must not be violated. Hospitality is something extended only to males. The men refer to each other as brothers; the father-in-law lavishly entertains the Levite.

The women's role in this story is object, victim, and ultimately sacrifice. Her role exemplifies violence against women and hammers home the message that women's bodies are men's property. Though the sacrifice of the innocent woman seems indefensible, certainly in the twentieth century, there is a long history of offering up one's wife or daughter to protect oneself.[25] It

---

22. *Dafak* has a sexual connotation today, similar to "screwed."

23. Susan Niditch, "The Sodomite Theme in Judges 19–20: Family, Community, and Social Disintegration," *Catholic Biblical Quarterly*, no 44:3 (1982): 365–378.

24. *Ibid.*, p. 369.

25. This is not to equate the wife-sister story of Genesis 12 with this one. Niditch (*ibid.*, p. 370) points out that "Abraham does not hand over Sarah to an angry mob. Rather, he acts in fear for his life and in consultation with Sarah. . . . In contrast . . . the Levite does not consult with his concubine or even speak to her. The language conveys the unconsidered swiftness with which he gives her up and the harshness."

certainly seems acceptable to the Levite who, not only does not protest, but in unseemly haste:

> seized [yehazek] his concubine and pushed [her][26] out to them. They raped her and abused her all night long until morning; and they let her go when dawn broke (Judges 19:25).

There are no gory details about what she suffered. The three verbs are *yadah, allal, shalach,* "knew her" (in the sexual sense), "tortured or abused her," and "sent her away" (when they had no more use for her). The three verbs though brief are graphic enough, they tell it all.

> Toward morning the woman came back. She collapsed at the doorway of the man's house where her master (*adon*) was [sleeping] until it was light (Judges 19:26).

The despicable cold-bloodiness of the husband, who is now referred to for the first time as master [*adon*], can no longer be hidden. Until now he was husband [*ish*], but from this point on he is only the master. The narrator writes that the master "gets up" in the morning, apparently having slept calmly and without dreams throughout the night. He prepares to leave and then discovers the woman, his concubine, fallen on the doorstep with her hands on the threshold (v. 27). When he commands her "get up, let's go," she doesn't answer. So he picks her up like an object and puts her on his donkey and without any remorse or apologies sets out for home.

It is not clear if she is alive or dead. Trible points out that the Septuagint adds "for she was dead" whereas the Hebrew text "is silent, allowing the interpretation that this abused woman is yet alive."[27] The account we have in the biblical text allows us to think that the Levite is the murderer of the woman and not the rapists of Gibeah.

> When he came home, he picked up *the* [emphasis Trible's] knife [ma-achelet][28] and took hold [yachzek] of his concubine and cut her up limb

---

26. Trible (*Texts of Terror*, p. 76) points out that the Hebrew omits the direct object *her* for the second verb.

27. *Ibid.*, p. 79.

28. The only other use of this word is the knife Abraham intended to use to slaughter Isaac in Genesis 22:10.

by limb into twelve parts. He sent them throughout the territory of Israel. And everyone who saw it cried out, "Never has such a thing [*zot*] happened or been seen from the day the Israelites came out of the land of Egypt to this day!" (Judges 19:29–30).

The vagueness of this account contrasts strongly with the Levite's later account in which he states that the men of Gibeah raped her and she died. Is this to allay any suspicions that he did indeed kill her? It would seem to me that there is enough textual evidence to assume that she was alive. The use of the *ma-achelet*, which is used for sacrificial purposes and the fact that the Levite lies about what happened leads me to see him as a cold-blooded murderer who used his wife's living body to avenge himself. Thus, when it is said "never has such a *thing* happened," the *zot*, which is "thing" in the feminine singular, is suggestive of more than one atrocity—the rape, handing her over to the men of Gibeah, and the chopping up of her body.[29]

The members of the assembly in true male-bonding fashion arise as "one man" (Judges 20:1) against their brothers, the Benjaminites, after hearing the Levite's speech. Further atrocities are committed, four hundred more women are raped and two hundred young women are abducted in the course of this civil war. In fact, the elders of Israel end up by behaving as abominably as the men of Gibeah and the Levite.

Although the Bible's ostensible purpose in telling this story is to show how Israeli society was lawless and needed a king, we can read this story as does Trible, as a story which "depicts the horrors of male power, brutality, and triumphalism; of female helplessness, abuse and annihilation."[30] The woman, dead or alive, raped and tortured, is in the power of men from beginning to end. No one intervenes to save her. She is not human. She is property, object, and tool. She has been passed back and forth. She has been obliterated and dismembered.[31] In short, she is woman as meat, not eaten, but with body butchered, cut up (*natach*) into parts like an animal, and distributed as a message to the tribes. No burial

---

29. Trible (*Texts of Terror*, p. 81), who reads the text similarly, translates 19:30 as follows: "And all who saw *her* said, '*She* was not, and *she* was not seen such as this from the day that the people came up out of the land of Egypt until this day.'" Her translation serves a hermeneutical emphasis: to highlight the woman who is the victim of terror.

30. *Ibid.*, p. 65.

31. *Ibid.*, pp. 80–81.

of her parts are mentioned in the text; this is a far cry from traditional Jewish respect for the dead.[32]

It is no coincidence that the instrument used to cut her up is called a *ma-achelet*, whose Hebrew root is the same as food (*ochel*). The Hebrew text of Judges 19 gave us the motive for the wife's leaving as *va-tizneh alav*,[33] which implies she played the harlot or was faithless and was thus implicated as the cause of her own physical endangerment. If this indeed is the reason for the violence that later befalls her, then this story can serve as a warning to all women to remain at home, even when things go bad with a marriage. That such violence can happen to women—even when one's husband is around—is functional to a patriarchal society. Fear of this violence forces women to restrict their movements. The message is that one should not stray (*va-tizneh*) from the private sphere of the home.

Abraham Sarteano, an Italian Hebrew poet of the Renaissance period and author of "The Misogynist,"[34] accuses the concubine "for the upheaval which followed her death and for the expulsion of the Benjaminites from the Hebrew nation." He also declares that Dinah deserved to be raped, and sympathizes with her rapist, blaming her for the destruction of the town of Shechem, all because "she went out." According to Adelman, not only do writers such as Sarteano "remove all male culpability from the biblical stories, but they often show more compassion for the male enemies of Israel than for the Jewish women, choosing male bonding over Jewish solidarity."[35]

In contrast to Sarteano's misogynist interpretation, the sages use this story as a warning to husbands not to terrorize their households. They comment on the text, "And his concubine played the harlot against him," to

---

32. See *ibid.*, p. 81 and footnotes 51 and 53 for more parallels.

33. Neither the Septuagint's reading of this as "she became angry with him" nor the English translation "she deserted him" do justice to the metaphoric sense of the word *zanah*. A woman who leaves her husband, is a *zonah*, just as Israel is a *zonah* when she leaves God. See the *She'ma*, which is recited daily. This will be developed in Chapter Four.

34. Sarteano is quoted by Howard Adelman in "Images of Women in Italian Jewish Literature," *Proceedings of the Tenth World Congress of Jewish Studies*, Division B, Volume II, *The History of the Jewish People* (Jerusalem: World Union of Jewish Studies, 1990), pp. 99–108.

35. *Ibid.*, pp. 100–101.

show the danger of the husband who finds too much fault with his wife,[36] thus causing her to run away from him and be guilty of harlotry.

R. Hisda said: A man should never terrorize his household. The concubine of Gibeah was terrorized by her husband and she was the cause of many thousands being slaughtered in Israel. Rab Judah said in the name of Rab: If a man terrorizes his household, he will eventually commit the three sins of unchastity (B. Gittin, 6b).[37]

The Sotah: The Case of the Jealous Husband

There is one more act of violence against women in the Pentateuch. It is found in a legal section of the Torah. In Numbers 5, we read the rule of the *sotah*, the case of the suspected adulteress.[38] The suspect is tested with an oath and an ordeal. First we are introduced to the case:

If any man's wife has gone astray and broken faith with him in that a man has had carnal relations with her unbeknown to her husband, and she keeps secret the fact that she has defiled herself without being forced, and there is no witness against her—but a fit of jealousy comes over him and he is wrought up about the wife who has defiled herself; or if a fit of jealousy comes over one and he is wrought up about his wife although she has not defiled herself—the man shall bring his wife to the priest . . . (Num. 5:12–15).

---

36. R. Abiathar said that the Levite found a fly with her, and R. Jonathan said that he found a hair on her. R. Abiathar soon afterward came across Elijah and said to him: "What is the Holy One, blessed be He, doing?" and he answered, "He is discussing the question of the concubine in Gibeah." "What does He say?" said Elijah: "[He says], My son Abiathar says So—and—so, and my son says So—and—so." Said R. Abiathar: "Can there possibly be uncertainty in the mind of the Heavenly One?" He replied: "Both [answers] are the word of the living God. He [the Levite] found a fly and excused it, he found a hair and did not excuse it." Rab Judah explained: He found a fly in his food and a hair *in loco concubitus*; the fly was merely disgusting, but the hair was dangerous. Some say, he found both in his food; the fly was not her fault, the hair was.

37. This *midrash* (B. Gittin, 6b) is referred to in Chapter Eight, since R. Hisda is quoted by Binyamin Ze'ev and others who oppose wifebeating or the terrorizing of one's household.

38. Although *halakha*, not narrative or metaphor, the assumption of this rule is related to the metaphor of man's control over women.

Thus, whether the wife is innocent or not—when there is no proof one way or the other—the jealous husband is told to bring his wife to the high priest. Then the ritual ordeal is prepared.

> The priest shall bring her forward and have her stand before the Lord. . . . [He] shall bare the woman's head and place upon her hands the meal offering of remembrance, which is a meal offering of jealousy. And in the priest's hands shall be the water of bitterness that induces the spell (Num. 5:16–18).

Before administering the waters, the priests takes an oath saying that if no man has lain with her, she will be immune to harm (and able to retain seed), but if she has gone astray and defiled herself

> "may the Lord make you a curse and an imprecation among your people, as the Lord causes your thigh to sag and your belly to distend; may this water that induces the spell enter your body, causing the belly to distend and the thigh to sag." And the woman shall say, "Amen, amen!" (Num. 5:21–22)

Thus according to the text the curse derives its strength from God, not the water, and the woman has to cooperate against herself in this ceremony. In baring her head, she is forced to perform an immodest act. In a sense she is being prejudged and there are no apologies if she is innocent. If she is guilty, the waters will work their effect within her causing "her belly to distend and her thigh shall sag; and the woman shall become a curse among her people" (Num. 5:27). If she is innocent, she passes the test and is cleared: "she shall be unharmed and able to retain seed" (Num. 5:28). The passage ends by stating:

> This is the ritual in cases of jealousy, when a woman goes astray while married to her husband and defiles herself, or when a fit of jealousy comes over a man and he is wrought up over his wife: the woman shall be made to stand before the Lord and the priest shall carry out all this ritual with her (Num. 5:29–30).

The priest is the medium through whom the sacred waters enter the *Sotah's* body. This case is reminiscent of the water test of a suspected witch: if the witch sinks, she is innocent; if she doesn't then she is guilty and sentenced to death.

In a postscript to this section it states that "the man shall be clear of guilt; but that woman shall suffer for her guilt" (Num. 5:31). According to Wegner, since only a wife can commit adultery, not the husband, it is a clear case of a double standard in action and the only case where rules of evidence are circumvented.[39] The husband is protected by the law; he has nothing to lose, only something to gain, by subjecting his wife to the ordeal. Either his suspicions will be proved and she will be punished, or his suspicions will prove to be false and then they can live happily ever after. No matter what, the woman will suffer for her alleged guilt. No thought, however, is given to her physical and mental anguish from the aftereffects of the ordeal and her husband's mistrust of her, and the "ganging up" on her by the community, priests, and God.

The Mishnah, in cognizance of a double standard, attempts to soften the effect of this law. Rabbi Yohanan ben Zakkai suspended the *sotah* ordeal because adulterers became too numerous to control.[40] Whatever the reason, the practice certainly fell into disuse after 70 C.E. when the Temple was destroyed, if not before. The rabbis in the first three chapters of Tractate *Sotah* argue that an accused woman should not have to drink the bitter waters, and even if she does have to drink them, she may have some merits that make the waters inoperative. Thus a woman who educates her children, supports her husband in his studies or who herself studies Torah might be able to ward off the effects.[41]

One might argue that this is not actually an act of violence against women[42]—that it is in fact a way of preventing violence, since in ancient times (and even today) a man who suspects his wife of betraying him will often kill her. Thus the woman is better off, since she "only" has to drink the bitter waters. Rachel Biale writes that

---

39. Judith Romney Wegner, *Chattel or Person? The Status of Women in the Mishnah* (Oxford: Oxford University Press, 1988), pp. 52–54.

40. B. Sotah 27b, M. Sotah 5:1.

41. See M. Sotah 3:4 and B. Sotah 20a about whether a woman should be taught Torah by her father. Learning might empower her with (dangerous) knowledge; thus she might not fear the consequences of adultery.

42. See H.C. Brichto, "The Case of the Sotah and a Reconsideration of Biblical 'Law'," *HUCA* 46: (1975): 55–70

the real purpose of the ordeal is not to convict adulterous women . . . but primarily to afford a way for women to clear themselves of suspicion. . . . The ordeal of the "bitter water" allows a fairly simple, safe way for a woman to clear her name with divine approval, sanctioned by the priest and the Temple ritual. . . . The ordeal is changed from a measure threatening women to a mechanism for their protection.[43]

Despite Biale's point, what we have here is a form of institutionalized violence, humiliation, and violation of a woman's body.

Women are threatened in any case. But, most importantly, this "law" is based on the metaphor of the husband's "owning" his wife and his power over her. The reason that only the wife is considered to have committed adultery is because the relationship is only one way: she is a possession. It is a concrete legal expression of all we have spelled out so far, and it is the first example of law reflecting metaphor. (See Chapter Four.)

Both God and the priest take the husband's side (even if it is ostensibly to protect a suspected adulteress from a jealous husband's vengeance) and force her, not him, to acquiesce and partake in this degrading and possibly painful ritual. To understand the psychological, if not physical, harm done a woman by this ritual, we should think of a modern day situation such as husbands returning from the battlefield routinely demanding to have their wives tested with a polygraph to determine if they were faithful while they were gone.[44]

The description of the suspected adulteress in the Bible demonstrates once again that the wife is the husband's sexual property[45] and that there is a lack of symmetry in the laws that pertain to husband and wife. She is publicly humiliated and has no alternatives but to acquiesce and undergo the ordeal.

We have seen woman as sex objects, woman as property, woman as tool. The image of the helpless woman of no intrinsic worth in relationship to a male lord and master becomes the image of the chosen people of Israel in relationship to an omnipotent god. This image is further developed in the prophetic writings to which we now turn.

---

43. Rachel Biale, *Women and Jewish Law* (New York: Schocken Books, 1984), p. 187.

44. See *Yoman haShavua* [Night News] August 20, 1982. During an evening of interviews, a polygraph was used to test Israeli wives and found them innocent.

45. Wegner, *Chattel or Person?*, p. 50.

3

A Prophetic Metaphor: God Is to Israel as Husband Is to Wife—The Metaphoric Battering of Hosea's Wife

The prophets hold a special and prominent place in Jewish tradition. Each week after the reading from the Five Books of the Torah (the Pentateuch) in the synagogue, an additional section is read, usually from the prophets, called the haftara. This tradition turns these prophetic selections into "liturgy," sections which are constantly repeated and known by all. The rabbis who initiated the custom may have wanted to make a religious statement that the writings of The Prophets, not only the Torah, are divinely inspired.[1] When the weekly portion became standardized, the haftara also became fixed. It served, among other things, as a sort of internal commentary on, or an elucidation of, the Torah portion itself.[2]

---

1. See the blessings surrounding the haftara reading.

2. For detailed information on the haftara tradition, see Joseph Jacobs, "Triennial Cycle," in *The Jewish Encyclopedia*, vol. 12 (New York: Funk and Wagnalls, 1917), pp. 254–257; Louis I. Rabinowitz, "Haftarah," in the *Encyclopedia Judaica*, vol. 6 (Jerusalem: Keter, 1971), pp. 1342–1345. Both entries have excellent bibliographies. See also Jacob Mann, *The Bible as Read and Preached in the Old Synagogue* (Cincinnati OH, Union of American Hebrew Congregations, 1940).

An example of this is the haftara accompanying the first portion of Numbers. The opening chapter of Numbers, *bammidbar* ("in the wilderness"), is a census of the Israelites during the wilderness period. The haftara, from Chapter 2 of Hosea, refers to "the multitudes of the people who are as the sands of the sea." Hosea's message is that the people no longer listen to God's word (*dabar*) and, if they do not shape up, they will be in danger of entering a spiritual wilderness (*midbar*). However, when (and if) the people of Israel will again be faithful to God (as they were during the period of the wilderness (*bammidbar*), God will renew His covenant with them. Hosea speaks for God and says:

> Assuredly, I will speak coaxingly to her
> And lead her through the wilderness [*midbar*]
> And speak [*dibbarti*] to her tenderly (Hos. 2:16).

There is an integral connection between the associative wordplay of the root *dbr*, which has to do with God's word, and the wilderness. The wordplay echoes important themes and serves as a rhetorical device that unites and connects the Haftara from Hosea with the Torah portion from Numbers.

THE MARRIAGE METAPHOR

Hosea was a prophet of the eighth century B.C.E. who, most commentators[3] believe, addressed himself to the Northern Kingdom of Israel. This kingdom, according to the Bible, was destined to be exiled because of its sins. Hosea describes God's relationship to Israel in metaphorical terms as a marriage. According to Gerson Cohen, such a marriage metaphor is not found in the literature of any other ancient religion besides Israel's. He writes, "The Hebrew God alone was spoken of as the lover and husband of His people, and only the house of Israel spoke of itself as the bride of the

---

3. We know next to nothing of Hosea ben Beeri's background, lineage, or locality—only the name of his father. Scholars who study these early periods have difficulties dating the work and identifying people, places, and events. It was common practice among some scholars to remove references to Judah in this book, since the consensus among scholars is that Hosea's audience is Israel and not Judah. See the "Introduction" in Francis I. Andersen and David Noel Freedman, *Hosea: A New Translation: The Anchor Bible* (New York: Doubleday, 1980), pp. 31–77, for a detailed background to this book.

Almighty."[4] Hosea's protagonist is himself, the husband who casts out his wife for being unfaithful to him and then takes her back—with the understanding that "she" will behave herself.[5]

Benjamin Scolnic, paraphrasing Gerson Cohen writes:

> God, not Ba' al, is Israel's husband and lover. . . . Since a wife's loyalty to her husband must be absolute and unwavering, it is a powerful analogy to the complete loyalty that God demands of the Israelites. The covenant between God and Israel made at Mount Sinai is a marriage; idolatry, which breaks the covenant, is adultery.[6]

God orders Hosea to marry Gomer, daughter of Diblaim, a promiscuous woman (*eshet zenunim*)[7] who, metaphorically speaking, is Israel, while Hosea is placed in the position of God. God/Hosea punishes Israel/Gomer for worshipping/committing adultery with other gods. However, because of "his" great love for "her," and "his" commitment to the covenant of marriage, "he" begs "her" to come back and restores "her" to "her" former state. Thus we have a male prophet, who represents a male God.[8]

This God, however, threatens the people for not worshipping Him exclusively. Though presumably the entire community, male and female

---

4. Gerson Cohen, "The Song of Songs and the Jewish Religious Mentality," *Studies in the Variety of Rabbinic Cultures* (Philadelphia: Jewish Publication Society, 1991), p. 6.

5. According to Harold Fisch, "Hosea more than any other book of the Bible . . . gives us God's side of the relationship. It is dominated by the first-person mode of address as God himself cries out, cajoles, reprimands, mourns and debates with himself. . . . Hosea gives us fundamentally the prophet's reflection of, or participation in, the divine pathos, as that pathos is directed toward man," who, in this case, is depicted as woman. (Fisch, "Hosea: A Poetics of Violence," *Poetry With a Purpose* (Bloomington, IN: Indiana University Press, 1990), p. 141. Fisch calls our attention to A.J. Heschel, *The Prophets* (Philadelphia: Jewish Publication Society, 1962), p. 27.

6. Benjamin Scolnic, "Bible Battering," *Conservative Judaism* (Fall 1992): 43.

7. See Phyllis Bird, "'To Play the Harlot': An Inquiry Into an Old Testament Metaphor," in *Gender and Difference in Ancient Israel*, ed. Peggy L. Day (Minneapolis, MN: Fortress Press, 1989), pp. 75–94. Bird writes, "Although the underlying metaphor is that of marriage, the use of the root *znh* rather than *n"p* serves to emphasize promiscuity rather than infidelity, 'wantonness' rather than violation of marriage contract or covenant" (p. 80).

8. Gerson Cohen writes, "The Bible unquestionably affirmed the masculinity of God and spoke of Him graphically as the husband. . . . By proclaiming His masculinity . . . Judaism affirmed His reality and . . . potency. . . . To such a person one could proclaim fealty, submission and love" ("The Song of Songs," p. 15).

alike, sins against God, the prophet has chosen to describe the people of Israel exclusively in terms of imagery which is feminine.

The standard interpretations of Hosea sympathize with the husband, who has put up with so much from this fickle woman and who desperately promises his wife everything if only she will return to him. The *midrash* depicts the relationship between God and His people in a poignant manner as a husband/master/God who cannot send His wife/subjects/people away, nor can He divorce her, for she, like Hosea's wife, has borne Him children. God says to Hosea that if

> Thou cannot even be sure that her children are yours, and yet you cannot separate from her, how, then, can I separate Myself from Israel, from My children. . . .[9]

God is seen here as all-forgiving, and the husband who cannot separate himself from his wife is the model after which Hosea is expected to pattern himself. In the *midrash*, there are several fables that depict God as a king who is angry with his wife, or as a father who is angry with his son. In these stories, there are "happy endings": the king buys his wife some jewelry and they presumably kiss and make up, despite his previous statements that he will divorce her; the father scolds his son for not going to school and then afterward invites him to dine with him.[10]

Despite the sympathetic overtones in the *midrash*, we see that in the biblical text the "poignant relationship" is achieved at a price. The possibility of violence in this intimate relationship is stated. We see it played out in a *midrash*, on the verse "If thou Lend money to any of My people" (Exod. 22:24), which compares God to a wifebeater. This *midrash* describes how, after Israel was driven from Jerusalem, their enemies said that God had no desire for His people. Jeremiah asked God if it was true that He had rejected His children:

> "Hast Thou Utterly rejected Judah? Hath Thy soul loathed Zion? Why hast Thou smitten us, and there is no healing for us?" (Jer. 14:19). It can

---

9. See B. Pesahim 87a-b. This passage is cited more fully in Chapter Four in the discussion of *kinyan*.

10. *Numbers Rabbah* 2:15, pp. 51–52. All English translations are from *The Midrash*, ed. H. Freedman and M. Simon (London: Soncino Press, 1983).

be compared to a man who was beating his wife. Her best friend asked him: "How long will you go on beating her? If your desire is to drive her out [of life], then keep on beating her till she dies; but if you do not wish her [to die], then why do you keep on beating her?" His reply was: "I will not divorce my wife even if my entire palace becomes a ruin." This is what Jeremiah said to God: "If Thy desire be to drive us out [of this world], then smite us till we die." As it says, "Thou canst not have utterly rejected us, and be exceedingly wroth against us!" [Lam. 5:22], but if this is not [Thy desire], then "Why hast Thou smitten us, and there is no healing for us?" God replied: "I will not banish Israel, even if I destroy my world," as it says, "Thus saith the Lord: If heaven above can be measured . . . then will I also cast off all the seed of Israel . . . [Jer. 31:37].[11]

This *midrash* depicts a zealous emotional bond that has developed between God and His people, which can be seen as resulting in Israel's being gradually taken prisoner during a pathological courtship that may result in annihilation.

The psychiatrist Judith Herman, in *Trauma and Recovery*,[12] describes a woman who becomes involved with a batterer and interprets his attention as a sign of love. The woman minimizes and excuses his behavior, because she cares for him. To avoid staying in this relationship, she will have to fight his protestations that "just one more sacrifice, one more proof of her love, will end the violence and save the relationship."[13] Herman writes that most women are trapped by the batterer because he appeals to "her most cherished values. It is not surprising, therefore, that battered women are often persuaded to return after trying to flee from their abusers."[14] This is precisely what the *midrash* has expressed in its interpretation of Jeremiah.

Turning back to Hosea, we see that our text details very explicitly a case of domestic abuse. We see this in the punitive measures Hosea plans to take. In verse 5, God/Hosea threatens to

---

11. *Exodus Rabbah* on Mishpatim 31:10, pp. 388–389. I am grateful to Howard Adelman for bringing this *midrash* to my attention.

12. Judith Herman, *Trauma and Recovery: The Aftermath of Violence From Domestic Abuse to Political Terror* (New York: Basic Books, 1992).

13. *Ibid.*, p. 83.

14. *Idem.*

strip her naked and leave her
as on the day she was born;
And I will make her like a wilderness,
render her like desert land,
and let her die of thirst.

In verse 8, God/Hosea threatens to

hedge up her roads with thorns
and raise walls against her.

In verse 11, God/Hosea says he will humiliate her by taking back

My new grain in its time
and My new wine in its season,
And I will snatch away My wool
and My linen that serve to cover her nakedness.

If this depicts the real state of Hosea/God's and Gomer/Israel's relationship, we have here a very troubled marriage. Gale A. Yee, in the new *Women's Bible Commentary*, writes that "Chapter Two pushes the marriage metaphor to dangerous limits, whereby [God's] legitimate punishment of Israel for breach of covenant is figuratively described as threats of violence against the wife."[15] Hosea begins with the threats to strip her naked. These threats escalate with the children being abused by association with the mother's shamelessness. The next thing he does is to isolate his wife from her lovers by "building a wall against her," so that she is totally dependent on her husband. Then he withholds food from her and publicly humiliates her by uncovering her nakedness.[16]

---

15. Gale A. Yee, "Hosea," in *The Women's Bible Commentary*, ed. Carol A. Newsome and Sharon H. Ringe (Louisville, KY: Westminster, 1992), p. 199.

16. Ilana Pardes, *Countertraditions in the Bible* (Cambridge, MA: Harvard University Press, 1992), writes, "To further understand the sin and punishment, one needs to bear in mind that 'uncovering the nakedness' is a biblical expression designating illicit sexual relations (from incest to adultery). Conversely, 'covering the nakedness,' as is evident in both Hosea 2:11 and Ezekiel 16:8, is a synonym for marriage" (p. 134).

Many biblical scholars and rabbis do not view this harshly. For example, Benjamin Scolnic's reaction to Hosea 2 is that it is "just a metaphor" never intended to be taken seriously or carried out.[17]

However, F.I. Andersen and D.N. Freedman, the commentators on Hosea in the Anchor Bible series, are not so sure that Hosea's threats are benign. They hint that God's threats of death in Hosea 2:5 (see above) might have been carried out when the people betrayed God in Hosea 6:5.[18]

That is why I hacked them with my prophets;
I killed them with the words of my mouth.
My judgment goes forth like the sun (Hos. 6:5).

Scolnic, however, minimizes these threats, viewing them as an act of prophetic desperation. These threats, he writes, are "about love, not wife-battering. They are about forgiveness, not punishment . . . [The perspective is] of a man who has the right to . . . strip her, humiliate her, etc., but doesn't and, instead, seeks reconciliation."[19] The commentators of the Anchor Bible disagree that these passages are just some mild form of verbal abuse. They write, "the passage expresses both an ardent will to reconciliation and an indignant determination to use coercive or punitive measures to correct or even to destroy her."[20]

One can argue that by using the marriage metaphor we are allowed to glimpse the compassionate side of God.[21] Because of the intimate relation-

---

17. "I don't mean to pretend that this isn't rough stuff. But we must remember that this really is a metaphor understood . . . by the Israelites *as a metaphor.* . . . I will not hide behind the notion that since this is all 'just a metaphor' or polemic against *Ba'al* worship, we don't have to take the words themselves seriously. But there is never a chance that any of the things threatened here will be carried out" (Scolnic, "Bible-Battering," pp. 47–48). Scolnic's article was written as a response and companion piece to my article "The Haftorah Tradition and the Metaphoric Battering of Hosea's Wife," *Conservative Judaism* (Fall 1992): 29–42. This article was later revised and appears in *A Feminist Companion to the Latter Prophets*, ed. A. Brenner (Sheffield, UK: Sheffield Academic Press, 1995), pp. 126–145.

18. Andersen and Freedman, write about Hosea 2:5 that "A fourth possible stage, death, threatened in verse 5, is apparently never reached (but see 6:5)" (F.I. Anderson and D.N. Freedman, Hosea, p. 129).

19. Scolnic, "Bible Battering," p. 48.

20. Andersen and Freedman, Hosea, p. 128.

21. We can only guess what the marriage metaphor meant in Hosea's day. We, however, view the marriage metaphor through our eyes and see how it came to be used and abused in later generations.

ship, God is more accessible to His people. Not only do we have descriptions of an intimate relationship with God, but, also, we have allusions to the idyllic, pre-expulsion relationship of equality between God and humanity.[22]

> In that day, I will make a covenant for them with the beasts of the field, the birds of the air, and the creeping things of the ground. . . . And I will espouse you with faithfulness; then you shall [know (*yada*) God intimately] (Hos. 2:20-22).

However, unlike the relationship between Adam and Eve, the relationship between God and Israel is one-sided. God would like the uncomplicated pre-expulsion relationship, before the people "knew" (*yada*) about choice. God promises the returning nation an intimate covenantal relationship with Him despite the fact that knowledge (*da'at*) was the reason Adam and Eve were punished (see Gen. 3).

Jeremiah, too, depicts a God who loved his young, eager, naive Israel, yet turns on His people when "she" grows up and wants some independence. When God decides to espouse Israel forever with faithfulness, it is so that the people will "know" (*yada*) only God. If Israel wants to know more than just God, if she wants to take fruit from the tree again, the implication is that she will again be expelled from the Garden of Eden, stripped naked and left as on the day "she" was created—with nothing (Hos. 2:5). God is telling Israel/Gomer that she can either be intimate with Him (her husband) or with other gods/lovers but not with both of them at the same time. She can have knowledge of good and evil from Him or from others. If she chooses others, He will destroy her. So despite the potential glimpse of a compassionate God, He is accessible to His people only on His own terms.[23]

---

22. In Genesis 1:27, male and female are created in one act. I am not in complete accord with Trible's "depatriarchalizing" of Genesis 2–3. See Phyllis Trible, "Depatriarchalizing in Biblical Interpretation," in *The Jewish Woman: New Perspectives*, ed. Elizabeth Koltun (New York: Schocken Press, 1976), pp. 217–240.

23. It is worthwhile comparing Hosea to the *Song of Songs*, which is probably the only completely nonsexist account of a relationship between a man and a woman. There are echoes of this relationship in Hosea 2:9. Van Dijk-Hemmes argues that there is an intertextual relationship between the two texts and that, if we "re-place the 'quotations' back into the love-songs from which they were borrowed, the vision of the woman in this text is restored." To see how she develops this idea, see Fokkelien Van Dijk-Hemmes, "The Imagination of Power and the Power of Imagination: An Intertextual Analysis of Two Biblical Love Songs: The Song of Songs and Hosea 2," *Journal for the Study of the Old Testament*, no 44 (1990): 86.

Finally, one can argue that the marriage metaphor is "only a metaphor" and the motif of sexual violence is "only a theme of the metaphor." H.L. Ginsberg, in his articles on Hosea,[24] has pointed out that Hosea's important innovation is the "husband and wife allegory."

> The doctrine of God's jealousy and His insistence that His covenant partner Israel worship no other gods beside Him [is a] factor favorable to the birth of such an allegory. . . . This, however, was heavily outweighed by a horror of associating sexuality with God, and only the need of the . . . hour overcame this inhibition to the extent of giving rise to the wife metaphor, or allegory. . . .[25]

In his discussion of the commentators on Hosea, Ginsberg writes that the rabbis of the Talmud "accepted literally the divine command to Hosea to marry a prostitute,"[26] and that Rashi was still satisfied with such a view. But Ginsberg's sympathy is clearly with Ibn Ezra, Kimhi, and Maimonides, who maintained that the story was "but accounts of prophetic visions."[27] Even if we accept Ginsberg's view that Hosea is not a real description of a husband/wife relationship but *only* a metaphorical, allegorical vision, that does not mean that such metaphoric imagery has no power, no force. As many have pointed out, it is no longer possible to argue that a metaphor is less for being a metaphor. On the contrary, metaphor has power over people's minds and hearts. As Lakoff and Turner write,

> . . . For the same reasons that schemas and metaphors give us power to conceptualize and reason, so they have power over us. Anything that we rely on constantly, unconsciously, and automatically is so much part of us that it cannot be easily resisted, in large measure because it is barely even noticed. To the extent that we use a conceptual schema or a conceptual metaphor, we accept its validity. Consequently, when someone else uses it, we are predisposed to accept its validity. For this reason, conventionalized schemas and metaphors have *persuasive* power over us.[28]

---

24. H.L. Ginsberg, "Studies in Hosea 1–3," in *Yehezkel Kaufmann Jubilee Volume*, ed. Menachem Haran (Jerusalem: Magnes Press, 1960), pp. 50–69, English Section; *JBL*, 80 (1961): 339–347, "Hosea, Book of," in *Encyclopedia Judaica*, vol. 8 (Jerusalem: Keter Publishing House, 1972), pp. 1010–1025.

25. H.L. Ginsberg, "Hosea, Book of," p. 1016.

26. *Ibid.*, p. 1011.

27. *Ibid.*, p. 1012.

28. George Lakoff and Mark Turner, *More Than Cool Reason: A Field Guide to Poetic Metaphor* (Chicago, IL: University of Chicago Press, 1989), pp. xi, 9, 63.

One of the side effects of thinking metaphorically is that we often disregard the differences between the two dissimilar objects being compared. One source of metaphor's power lies precisely in that we tend to lose sight of the fact that it is "just" a metaphor. What this means in our case, writes Renita J. Weems, is that "God is no longer *like* a husband; God *is* a husband." If "God's covenant with Israel is like a marriage, . . . then a husband's physical punishment against his wife is as warranted as God's punishment of Israel."[29]

DANGEROUS ASSUMPTIONS

In this case, the marriage metaphor became part of Jewish religious understanding and rhetoric to account for Israel's destiny: her being chosen by God and her later exile from the land. Jewish theology attempts to comfort the people by linking her behavior (idolatry) to her punishment. Thus God's actions are not arbitrarily cruel. There is a reason for them: the people have sinned. However, what may work as a theological explanation is bad for human relationships, especially when one partner is stronger than the other.

We have already seen two aspects of the metaphor used by the prophets as inherent in the halakhic conception of marriage; namely, that only the wife/Israel can go astray, and that the husband/God, in some sense "owns" the wife as a result of the marriage bond. The marriage metaphor became a favorite both in the classic period and in contemporary times. The first classic example appears in a *midrash* that connects the Torah portion of Numbers to the Haftara from Hosea. The purpose of this *midrash* is to describe God's unquenchable love for Israel.

R. Hanina said, "Only in ignorance could one think that what He meant by saying 'I will not be to you' was that He would not be to you for a God. That is certainly not the meaning; what then does the phrase, 'and I will not be to you,' mean? It means that even though you would not be My people and would seek to separate yourselves from Me, yet 'I will not be to you'; i.e., My mind will not be the same as yours, but in spite of yourselves you will be My people . . . 'As I live, saith the Lord God, surely with a mighty hand, and with an outstretched arm, and with fury poured

---

29. Renita J. Weems, "Gomer: Victim of Violence or Victim of Metaphor?" *Semeia,* no 47 (1989): 100. She is quoting Sally McFague, *Metaphorical Theology* (Philadelphia: Fortress, 1982).

out, will I be king over you' (Ezek. 20:33). All this teaches us of God's affection for Israel.[30]

One can look at this extraordinary proclamation in two ways:

1. Positively, as a sign of God's devotion; no matter what the people does He still loves them. Or:
2. Negatively, as a sign of psycho-pathology. God's sense of selfhood is so entangled with controlling his people that the possibility that they might reject him cannot be countenanced. There is no mutuality or room for dialogue.

This is all against "her" (the people's) will. There has been no discussion, no ending of mutual recriminations. "He" does not recognize the writing on the wall. "She" does not want "him," she has had it with "him"; sick of "his" mighty hand, outstretched arm, and fury. She has decided to leave him, but he refuses to face facts. To him marriage means "I will espouse you to me forever," even if it does not work out. She feels she has no option, that she is trapped in the marriage.

The contemporary *midrash* is that of Rabbi Shlomo Riskin.[31] His *midrash* is on *The Song of Songs*, generally considered to be an allegorical depiction of the mutual love of God and Israel:

> When God knocks in the middle of the night, He wants the Jewish people to let Him in and end their long exile. . . . But the nation answers . . . that it is too difficult to dirty oneself by joining God in His Land, stepping into the "mud" of a struggling country. . . . Rejected, God removes His hand from the latch. . . . Only then does the nation grasp the significance of her hesitation and her innards begin to turn as she rises to open the door. Unfortunately, her actions, because she is smothered in perfume, are dull and heavy, her arms and fingers dripping with cold cream and Chanel No. 5. By the time the latch is opened, God is gone, and she goes on searching desperately everywhere for her beloved.[32]

---

30. *Numbers Rabbah* (Vilna) 2:16 (p. 53 in Freedman and Simon, *The Midrash*).

31. Riskin writes a weekly column "Shabbat Shalom" for *The Jerusalem Post*, which at the time was the only daily English newspaper in Israel. Riskin's weekly column appears in the popular overseas edition as well.

32. *The Jerusalem Post* (13 April 1990). ·

Here Riskin, in his reading of the *Song of Songs*, has chosen to use the metaphor of a sinning woman to depict the entire nation (both men and women!), which does not heed God's call to settle in the Land of Israel. He does this without being in the least cognizant of the antifemale bias of the metaphor. The ancient metaphor—God as male and the sinning people as female—is alive and well in present day rabbinical thinking.[33]

Behind all of these passages is the assumption that God is an aggressive, domineering being who is master over His passive, female, adoring people. There is a need to eradicate the self through an intense sexual relationship. The implication is that in order to find God one must sacrifice one's sense of self-hood.[34]

But this type of thinking is dangerous both to women and to society in general. I argue, along with other feminist commentators,[35] that the language of Hosea, and the other prophets and rabbis who use "objectified female sexuality as a symbol of evil,"[36] has had damaging effects on women. Women who read of God's relationship with Israel through the prism of a

---

33. Shlomo Riskin in "The Almighty waits for our return," in his "Shabbat Shalom" column of *The Jerusalem Post* (23 August 1996) suggests that there might be some problems with the God-Israel relationship being akin to a groom-bride relationship. Riskin hints at the theological problematics of the analogy of the husband/wife relationship and the impossibility of divorcing (or being divorced by) God and the halakhic problem of "our being taken back by God after having betrayed Him." He suggests instead that "we can always be comforted by a God-Israel relationship akin to parent-child, secure in the knowledge that, despite our immoral backsliding, the God of the Covenant waits with outstretched arms for us to return to an ever-ready embrace."

34. This message is familiar to women.

35. See J. Cheryl Exum, "The Ethics of Biblical Violence Against Women," in *The Bible in Ethics*, ed. John W. Rogerson, et al., *JSOT* Supplement Series 207 (Sheffield, UK: Sheffield Academic Press, 1995), pp. 248–271.

36. T. Drorah Setel, "Prophets and Pornography: Female Sexual Imagery in Hosea," in *Feminist Interpretation of the Bible*, ed. Letty Russell (Philadelphia: Westminster, 1985), p. 86. Tikva Frymer-Kensky recognizes the problematic nature of our text and the marriage metaphor, but is not willing to accept that the negative portrayal of Israel-as-wife rises from misogyny. She writes that, except for Ecclesiastes, "there are no overt anti-woman statements in the Hebrew Bible. . . . [although] the depiction of the Wanton City-woman is the most truly negative portrayal of any female in the Bible." But she stresses that the prophets' anger is directed against the people (city) and not the women. She admits, however, that "the intensity of these passages and their sexual fantasies of nymphomania and revenge seem to be fueled by unconscious fear and rage" [p. 150 of "The Wanton Wife of God," *In the Wake of Goddesses* (New York: The Free Press, 1992), pp. 144–152].

misogynist male prophet or rabbinical commentator, and have religious sensibilities, are forced to identify against themselves.[37] Fokkelien van Dijk-Hemmes asks the salient question:

> Why is Israel, first the land but then also the nation, represented in the image of a faithless wife, a harlot and not in the image of e.g. a rapist? This would have been more justified when we look at Israel's misdeeds, which YHWH/Hosea points out in the following 4:1–5:7. . . . And beyond that, it is the men who are held responsible for social and religious abuses; it is the priests who mislead the people (4:4–6) and the fathers who force their daughters to play the harlot (4:13–14).[38]

Why did it not occur to Riskin to say that "Israel was too busy fiddling with his computers or tinkering with his cars or watching football on the Sabbath to have time to pay attention to God"?

The problem is that the ancient metaphors of marriage, in order to emphasize God's love, take for granted the patriarchal view of women's subservient role. They represent God's punishment of Israel as justice. According to Ilana Pardes, God's severe response to Israel is "almost moderate, given her ingratitude. One is expected to take pity on God for having to play such a violent role, for having to suffer so for the sake of Law and Order."[39] Prophets and rabbis should not be enshrining the legal subordination of women in metaphor.[40] In my view, love, punishment, and subservience are not compatible concepts.

Why should this concern us at all, since presumably the metaphor *only* expresses the social reality of the biblical period? In fact one can argue that

---

37. Mayer I. Gruber, "The Motherhood of God in Second Isaiah," *Revue Biblique* 3 (1983): 358, writes that Jeremiah and Ezekiel "intimated that in the religion of Israel maleness is a positive value . . . while femaleness is a negative value with which divinity refuses to identify itself." In "The Wanton Wife of God," p. 152, Frymer-Kensky writes that "the marital metaphor reveals the dramatic inner core of monotheism: the awesome solo mastery of God brings humans into direct unadulterated contact with supreme power . . . in this relationship, the people stand directly before and with God. . . . There is only us and God." Clearly the relationship is awesome, but to the battered wife/people, there is something frightening about there being no buffer or intercessor between us and a God who is depicted as a vengeful husband.

38. van Dijk-Hemmes, "The Imagination of Power," p. 85.

39. Pardes, *Countertraditions*, p. 136.

40. Judith Plaskow, *Standing Again at Sinai: Judaism From a Feminist Perspective* (San Francisco: Harper and Row, 1990), p. 6.

understanding "the historical setting of prophetic texts may provide a perspective of 'moral realism' which allows them to be read as sacred writing."[41] However, the argument for an historical setting recedes if we realize that, because of the sanctification of Hosea 2 in a fixed haftara, it plays a role in perpetuating biblical patriarchalism into our own day.[42] Because of its morally flawed allegory, the message of the prophets can be understood as permitting husbands to abuse their wives psychologically and physically.[43]

PROBLEMATIC RELATIONSHIP

An argument for the continuance of this fixed haftara in the tradition might be that of its so-called "happy end." If we examine God's declaration of love to "his" people superficially, it appears to be a monogamous declaration by God to "his" formerly faithless people. Hosea 2:16-22 goes as follows:

> I will speak coaxingly to her
> and lead her through the wilderness
> and speak to her tenderly. . . .
> There she shall submit[44] as in the days of her youth, when she came up
> from the land of Egypt.
> And in that day—declares the Lord—

---

41. Setel, "Prophets and Pornography," p. 95.

42. In "The Haftarah Tradition and the Metaphoric Battering of Hosea's Wife," *Conservative Judaism* (Fall 1992): 40, I suggested a possible alternative reading, based on the triennial list available to us from the *Genizah*. Isaiah 43:19–21 is a non-sexist account of God's relationship with Israel and refers to the desert period in the context of God's lining the desert with rivers for His chosen people.

43. See Plaskow, *Standing Again*, p. 6. See also Gruber, "Motherhood of God," who concludes his article by saying: ". . . a religion which seeks to convey the Teaching of God who is above and beyond both sexes cannot succeed in conveying that Teaching if it seeks to do so in a manner which implies that a postitive-divine value is attached only to one of the two sexes" (p. 35).

44. The usual translation of this word is "respond." However, Pamela Gordon and Harold C. Washington, "Rape as a Military Metaphor in the Hebrew Bible," in *A Feminist Companion to the Latter Prophets*, ed. Athalya Brenner (Sheffield, UK: Sheffield Academic Press, 1995), argue that we can translate it as submit, be humbled, be bent (p. 314). I tend to agree, having myself understood the root *ayin, nun, heh* to have the meaning of rape. See Naomi Graetz, "Dinah the Daughter," in *A Feminist Companion to Genesis*, ed. Athalya Brenner (Sheffield, UK: Sheffield Academic Press, 1993), p. 307, note 1.

you will call [Me] *Ishi* [husband],
and no more will you call Me *Ba'ali*.
For I will remove
the names of the *Ba'alim* from her mouth,
and they shall nevermore be mentioned by name.
In that day, I will make a covenant for them with the beasts of the field, the
birds of the air, and the creeping things of the ground; I will also banish
bow, sword, and war from the land. Thus I will let them lie down in safety.
And I will espouse you forever:
I will espouse you with righteousness and justice,
and with goodness and mercy,
and I will espouse you with faithfulness;
Then you shall be devoted to [*yadat et*] the Lord.

One might claim that in a polytheistic society, the assumption of total
faithfulness on God's part and the demand of faithfulness to a single God on
the people's part was revolutionary. The prophet's use of the marriage metaphor, "You will call [Me] *ishi* [my man/husband], is a new vision of a God
who will not tolerate a polygamous association. And no more will you call
me *Ba'ali* [my husband/lord/master]. For I will remove the names of the
Ba'alim [pagan gods]. . . ."[45] The monogamous aspect of marriage on the
part of the husband is clearly unusual, but it still does not address the problematics involved in monogamy when one side controls the other.

> Mary Joan Winn Leith argues that
> The rejected form of address, *Ba'al*, implies not only a different deity,
> but also a different, more dominating relationship. . . . God's new title,
> "husband" [*ishi*], signals a new beginning, a new betrothal, and a
> (re)new(ed) covenant, whose inauguration sounds strikingly like a
> (re)creation of the world.[46]

There is a terrible assumption here in Leith's argument. Israel has to *suffer* in order to be entitled to this new betrothal: "she" has to be battered into
submission in order to kiss and make up at the end. She has to agree to be on

---

45. There is a *double entendre* here, since *Ba'al* can be also understood to mean husband.

46. Mary Joan Winn Leith, "Verse and Reverse: The Transformation of the Woman,
Israel, in Hosea, 1–3," in *Gender and Difference in Ancient Israel*, ed. Peggy L. Day (Minneapolis, MN: Fortress Press, 1989), p. 101.

the receiving end of her husband's jealousy. The premise is that a woman has no other choice but to remain in such a marriage. True, God is very generous to Israel. He promises to espouse her forever with righteousness, justice, goodness, mercy, and faithfulness. But despite the potential for a new model of a relationship between God and Israel, it is not a model of real reciprocity. It is based on suffering and the assumption that Israel will submit to God's will. Hosea, however, rejoices in this transformation and in the "ordeal [which] has fit the woman for a new, enhanced relationship with God."[47]

The reader who is caught up in this new betrothal and renewed covenant overlooks the fact that this joyous reconciliation between God and Israel follows the exact pattern of abusive relationships that battered wives know so well.[48] Israel is physically and psychologically punished, abused, and then seduced into remaining in the covenant by tender words and caresses. The religious images may be as beautiful and profound as Leith has pointed out, but, as Yee writes,

> studies have shown that many wives remain in abusive relationships because periods of mistreatment are often followed by intervals of kindness and generosity. This ambivalent strategy reinforces the wife's dependence on the husband. During periods of kindness, her fears are temporarily eased so that she decides to remain in the relationship; then the cycle of abuse begins again.[49]

God is not suggesting a full-fledged partnership, despite his declarations. Hosea's portrayal of Israel as a sinning woman returning abjectly to the open arms of her husband who graciously accepts her—after her great suffering, and providing she repents—has limited the potential of the relationship. Thus, the prophet's marriage metaphor is problematic. It makes its theological point at the expense of women and contracts rather than expands the potential of partnership.

---

47. *Ibid.*, p. 103.

48. See Vietta Helm's "New Domestic Violence Wheel," in which she re-examines the cycle of violence in all its phases. An electronic mail communication dated Tue, July 2, 1996, from fivers@athens.net (a moderated list for professionals and interested scholars in domestic violence).

49. Gail A. Yee, "Hosea," in *The Women's Bible Commentary*, ed. C.A. Newsom and S.H. Ringe (Louisville, KY: Westminster, 1992), p. 200.

One might argue that Jewish tradition did try to expand the potential partnership. This can be seen in the assumption that Jewish males gain sensitivity from their obligation to recite the concluding phrases from the haftara (Hos. 2.21–2) when they put on their *tefillin* [phylacteries] every morning.

What does it mean to daily identify with a woman's position? For that is what the male does. The male wraps the bands of the *tefillin* around his middle finger—almost like a wedding ring. He repeats the words God says to his bride. He affirms and re-affirms his binding relationship with God. Clearly God is binding Himself to Israel as a groom binds himself to his bride. The male who puts on *tefillin* identifies with the bride. Since the male (identifying with the female) is in a subservient relationship to God in this daily re-run of the ritual of marriage, does he gain any insight from this experience which forces him to subconsciously reverse roles? Can this ritual act be a basis for re-interpreting Hosea?

REINTERPRETING HOSEA

There are two midrashim that shed light on this question. One of them, a *midrash* on a verse from Parashat Ekeb (Deut. 7:12), looks promising as a basis for reinterpretation. This *midrash* connects the covenant between God and Abraham with the marriage of a king and a noble lady who brings two valuable gems into the house. In this partnership type of relationship she brings gems and he also brings gems. When she loses the gems, he takes away his. When she finds them, he restores his and decrees that,

> a crown should be made of both sets of gems and that it should be placed on the head of the noble lady. . . . God, too, set up two gems corresponding to them, namely, loving kindness and mercy. . . . Israel lost hers. . . . God thereupon took away His. . . . And after Israel has restored hers and God has given back His, God will say, "Let both pairs be made into a crown and be placed on the head of Israel," as it is said, "And I will betroth thee unto Me, yea, I will betroth thee unto Me in righteousness and in justice, and in loving kindness, and in compassion. And I will betroth thee unto Me in faithfulness; and thou shalt know the Lord" (Hos. 2:21).[50]

---

50. *Deuteronomy Rabbah* (Ekeb) 3:7, in *The Midrash*, ed. Freedman and Simon, pp. 75–76.

The greater context of this *midrash* is that of Deuteronomy. In this book Israel is constantly being berated and threatened by God. If Israel behaves as God demands, Israel will be treated well. If Israel strays from the narrow path, Israel will be punished. However, the rabbis have made a tremendous conceptual leap forward by allowing us to imply from the relationship that God has with Abraham a potential relationship a man might have with his wife.[51]

However, in another, less-promising *midrash*, which connects the passage "For the Lord your God is a consuming fire, an impassioned God [*el kana*]" from Deut. 4:24 with the passage, "I will espouse you with faithfulness" (Hos. 2:21), we have a different kind of relationship: God as a jealous husband. In contrast to those who merit the next world [*olam habba*] are those who are consumed by a great fire. The rabbis ask, How do we know that God is jealous? The answer is, just as a husband is jealous of his wife, so is the God of Israel.[52] Thus, the use of the *tefillin* ritual could become a means of reinterpreting the haftara from Hosea only if it is accompanied by specific interpretation.

THEOLOGICAL IMPLICATIONS

It is almost a truism to speak of God as having the power and authority to control and possess. However, it is theologically debatable whether God wants to use this power to interfere in our lives. Unfortunately, the prophets persisted in representing God as having and wanting the same authority to control and possess that a husband has traditionally had over his wife, including control over her food, possessions, and earnings. This metaphor expressed the hierarchy of husband and wife in the patriarchal society, and elevated that hierarchy to a theological tenet, a description of how God meant the world to be. In this hierarchy, the woman can always be suspected, as we saw in the case of the *sotah* (Chapter Two). The assumption is that the husband can use the absolute and arbitrary power entrusted to him to question his wife's loyalty. These biblical metaphors are basic to the mentality of men and women in Jewish society and can find concrete expression in Jewish law, *halakha*, which rules their lives.

---

51. See a forthcoming work by Michael Graetz for further discussion and development of this *midrash*.

52. Midrash Tanhuma (Warsaw), Parashat *t'zav* 14:1 [Hebrew].

4

The Connection Between Metaphor and Halakha

FORMATION OF METAPHOR

Myth [*aggadah*], narrative, or metaphor play a central role in forming the mindset of rabbis who create and apply Jewish law [*halakha*] or *nomos* to the life of the Jewish community.[1] The reciprocal relationship between *aggadah/* narrative/metaphor and *halakha*/Jewish law/*nomos* is a central issue in this book. Robert Cover, in his article "*Nomos* and Narrative" insisted that, "for every constitution there is a epic, for each decalogue a scripture."[2] Rules are embedded in the narrative and are equal partners in the evolution of law and

---

1. Robert Cover discusses the categories "nomos" and "narrative" in his seminal paper, "The Supreme Court, 1982 Term-Foreword: *Nomos* and Narrative," *Harvard Law Review* 97:1 (1983). Rachel Adler summarizes part of Cover's article in "Feminist Folktales of Justice: Robert Cover as a Resource for the Renewal of Halakha," *Conservative Judaism* XLV:3 (1993): 41. "Law is not reducible only to formal lawmaking, Cover maintains, because it is generated by a *nomos*, a universe of meanings, values and rules, embedded in stories. A *nomos* is not a body of data to master and adapt, but a world to inhabit. Knowing how to live in a nomic world means being able to envision the possibilities implicit in its stories and norms and being willing to live some of them out in praxis."

2. Cover, as cited in Gordon Tucker, "The Sayings of the Wise are Like Goads: An Appreciation of the Works of Robert Cover," *Conservative Judaism* XLV: 3 (1993): 4.

custom. Law does not exist in a vacuum. It is given guidelines by the beliefs and metaphors that constitute our shared experiences; that is, our communal "script."[3]

Metaphor is not only words, and it is not only similarity. It is basic to how we think about all human concerns and a necessary tool that we use automatically to express our thoughts. Conceptual metaphors about life, love, death, and relationships are "part of the way members of a culture have of conceptualizing their experience."[4]

Prophets and law-makers, among others, as members of their cultures, use metaphors to communicate. Successful communication and the vitality of metaphor depend on "its reliance on shared moral assumptions, and its ability to convey to the reader or hearer the existence of some similarity between the metaphorical image and what it is meant to explain."[5] The success of the prophets and law-makers depends on their ability to extend their "moral revulsion from the primary realm of the metaphor to the realm it represents—that is, from the relations among human beings to the relations between them and God."[6] In the process, there is an intentional blurring of the "primary distinction that ostensibly exists between them and God [which] transforms God into a fellow human being."[7]

The beliefs of prophets and law-makers are part of the formulation of metaphor. Metaphor is a basic building block of the description of and the human conception of reality. Behavior is predicated on an understanding of reality. People do what they think is expected of them to live out their lives in accordance with their vision of "what should be." Behavior in relations between men and women are highly dependent on perceptions of the other as "male" or "female," and thus our basic metaphoric handling of these categories informs all behavior.

Why does a writer choose a particular metaphor? A metaphor is useful only if it expresses the author's perception of reality and human interaction. The right metaphor sharpens and organizes thoughts, which the author then

---

3. *Ibid.*, p. 24.

4. George Lakoff and Mark Turner, *More Than Cool Reason: A Field Guide to Poetic Metaphor* (Chicago: University of Chicago Press, 1989), p. 9.

5. Moshe Halbertal and Avishai Margalit, "Idolatry and Betrayal," in *Idolatry*, trans. Naomi Goldblum (Cambridge, MA: Harvard University Press, 1992), p. 10.

6. *Ibid.*

7. *Idem.*

uses to influence his audience so that they will adopt his perspective. The belief system is often shared by the audience, otherwise the metaphor doesn't usually work.[8]

Once the metaphor has been composed, it is learned and gets to be used "automatically, effortlessly, and even unconsciously."[9] The metaphor becomes so much part of us that "we accept its validity. Consequently, when someone else uses it, we are predisposed to accept its validity. For this reason, conventionalized schemas and metaphors have *persuasive* power over us."[10] It is often impossible to distinguish between the metaphor and reality.

According to Lakoff and Turner, there are five sources of the power of metaphor: the power to structure; the power of options; the power of reason; the power of evaluation; and, the power of being there.[11] Because they are there, available as tools, they are hard to question. Once in the public domain, metaphor is out of control of its creator, and, according to Moran, "will lead the mind in unanticipated directions. It is possible to get more out of it than one has explicitly put into it. The audience as well may engage in interpretation of the metaphor that is an exploratory elaboration of it, and which involves attention to the word rather than to the speaker."[12]

The sociologist Nisbet wrote of "the power and danger of metaphor when taken not as analogy but as attribute of reality,"[13] and Moran wrote that "part of the dangerous power of a strong metaphor is its control over one's thinking at a level beneath that of deliberation or volition."[14] Metaphor works by moving from the better-known concrete object to the lesser-known abstraction. It is a process that compares and extends meaning to encompass

8. Richard Moran, "Seeing and Believing: Metaphor, Image, and Force," *Critical Inquiry,* no 16:1 (1989): 107-109.

9. Lakoff and Turner, *More Than Cool Reason*, p. 62.

10. *Ibid.*, p. 63.

11. *Ibid.*, pp. 64–65.

12. Moran, "Seeing and Believing," p. 109.

13. Nisbet (1969:6), quoted in Tom Craig Darrand and Anson Shupe, *Metaphors of Social Control in a Pentecostal Sect* (Lewiston, NY: Edwin Mellen Press, 1983), p. 20.

14. Moran, "Seeing and Believing," p. 90.

the similarity of difference.[15] Yet, metaphor is doomed to fail in its attempt to describe the lesser-known (in our case, the divine), and ultimately highlights the disparity of the two realms being depicted.[16]

According to Susan Niditch:

> . . . metaphoric texts are rich indicators of their composers' mythology, of shared cultural values and aspects of world-view symbolically represented. Myths and metaphors if properly read may be the truest indicators of essential perceptions of existence.[17]

METAPHOR AND BATTERING

In Chapters Two and Three, we saw examples of the metaphoric abuse of women in the Jewish tradition. It does not matter that some of these texts do not deal with *actual* battering of woman. Carol Newsom, in an article dealing with female imagery, writes that texts that use symbolic language referring to women influence the behavior of the group of people that reads these texts.[18] The institution of marriage is the context in which wifebeating takes place, and the history of marriage allows for, and sanctions, a relationship between a submissive wife and a demanding husband. According to Andrea

---

15. "This semantic process involves the cooperation of two elements, a vehicle and a tenor. The vehicle is the base of metaphor, the better known element, while the tenor is its underlying (or overarching) subject, the lesser known element. The sense of the metaphor results from the interaction of vehicle and tenor, an interaction that varies with different metaphors. For instance, vehicle and tenor may call attention to each other equally, or one may highlight the other. Nevertheless, both are essential for the comparison; neither is an embellishment. Together they produce new meanings that are not available through the individual elements. Though clearly distinguishable, vehicle and tenor constitute the unit that is itself a metaphor." [(Phyllis Trible, *God and the Rhetoric of Sexuality* (Philadelphia: Fortress Press, 1978), p. 17. She uses I.A. Richards, *The Philosophy of Rhetoric* (London: Oxford University Press, 1936), pp. 89–138; and Philip Wheelwright, *Metaphor and Reality* (Bloomington, IN: Indiana University Press, 1962), pp. 70–91)].

16. See Trible, *God and the Rhetoric of Sexuality*, p. 20 (using I.A. Richards, see note 12).

17. Susan Niditch, *War in the Hebrew Bible* (New York: Oxford University Press), p. 37.

18. Carol Newsom, "Woman and Patriarchal Wisdom," p. 155, as quoted by Mary E. Shields in "Circumcision of the Prostitute," *Biblical Interpretation*, no 3:1 (1995): 72. Shields does not list a journal for Newsom.

Nye, there is an "oppressive dynamic" at work in which a wife is expected to stay put until she cannot stand it any longer, and

> then is punished and then is forgiven because she cannot be allowed to leave but must be made to stand back out of the way, be there and not there at the same time, obedient to the will of her husband but at the same time a presence that reassures him that he is not alone as he attempts time after time to discipline her and break her will, but not destroy her or allow her to leave, because without her he could not live.[19]

In my reading of the biblical and midrashic texts I found that the values that are implicit in these texts reflect a climate of social conventions that accept or condone *real* battering. I also found that there was an ambience of explicit and implicit family violence in seemingly unconnected episodes about Cain, Hagar, Lot's daughters, the Concubine at Gibeah, and the law of the *sotah*.[20] These five passages demonstrated how easy it is to perform violent acts against women in a patriarchal society in which women have little power and intrinsic value, as defined in terms of that society's needs. These very texts became the metaphors of Western society.

In the previous chapters, I have shown how the prophets used the image of the helpless woman of no intrinsic worth in relationship to a male lord and master who becomes the image of the chosen people of Israel in relationship to an omnipotent god. Although this metaphor expressed the reality of the hierarchical relationship between a husband and his wife in patriarchal society, the prophets elevated that hierarchy to a description of how God *meant* the world to be. Northrop Frye writes that we should "consider the possibility that metaphor is not an incidental ornament of biblical language, but one of its controlling modes of thought."[21]

How is it that the same prophets who speak so persuasively of social justice are themselves responsible for some of the worst examples of misogynistic texts in the Bible!? Part of any explanation will have to take into account that the prophets chose to use the marriage metaphor and female

---

19. Andrea Nye, *Words of Power: A Feminist Reading of the History of Logic* (London: Routledge, 1990), p. 150.

20. The laws of *sotah* are considered to be *halakha*, yet they have narrative or metaphoric nuances.

21. Northrop Frye, *The Great Code: The Bible and Literature* (New York: Harcourt Brace Jovanovich, 1982), p. 23.

imagery to depict relationships that could be understood in the historical context of the patriarchal society in which they lived. At the same time, however, there were other conceptions and relationships in the social structures of their time[22] against which the prophets rebelled.

Similarly we need to explain the paradox of legal codes, which on the one hand assume that women are the chattels of their husbands or fathers, yet, on the other hand, are concerned with the protection of the poor, the orphans, widows, and strangers in their midst.

Beyond that, of course, is the fact that both the prophets and the rabbis used female sexual imagery, and the violence that often accompanies it, because of their lack of ease with female sexuality and their desire to control it.[23]

METAPHOR AND HALAKHA: THE METAPHOR OF *KINYAN*[24]

The biblical metaphors, which are basic to the mentality of men and women in Jewish society, find concrete expression in *halakha* (Jewish law). The previous metaphors of male control, sanctity of family, women having to "take it" for the future of the group, all find concrete expression in rulings and principles of the halakhic corpus and codex. For example, the basic halakhic concept applying to marriage is *kinyan* [acquisition].

Kinyan is an act in which a person obtains rights of ownership or use in exchange for monetary (or other) payment. There are two major types of *kinyan*: original acquisition, and derivative acquisition. The former is when the "property" being acquired is not owned by anyone else, and the latter is when the property is acquired from a previous owner. It would seem that the "purchase" of a bride is a form of derivative acquisition, since she "belongs" to her father until her marriage. The function of *kinyan* is to demonstrate that the acquirer and the object of his acquisition are performing a transaction in which mutual benefit is being derived. The act of *kinyan* indicates that the two parties have made up their minds to conclude the transaction and the person who acquires the bride has to indicate his intention in the

---

22. See T. Drorah Setel, "Feminist Insights and the Question of Method," in *Feminist Perspectives of Biblical Scholarship*, ed. Adela Yarbro Collins (Chico, CA: Scholars Press, 1985), p. 41.

23. Katheryn Darr, "Ezekiel's Justifications of God," *JSOT*, no 55 (1992): 97–117.

24. "Is 'Kinyan' Only A Metaphor?" was the topic of a study session I lead at the Rabbinical Assembly Convention in Jerusalem (February 1998).

contract by mentioning an agreed monetary price (*kinyan kesef*). According to the Talmud (B. Kiddushin 2a-b), the bride cannot be acquired if she does not voluntarily agree to the act of betrothal.[25]

Rachel Biale, in her discussion of the *mishnah* and *gemara* text, "A Woman is acquired in three ways . . ." (B. Kid. 2a-b), points out that the acquisition of a woman by money is not purchase of property, since a man may not sell the woman he "acquires" and the amount of money is so small that it is not a "regular financial transaction." The amount of money is immaterial, because "the acquisition is symbolic," she states, and then asks, "If the exchange of money is not an actual purchase, what then is the 'real' meaning of acquiring a woman in marriage?"[26]

Although Biale dismisses the acquisition as a "symbolic" purchase, Judith Romney Wegner reads the same text of the Mishnah differently. She writes that the Mishnah prescribes the same modes of acquisition for wives as for Canaanite slaves and real property, and that marriage is a "formal sale and purchase of a woman's sexual function—a commercial transaction in which a man pays for the bride's virginity just as for any other object of value."[27] Wegner points out that the husband's purchase of his wife's biological function means that he has full legal claim on her sexuality; so much so that this claim overrides the woman's rights of personhood and makes her a form of chattel. We have seen what this means in the discussion about the *sotah* in Chapter Two, where the husband can use the threat of the "trial by ordeal" of the bitter waters to control his wife's sexual behavior.

Symbolic or metaphoric acquisition continues to have a place in the marriage ceremony, and the bride's virginity is mentioned in the marriage contract [*ketubah*] as well as the symbolic sum of money, which becomes hers if the marriage ends due to a fault of the husband's. Although the bride stands under the bridal canopy [*huppah*], it is the husband who recites the formal declaration of espousal, not the woman, nor does she say "I do" or "I

---

25. Although it is ideal that the bride agree, it is possible that the bride be "purchased" through an agent, since it is better for a woman to be unhappily married than to be single (B. Kiddushin 41a-b). For more details, see the entry, "Acquisition," in the *Encyclopedia Judaica*, vol. 2 (Jerusalem: Keter, 1971), pp. 216–221.

26. Rachel Biale, *Women and Jewish Law* (New York: Schocken Books, 1984), p. 48.

27. Judith Romney Wegner, *Chattel or Person? The Status of Women in the Mishnah* (New York: Oxford University Press, 1988), p. 42.

am espoused to you," since *he* formally acquires her. Although she has to agree, she does not give herself to him.

We see a merge of legal literature with midrashic material in another talmudic text. In a discussion of Hosea's relationship to his wife and children (God to Israel), Hosea complains to God that it is difficult for him to separate himself from his wife and divorce her. God asks, why should it be a problem since she's a prostitute and his children are the fruit of prostitution? How do you know whether they are yours or not? And, I, God (in contrast to Hosea), know that the people of Israel are My children ". . . one of four possessions (*kinyanim*) that I purchased in this world. The Torah is one possession (purchase) . . . heaven and earth is another . . . the temple is another . . . and Israel is another. . . ." (B. Pesachim 87b).

It is interesting that the marriage ceremony is likened to *kinyan*. Also, note the four categories of *kinyan* in this text—they are all instances of eternal possession and mastery over someone/thing else. These four cases (Israel being the fourth) all are based on an inherent, not acquired "ownership." Despite all protestations that *kinyan* in marriage does not give the husband possession of his wife, the metaphor suggests otherwise. Israel (the wife) is God's property to do with as He pleases. In a *midrash* in which God is likened to a heroic figure with great strength, we see an acceptance by the sages that Israel is God's possession, to do with her what he pleases.

> The hero hits another man and the man is killed immediately from the power of the one blow. He then goes into his house and hits his wife, also with one blow, and she is not killed. Her neighbors ask her, "How is it possible that all the great athletes have been killed from one of the hero's blows, and you are able to survive more than one blow?" She answers, "He hit the others with all his might, out of anger, but me he hits according to what I can take (and presumably out of love), and that is why I can take it."[28]

The wife (Israel) is justifying her husband's (God's) abuse to her. The *midrash* continues and asks, "How do we comfort ourselves and how is it that

---

28. Legend on Bereshit (Buber Version), Chapter 8:3. (*Bar-Ilan University Responsa Project: The Database for Jewish Studies*). For further discussion of this *midrash*, see my forthcoming article "Jerusalem the Widow," in *Women in Jewish Life and Culture*, a special issue of *Shofar* (Fall 1998).

we can stand against God's anger. Because although He hits us, He repents and creates us anew."[29] Implicit in this is that Israel is owned by God.

Although male God-language may seem innocuous, we have seen that metaphors matter. Though we have become desensitized to their implications on an individual and social level, through their long and established usage, we should remember that religious symbols are chosen carefully to communicate to society its values and help the community to understand itself and its conception of the world.[30] Thus if God is perceived as a father or a husband ruling and controlling "his" people, then the "nature of things" and the "divine plan," and even the "order of the universe," will be understood to be male dominated as well.[31]

We will now turn to the vast corpus of Jewish law, known as *halakha,* to see this metaphoric principle at work.

---

29. *Ibid.,* Chapter 8:4.

30. Judith Plaskow, *Standing Again at Sinai* (San Francisco: Harper & Row, 1990), p. 125.

31. Mary Daly, *Beyond God the Father* (Boston: Beacon Press, 1973), p. 13, as quoted in Plaskow in *Standing Again at Sinai,* p. 126.

5

Formative Laws and Principles in Support of Wifebeaters

Jewish law, which has continued to develop and change since biblical times, is called *halakha*. This word, which is derived from the root "*h-l-kh*" (to follow a path), is used in different ways—some broad and general, others narrow and restricted. It is beyond the scope of this book to give a comprehensive background on *halakha*, but there are excellent books and articles covering this topic.[1]

The salient point for our purpose is that Jewish society was fashioned and ruled by *halakha* as a legal system that pervaded all aspects of life, and whose functions, both judicial and legislative, were performed by rabbis whose authority was recognized by the Jewish community. Moreover, *halakha* was a "religious" system as well, and, as such, its influence was much more pervasive than an ordinary legal system, for it prescribed norms not only of legal behavior, but also of ethical behavior and standards. It molded the major institutions of Jewish life, including marriage and the family,

---

1. For more about *halakha* see the *Encyclopedia Judaica* entry on "*Halakha*," vol. 6 (Jerusalem: Keter, 1971); Elliot N. Dorff and Arthur Rossett, *The Living Tree* (Albany, NY: SUNY Press, 1988); Menachem Elon, *Mishpat Ivri* [Jewish Law], 3 Volumes (Jerusalem: Magnes Press, 1973) [Hebrew].

according to rabbinic religious tradition—a tradition that was based not only on interpretation of the words of the biblical texts, but also on the understanding of its intentions and values as transmitted in a chain of tradition throughout Jewish history.

Judaism is based on the doctrine that there are two sacred Torahs—the Written Torah (the Bible) and the Oral Torah (the traditions, including the rabbinic ones)—from which the halakha develops. Eventually the Oral Torah, which was based on human study of the sacred texts combined with practices that had flourished in Jewish society, was written down and became part of Jewish Sacred literature. But since the Oral Torah was based on learning and discussion among sages—rabbis who devoted their life to study and clarification of the Written Torah—it was never monolithic in its decisions. Just as in any legal system there can be different legal decisions based on similar cases, so it is in halakha.

DEVELOPMENT OF HALAKHA

TIME	NOMENCLATURE	MAIN WORKS	DESCRIPTION
70 C.E. – 250 C.E	Tannaitic Period (*Tanna, Tannaim* = rabbis of earliest period)	*Mishnah* (c.200 C.E.) *Tosefta* (c. 240 C.E.)	The main codifications preserve minority as well as majority opinions.
250 C.E. – 600 C.E.	Amoraic Period (*Amora, Amoraim* = rabbis of second period)	Babylonian Talmud (c. 500 C.E.) Jerusalem Talmud (c. 400 C.E.)	preserve minority as well as majority opinions
7–10 C.E.	Geonim		
CENTURY 11th 11th (end) 12th 12th–13th	*Rishonim* [lit. first ones]: Rashi R. Isaac Alfasi (Rif) R. Moses ibn Ezra *Tosafot*	on Talmud *Sefer ha-Halakhot* on Bible on Talmud	Commentary abridged Talmud French/German Commentators
12th–13th 14th 16th	Maimonides Jacob ben Asher ben Jehiel Joseph Caro	*Mishneh Torah* *Sefer ha-Turim* Shulhan Arukh	Codification
	Aharonim [lit. last ones] Responsa, etc.		No alternate opinions

Still, *halakha* has shown amazing flexibility and staying power by being able to accommodate disagreement. The earliest codifications and interpretations of *halakha*—the Mishnah (c. 200 C.E.), the Tosefta (240 C.E.), and the Talmud (Jerusalem c. 400 C.E. and Babylonian c. 500 C.E.)—preserve minority as well as majority opinions. These early strata are the formative building blocks of *halakha*. Their authority is, at least theoretically, the highest. Some rabbis have expressed the opinion that *halakha* should not contradict the Mishnah and Talmud; on the other hand, there is a principle that *halakha* is according to the latest authority.

The direct continuation of this formative period are the works of the geonim (7–10th century C.E. leaders of the rabbinic academies of Babylonia after the Moslem conquest in 634 C.E.). Among the many major medieval commentators on these works, there are Rashi (1040–1105) on the Talmud; Ibn Ezra (12th century) on the Bible; Maimonides (1135–1204) on the Mishnah; and Tosafot (a school of French and German commentators, 12th–13th century) on the Talmud.

Later attempts were made to codify all the preceding material, and Codes appeared, such as the *Yad he-Hazakah*, also known as *Mishneh Torah*, of Maimonides, the *Tur* of Jacob ben Asher (14th century), and the *Shulhan Arukh* by Joseph Caro (16th century). Finally, there is a vast collection of Responsa literature, which includes rabbinical rulings (responses) on specific questions. These responsa date back to geonic times and continue to be written today. By and large, these works are based on legal interpretation; a process that decides on modification or application of halakhic principles to specific cases, and, in turn, each responsum (*teshuva*) can serve as a precedent for future responsa. In the responsa literature, we find not only a history of *halakha*, but also instances of how Jews who were not scholars actually lived.[2]

Less frequent are *takkanot*, which are ordinances or rulings promulgated to meet a specific need and which, in effect, change the *halakha* by creating legislation. One might argue that Moses was the originator of *takkanot*—customs and laws—that were not written in the Bible, or that Ezra the Scribe ordained the first *takkanot* that included Torah readings on Mondays, Thursdays, and Sabbath afternoons.[3] Other rulings had to do with

---

2. For more on Spanish *responsa*, see Avraham Grossman, "Legislation and Responsa Literature," in *Moreshet Sepharad: The Sephardi Legacy*, ed. Haim Beinart, vol. 1 (Jerusalem: Magnes Press, 1992), pp.188–219.

3. Martin S. Jaffee, "The Taqqanah in Tannaitic Literature," *Journal of Jewish Studies* (Autumn 1990): 204, note 2.

instituting marriage contracts, outlawing polygamy, prohibition of giving too much money to charity, child support, and so on. These *takkanot* were ordained by sages to regulate life and to radically alter, or amend an existing law. When they are contrasted with the "normal" halakhic process that extends Torah laws, *takkanot* can be described as revolutionary rather than evolutionary.[4]

The plurality of opinion and interpretation that constitutes *halakha* also applies to its treatment of women. The attitude of *halakha* toward women can be characterized as ambivalent rather than monolithic. The claim is often made that *halakha* has attempted to "redress the fundamental imbalance in power between men and women which characterizes biblical law,"[5] and that *halakha* often is in the vanguard in its "liberal, compassionate attitude toward women."[6]

According to Biale, *halakha* does not always reflect reality, in that it is often "more permissive and more generous to women than life itself."[7] However, input of women into the halakhic process is rare, and it is almost always men who have the authority to make halakhic decisions. In addition, social and cultural needs are major factors in determining the stance of *halakha*. The metaphoric status of women discussed in Chapters Two, Three, and Four are part of the *weltanschauung* of the males who created *halakha*. The metaphoric modes of thought led to "a particular mind-set, unfavorable to women [which] predominated in classical thinking and determined the ensuing halakhic disabilities which prevailed throughout the Middle Ages."[8] These facts must be kept in mind as we view the halakhic principles that have bearing on the case of the battered woman.

---

4. For more on *takkanot*, see Simcha Goldin, "The Role and Function of the *Herem* in the Medieval Ashkenaic Community," *Proceedings of the Eleventh World Congress of Jewish Studies*, Division B, vol. I (Jerusalem: World Union of Jewish Studies, 1994), pp. 105–112; see also Jaffee, "The Taqqanah in Tannaitic Literature," and Chapter Eleven and the Appendix written by Michael Graetz in this book.

5. Rachel Biale, *Women and Jewish Law* (New York: Shocken Books, 1984), p. 5.

6. *Ibid.*, p. 7.

7. *Idem.*

8. Phillip Sigal, "Elements of Male Chauvinism in Classical Halakha," *Judaism* 24:2 (1975): 226.

THE HUSBAND AS LORD, MASTER, AND OWNER: THE BIBLE

We have discussed the metaphor of man as master over woman. The analogy in biblical law is the perspective of women as chattel. In the tenth commandment in Exodus we are told not to covet our neighbor's house, wife, slave, maid, ass, ox, or anything that *belongs* to our neighbor (Ex. 20:14).[9] Monetary transactions accompanied many changes of a woman's status. A *mohar* (price of virginity) had to be paid by a rapist to the father of the "bride" (see Gen. 34:12; Ex. 22:15–16).

The word *ba'al*[10] implies ownership as well as lordship; as in the law about the *ba'al* of the ox spelled out in Biblical law (Ex. 21:28). When a woman gets married, the father's property rights are transferred to the husband. When she is divorced, the husband renounces his right to his (sexual) use of the property and announces that she is "now permitted to any man."[11] If the husband's property is damaged, compensation is paid to *him*. Thus:

> When men fight, and one of them pushes a pregnant woman and a miscarriage results, but no other damage ensues, the one responsible shall be fined according as the woman's husband may exact from him, the payment to be based on [calculating the degree of the woman's pregnancy] (Ex. 21:22).[12]

Thus he is not only the owner of his wife, he is also the owner of her pregnancy, even if the pregnancy is a result of lewdness.[13] The husband's

---

9. Compare with the list in Deuteronomy 5:18, where the wife precedes the house, field, slave, maid-servant, ass, ox, and everything that belongs to the man.

10. The husband is the master [*ba'al*], whose permission to rule over his wife originates in Genesis 3:16, where God tells the first woman that her husband shall rule over her.

I will make most severe
Your pangs in childbearing;
In pain shall you bear children.
Yet your urge shall be for your husband,
And he shall rule over you.

11. M. *Gittin* 9:3.

12. This is Speiser's suggestion of the meaning of the Hebrew *be-plilim*; see note 22 in Gunter Plaut, *The Torah: A Modern Commentary* (New York: Union of American Hebrew Congregations, 1981), p. 568.

13. B. *Baba Kama* 43a.

right to perform sexual intercourse, is called *liv'ol* (to take what is one's property) and the wife's status of "married woman" is referred to as *be'ulat ba'al* (i.e., she belongs to the owner).[14]

Taking a Wife

There are other biblical sources that support the view of woman as chattel. The first has to do with the description of how a man comes to get a wife. The verbs describing this act are *lakach* (to acquire)[15] and *ba'al* (to possess).[16] It is written that:

> a man acquires a wife and possesses her. [If] she fails to please him because he finds something obnoxious about her, [he can] write her a bill of divorcement, hand it to her and send her away from his house (Deut. 24:1).

Perhaps the legitimacy of his being able to discard her also stems from the dictum: "Yet your urge shall be for your husband, and he shall rule over you" (Gen. 3:16).

EARLY HALAKHIC STRATA

Although the bride was purchased in biblical times, "in the post-biblical era, the betrothal was realized by the performance of an act of acquisition (*kinyan*) and the making of a declaration by the bridegroom to the bride in the presence of two witnesses."[17] The Mishnah says that "a woman is acquired in three ways: with money (or something of nominal value), with a writ (of purchase), or by cohabitation; that is, sexual intercourse."[18] However, by Tannaitic times, according to Boaz Cohen, the understanding is that, although the word *kanah* (acquire) literally means to purchase, in the Mish-

---

14. In Gen. 20:3 Abimelech is told that Sarah belongs to Abraham.
15. Deut. 24:1.
16. Deut. 22:13.
17. Boaz Cohen, "Betrothal in Jewish and Roman Law," *Proceedings of the American Academy for Jewish Research,* no XVIII (1948–49): 75.
18. M. Kid. 1:1.

nah it means "a symbolical form of acquisition."[19] The bride price in the Tannaitic era was symbolic and was given to the bride, or to her father if she were a minor.

Marriage in Tannaitic times was more than a business arrangement—it was a religious institution and the word for betrothal was called *kiddushin* (lit. sanctification), as opposed to the biblical term of *erusin*.[20] The new term "*kiddushin*" also reflects the transition of the marriage "acquisition" from a private deal between two adults or between two families to a social and religious institution administered by the community and under rabbinic supervision. This change gives rise to rabbinic control over marriage and divorce, matters which in the biblical period were purely familial.[21]

Although the Mishnah does speak of the woman who is purchased (i.e., acquired), according to Cohen, "the noun *kinyan* is not used as a term for betrothal."[22] Through marriage, however, the woman becomes "the sacrosanct possession, *res sacra*, of her husband, or, as the Talmud puts it—*de'asar la achula alma ke-hekdesh*"—that is, she is forbidden to others as a sacred object is forbidden. This is the legal expression of the metaphor of marriage as sacred bond, which must be preserved at all costs as we have seen in Chapters Three and Four.

DAMAGE TO PROPERTY: THE INJURED WIFE: TANNAITIC STRATA

The earliest strata of *halakha*, the Mishnah and Talmud, do not discuss wifebeating overtly. However, the fact of wifebeating as part of society is established in that certain laws depend upon wifebeating as being part of the

---

19. Cohen, "Betrothal in Jewish and Roman Law," pp. 75–76.

20. In footnote 38 on p. 222 of *Chattel or Person? The Status of Women in the Mishnah* (New York: Oxford University Press, 1988), Wegner writes "Mishnaic marriage law employs three technical legal terms: *erusin*, here translated as 'betrothal'; *qiddushin*, here translated as 'espousal'; and *nissui'in*, here translated as 'consummation.' . . . In post-Mishnaic usage (e.g., at B. Qid. 12b), *erusin* and *qiddushin* are used interchangeably. However, the Mishnah's use of three technical terms must reflect a time when the first two denoted separate stages in the process." Thus, according to Wegner, the betrothed girl is not permitted sexually to the bridegroom. Contrast this with the expression we have already seen in Hosea "*ve-eyrastich li l'olam*," which is usually translated as espoused, since, in biblical times, the term *qiddushin* did not exist.

21. See Avraham Freiman, *Seder Kiddushin ve Nissuin* (Jerusalem: Mosad Harav Kook, 1964) [Hebrew].

22. Cohen, "Betrothal in Jewish and Roman Law," p. 77.

situation for which the ruling is stated. The Tosefta [lit. "additions"] is a source which is contemporaneous with the Mishnah and includes material which often parallels, but is not identical with, Mishnahic material.[23] In the text we have before us, the Tosefta deals with damages that have to be paid to those who are embarrassed or hurt in some way:

> [The case of] the man whose wife is injured—whether *he* inflicted the injury or whether someone else injured her—the damage money is held for the woman [lit. taken from him] (the husband?) and real estate is purchased for her, and *he* has access to the usufruct.[24]

To properly understand the place of wifebeating in this passage, we have to first understand something about the concepts of damages (*habalah*). A man is commanded not to injure or wound his fellow person, minor or adult, male or female, either accidentally or deliberately. If he does so, according to the Mishnah, he must reimburse the person or *the owner* of the person for the following: injury, pain, healing [medical costs], idleness [loss of livelihood] and humiliation.[25]

Because the wife is the husband's property, he administers his (and her) property. He benefits from the profits [fruits] of the land which belonged to her. If he or someone else damages his chattel or humiliates what is his, he (or someone else) has to pay the appraised value for damages in the form of reparation money. Land is usually bought for her. She is not given money, since any money or earnings a woman has belongs to the husband, whereas the land itself belongs to her. The closest the rabbis can come to compensate her for damages done to her is to award her land, which is hers and not her husband's. Yet, she cannot be fully compensated as an individual since the *halakha* says all of her (and the land's) earnings belongs to him. She is at once

---

23. For an intelligent discussion of what is essentially the age-old chicken-egg problem, see Peter Schaefer, "Research into Rabbinic Literature: An Attempt to Define the Status Quaestionis," *Journal of Jewish Studies,* 37:2 (1986): 139–152. On pp. 147–148, he writes that, although the Tosefta is usually considered to be the first commentary of the Mishnah, there are tractates in the Mishnah that antedate it. There are also Tosefta tractates that do not refer to the extant version of today's Mishnah, suggesting the knowledge of an earlier Mishnah than that known today.

24. This is translated from Lieberman, S. (1988). *Tosefta Ki-Peshutah: A Comprehensive Commentary on the Tosefta* (New York: JTSA), Baba Kama 9:14 (p. 45).

25. M. *Baba Kama* 8:1.

both chattel and free. The fact that a husband might beat his wife, give her property in compensation out of his estate and then benefit from the profits of this damage payment (to her) may have bothered the writer of this Tosefta, yet the husband was allowed by law to use the profits as he saw fit. The text of the Tosefta, however, continues:

> R. Judah b. Bathyra says: If the injury [Heb. *boshet*, humiliation] was done to a hidden part of her body, two-thirds of the compensation is hers and one-third goes to her husband; if the injury [*boshet*] was done to a visible part of her body, two-thirds falls to him and one-third to her.
>
> His share is given to him directly, but as for hers, land is bought with it, and he has the use (usufruct) of it.[26]

Thus R. Judah qualifies the full force of the first passage. He makes clear that the husband is entitled to some compensation, depending on the nature of the injury. If the injury is in a private part of the body, which is hidden and thus invisible to the public eye, she gets two-thirds of the compensation money and he one-third since most of the "humiliation" is hers. If, however, the injury is visible, in order for him to save face for *his* public humiliation, his payment is not deferred; it is "given to him directly [immediately]" and hers is given in the form of land, with his being able to use the earnings of the land as the law allows.

One would like to assume that R. Judah only means to qualify the case when the damage is *not* inflicted by the husband. But it is not clear. In a note to this passage, the modern Talmudic researcher Saul Lieberman (1898–1983) quotes Maimonides, who said in the name of the Geonim that, *if it was her husband who beat her, she can do what she wants with the money*; that is, she can give it away if she wishes.[27] The significance of what Maimonides is saying is that she does not have to consult her husband; she can act without his knowledge as an independent agent if he has beaten her. Clearly Maimonides, in qualifying the second half of the passage from the Tosefta, was appalled by the inequity of a husband using compensation money for injury *he* had done his wife.[28] There are others, however, who, assuming that the husband does not *mean* to harm her (as might happen during the passions of sexual intercourse), decree that he only has to pay her her share and not

---

26. This comes from Lieberman, Baba Kama 9 (p. 45).
27. Lieberman, notes to lines 42–44, p. 101. See Maimonides *Hilchot Hovel U-Mazik* 4:16.
28. For a fuller discussion of this, see footnotes 41 to note on line 43 in Lieberman, p. 102.

everything. No doubt it would have been a different matter if the husband's motivation was to deliberately inflict pain.[29]

When we turn to the Mishnah we find a passage whose second half is almost identical to the passage in the Tosefta. The first half, however, is different, since its focus is on the husband's rights to the woman's property and not on damages to her.

> Anything found by a wife and the proceeds of her labor belong to her husband; and during her lifetime he has the use (usufruct) of her inheritance. If she received compensation for indignity or disfigurement occurring to her though injury (by a third party), it is *hers*.[30]

This text does not suggest that the husband has injured her. Yet it says that whatever compensation she gets for indignity is hers. Not only is it highly unusual to give it to her, but it does not say what form: money or land? So it should not surprise us that R. Judah b. Bathyra uses similar language to that in the Tosefta to clarify (or object to) the contents of this half of the passage (as quoted above).[31]

Thus the first part of the Mishnah states that the woman gets the money directly and has full use of it, giving her full and unusually generous compensation for her injury—as if she is a person with rights. R. Judah b. Bathyra, however, in his minority opinion, relates to her in the traditional manner, as damaged property whose value is reduced if the injury is visible.[32]

The differences between the Mishnah and the Tosefta seem to be two-fold: on the one hand the Mishnah doesn't specifically[33] deal at all with a

---

29. For all the sources pertaining to this controversy, see the *Encyclopedia Talmudit* entry on "*Hovel*" [damages], vol. 12 (Jerusalem: Yad Harav Herzog, 1993); see especially pp. 729–732 [Hebrew].

30. Hebrew: *boshta u-pegama shela;* in most cases *boshet* and *pegam* are used together as compensation for rape and seduction; see B. Shevuot 33a; B. Arachin 15a.

31. M. Ketuboth 6:1 in Nashim, Third Division. See the translation of Herbert Danby, *The Mishnah* (Oxford UK: Oxford University Press, 1938), p. 253; see also Wegner's translation and discussion in *Chattel or Person?*, pp. 87–88.

32. In studying this text together with me, Judith Hauptman offered a working hypothesis that reads this passage as a way of protecting the woman by giving compensation to her in the form of land; that is, a safe investment, not to be "eaten up" by the husband.

33. Some scholars believe that the formulation in the Mishnah is meant to be understood as anyone causing bodily damage, including the husband. Since the Talmud, however, does not draw that inference, perhaps in this case the Mishnah did not mean to include the case mentioned in the Tosefta.

woman injured by her husband. On the other hand the Mishnah is also more liberal about her use of the damages awarded to her. The significance of the two sources is that they are only two.

The Mishnah sets the agenda for *halakha*, unless there are major external sources that the Talmud brings to illuminate the Mishnah and open it up for discussion. Thus, since, in the Mishnah, there is nothing about a battered wife, and only one *beraita* (a tannaitic tradition not included in the Mishnah), there is hardly a mention of the battered wife in the Talmud.[34]

In speculating about the subject of wifebeating in these sources, Judith Hauptman writes that, since

> the Jewish communities of Israel and Babylonia were not violent, not given, in general, to expressing anger physically . . . domestic violence was not common and hence not dealt with in the Talmud. . . . It is tempting to speculate that those matters that were common occurrences found their way into the law codes whereas those that were rare did not.[35]

I concur completely with her alternative speculation: "Wifebeating and other forms of domestic violence were standard and allowable, according to the majority of the rabbis, and, for that reason, the Talmud need say nothing on the subject."[36] Following this reasoning we can presume that wives may be beaten by their husbands. The only issue at stake is if, and in what manner, compensation for physical damage is to be administered.

Such a presumption may have been behind the thinking of Reish Lakish (a tannaitic rabbi of the mid-2nd century C.E.) when he quoted Rabbi Meir: "Since [a husband] has the right to compel her to work, his consecration is regarded as if he had said to her, 'May your hands, be consecrated to Him who created them.'"[37] It would appear that Reish Lakish believes that it is R. Meir's opinion that a husband has the right to compel his wife forcibly to work. What kind of force? We don't know.

Can we draw any conclusions about what Rabbis think about wifebeating from the Talmud; that is, whether they approve or disapprove? Can one

---

34. We will see the one example of that in Chapter Six.

35. I would like to thank Judith Hauptman for sharing with me her unpublished article, "Traditional Jewish Texts, Wifebeating, and the Patriarchal Construction of Jewish Marriage" (May 22, 1995).

36. *Ibid.*

37. *B. Ket.* 58b.

argue that since there is almost no discussion of the battered wife in these early sources, that wifebeating was not very widespread? There are many apologists who would say yes, but it might also be said that the phenomenon existed and the rabbis knew about it and chose to downplay it through a form of censorship.[38] One can get a sense of wifebeating as an existing phenomenon from the above comment of Reish Lakish and from some other statements that rabbis made that appear in the Talmud.

BETTER TO BE WED AND DEAD

Reish Lakish is also quoted as saying to women that "it is better to live [an unhappy life] in a married state than to live [a happy life] in solitude."[39] This is eerily reminiscent of the text from Isaiah, where the worst thing the prophet can possibly imagine is a woman without a husband. "Let us be called by your name—Take away our disgrace,"[40] the women cried as they grabbed hold of the last available male.

The idea that women have no means of protest against their husband's brutality, that they are occasionally considered "less than human, matter without spirit,"[41] can be attested to by the following quotation from the Talmud:

> An unhappy wife came to Rabbi Yohanan to complain and he answered that anything a man wishes to do to his wife he may do. "Meat which comes from a slaughter house, if he wishes, may be eaten with salt; it may be eaten roasted, it may be eaten boiled, it may be eaten cooked in a stew; and so it is with fish from the fisherman." [In a continuation of this source another rabbi answers the question] "Why are you different from a fish? You have no more right to complain against your husband's treatment than the fish has the right to object to the manner in which it has been cooked."[42]

---

38. Mordecai Frishtik, "Violence Against Women in Judaism," *Journal of Psychology and Judaism* 14:3 (1990): 131–153.

39. *B. Yebamot* 118b. This attitude is echoed in "Fiddler on the Roof" in the conversation between Golda and the matchmaker Yenta at the beginning of the musical.

40. Isaiah 4:1.

41. Susan Griffin, as quoted by Carol J. Adams, *The Sexual Politics of Meat* (New York: Continuum, 1990), p. 46.

42. B. Nedarim 20a-b.

The context of this passage has to do with a woman's complaint about nonmissionary sexual positioning! In this passage, a wife is compared to a piece of meat or fish; to something which can be kneaded, shaped, and knocked around at will by her husband. R. Yohanan's advice to the unhappy wife is remarkably similar to the advice given to women by Marabel Morgan, a modern proponent of marriage at all cost.[43]

Even though we have seen there is almost no direct mention of wifebeating in the tannaitic and amoraic materials, the statements we have just reviewed were applied like halakhic principles and allied to the legal situation of wifebeating. Even though aggadic in origin, these statements attained the status of quasi-halakhic statements and were so used.

Can violence ever be justified against a woman? We will see later that some rabbis do justify it if she is remiss in her duties. By virtue of the act of marriage, the husband has certain rights, responsibilities, and privileges. Four very specific privileges the husband has are:

1. the right to any income from her work;
2. the right to whatever she finds;
3. the rights to the fruits (interest) of her property and possessions; and,
4. the right to inherit her property.

These rights are not consensual. They exist in law by virtue of the act of marriage, and they do not have to be renewed or spelled out with every marriage contract. The same is true of the husband's obligations to his wife, which is discussed below.

Furthermore, the woman cannot initiate divorce, even if she is beaten. All of the principles we have seen take on even greater weight when viewed in the light of the fact that the woman's ability to demand or even initiate divorce is almost nonexistent. In the light of this, what happens if the woman rebels, or refuses to perform her obligatory duties to her husband?

---

43. "Like hamburger, you may have to prepare yourself in a variety of different ways now and then"; Marabel Morgan, "365 ways to Fix Hamburger," *The Total Woman* (Fleming H. Revell Co., 1976), p. 113, quoted in Carol J. Adams, *The Sexual Politics of Meat*, p. 46. Adams's comment about this is that hamburgers, like women, are "objectified . . . prepared, reshaped, acculturated to be made consumable in a patriarchal world" (p. 55).

The "Rebellious" Wife

Although the Bible does not mention the wife's obligations toward her husband, the rabbis ruled that, since the husband was obliged to care for his wife, he had to be compensated for his expenditure. This rabbinical ruling extended the husband's rule over his wife, which was ordained by God. Thus, in the Mishnah there is a list of the services a wife has to perform:

> These are the household duties a wife does for her husband: she grinds, bakes, and washes; she cooks and nurses her child; she makes his bed and spins wool. If [she brought into the marriage] one maid, she need not grind, bake, or wash; [if she brought into the marriage] two [maids], she need not make his bed or spin wool; [and if she brought] four [maids], she sits on her throne. R. Eliezer says: Even if she brings in one hundred maids, he must force her to spin wool, for inactivity leads to lewdness. Rabban Shimon ben Gamliel says: If a husband makes a vow to keep his wife from performing any tasks, he must grant her a divorce and give her the alimony provided for by the marriage contract, for inactivity leads to boredom.[44]

Maimonides explains the reasoning behind the ruling:

> Thus they [the scholars] commanded that the wife should honor her husband beyond any limit, and *his fear should be over her*, and everything she does should be according to his demands. He should be in her eyes like a prince or a king who behaves in accordance with his heart's desires. She should remove everything that is hateful to him, etc.[45]

In addition to the household duties, it is assumed that she willingly engages in sexual intercourse with him—or at least does not deny him his conjugal rights. If she does the latter, she is considered to be a rebellious wife. The "rebellious woman" (*moredet*) is a "woman who refuses to fulfill her obligations toward her husband." There is some debate among the sages about this, which is reflected in a *midrash* on *Genesis*. The *midrash* begins by defining a *moredet* as a woman who refuses to fulfill household obligations, but concludes with the view of R. Yohanan—a first-generation Amora in the Land of Israel—that a

---

44. M. Ket 5:5; see also B. Ketubot 59b.
45. Maimonides, Ishut 15:20.

moredet is a wife who refuses to fulfill her side of the sexual marital bond;[46] that is, a woman who refuses to have conjugal relations with her husband. Such a woman may be fined by having money deducted from her *ketubah* [marriage settlement], and her husband may force her to accept a divorce.[47] These obligations have been alluded to above.

SEXUAL ABHORRENCE

In the Bible, the husband's finding something "sexually abhorrent" (*ervat davar*) about the wife is grounds for divorce (Deut. 24:1). In the Mishnah, we read:

> The School of Shammai stated: "A man is not to divorce his wife unless he has found something *sexually abhorrent* about her, as the Torah says, '. . . because he has found something abhorrent about her,'" (Deut. 24:1). The School of Hillel stated: "Even if she burned his food, as the Torah says, '. . . because he found *anything* obnoxious about her.'" R. Akiba stated: "Even if he found one more attractive than her, as the Torah says, '. . . and if she did not find *favor* in his eyes.'"[48]

The key words here are *ervat davar*, something (or anything) sexually abhorrent or obnoxious. The Shammaite position allows limited grounds for divorce, while the Hillelite position allows for a greater variety of reasons, and Akiba's position seems to be totally subjective.

Though the *halakha* follows the School of Hillel, the sages indicated that one *ought* to act according to the School of Shammai. An example of this moral argument is to be found in an aggadic tale from the Talmud which states that "Whoever divorces his first wife even the altar of God weeps for him. . . ."[49] This is because God is personally interested in preserving the institution of marriage. Thus the *aggadah* has morally tempered the force of the *halakha* by

---

46. See Shlomo Riskin's *Women and Jewish Divorce: The Rebellious Wife* (Hoboken, NJ: K'tav Publishing House, 1989), p. 20.

47. See the entry in *The Talmud: The Steinsaltz Edition*, Israel Institute for Talmudic Publications (New York: Random House, 1989), p. 212.

48. M. *Gittin* 9:10, quoted by David Novack, *Law and Theology in Judaism* (New York: K'tav Publishing House, 1974), p. 6 (emphasis his).

49. B. *Gittin* 90b, quoted in *ibid.* p. 7. See B. *Sotah* 2a. Underlying this is a belief that the first marriage is made in heaven.

criticizing R. Akiba's subjective criteria for divorce. The sages protect the wife from the "anything goes" interpretation of *davar*; yet, by insisting that following the Shammaite position is righteous conduct, they close the doors temporarily to such criteria for divorce as mutual incompatibility.

THE CASE OF *SHALOM BAYIT*

The overwhelming need to preserve marriages, homes, and families leads us to a discussion of *shalom bayit*. The entire concept of *shalom bayit*—literally, peace in the home—is a slippery slope concept. It is referred to in order to hold marriages together. It works with a good marriage that just needs a little push to help it work, but unlike good marriage counseling, which is stopped when the marriage is so bad that nothing can help it work, *shalom bayit* is often invoked as a holy principle—one which overrides individual personal problems for the sake of the institution of marriage.

According to a *midrash*, Aaron (Moses' elder brother) is the consummate maker of peace, in particular between unhappy husbands and wives. The rabbis are told to be one of his disciples for that reason. Thousands of grateful couples named their babies after him. How did he manage to keep the peace? In an apocryphal story (usually associated with R. Meir) there is the case of the man who told his wife to spit in the high priest's face or else he wouldn't have her in his bed. Aaron, who was a high priest, heard of this and told the woman to spit in his face. Aaron's willingness to lose face and allow his official position to be disgraced saved the marriage.[50] The implication is that, since *shalom bayit* is the overriding principle, marriages must be preserved at all cost.

Thus, the configuration of halakhic principles that could support battering is as follows: the wife is property who is "bought," but who still has rights in that reparation for "damages" (to her) are sometimes paid her. The wife has certain duties toward her husband which, if not carried out, will lead her to be considered a "rebellious wife." The rabbis would seem to have preferred to have no grounds for divorce, because of the principle of *shalom bayit*, but, because they lived in a real world, not one of abstractions, they recognized that incompatibility was possible grounds for divorce and even annulment of the marriage.

---

50. Rashi on Avot 1:12; also J. Sotah 1:4, cited in "*Hava'at shalom*", in the *Encyclopedia Talmudit*, vol. 8, pp. 51–52 [Hebrew]; also *Avot de Rabbi Natan* B, chapter 24.

6

Formative Laws and Principles Opposed to Wifebeating

We have seen in the early halakhic strata laws that presume that wifebeating exists, and which seem to support its existence. An early source, in the Tosefta, reveals a background of wifebeating, but this case seems to oppose wifebeating on principle. It discusses whether during the menstruation period (*niddah*) and the seven following days it is improper to beat one's wife, since the husband might possibly become impure (*tameh*) through the stick. Menahem ben Solomon Meiri (1249-1316), one of the foremost rabbis of the fourteenth century comments that one should not hit her at any time, because it humiliates her, and not because she is in a state of ritual impurity.

> According to our opinion, what was said in *The Tosefta* that one should not beat her with a stick, is not the *halakha* here: Touching the skin is not the issue, there is no continuance of affection, but what matters is that it has to be completely forbidden, by virtue of the fact that it is wrong.[1]

---

1. Menahem Hameiri (Provence, first half of 14th century) quoted in Avraham Grossman, "Medieval Rabbinic Views of Wife Beating: (8th–13th Centuries)," *Tenth World Congress of Jewish Studies*, Division B, volume I (Jerusalem: World Union of Jewish Studies, 1990), p. 121; see also note 15 [Hebrew].

The answer assumes that the woman is a person with feelings that have to be taken into consideration.[2]

There are aspects of the *halakha* that seem to be aware of the woman as a "person." For example, since a *moredet* [rebellious wife] is liable to forfeit the entire alimony provision in her marriage contract, and ultimately be divorced, the rabbis are interested in understanding what her motivation might be in rebelling.

Starting in the 3rd century C.E. in the Land of Israel, there is recognition that a woman might grow to hate her husband (or vice versa), and that these are acceptable reasons for either party to initiate divorce proceedings. In some marriage contracts found in archives in Elephantine (Egypt, 5th century B.C.E.) there are prenuptial clauses taking this into account.[3] According to Riskin, the rabbis

> understood that it might be possible for a woman to come to hate her husband and prefer to live without him [contrary to Resh Lakish's above-stated assertion of a woman's preference for marriage under all circumstances]. In this case of true unhappiness, rather than sex as the tactical medium, the Rabbis ensured, by a special stipulation in the marriage contract, that the woman would receive at least partial alimony, and—more importantly—that she could virtually initiate the divorce herself.[4]

As Riskin rightly indicates, the latter point is a breakthrough. The fact that the rabbis recognize "true unhappiness" (the converse of true love) is interesting.

In the Talmud, the sages are sympathetic to a woman who finds her husband repulsive:

> What is to be understood by the term rebellious wife?
> Amemar said: She who says "I wish to remain married to him, but I want to cause him pain"; if she says, however, "He is repulsive to me," she is not forced [to resume sexual relations concurrent with the steady reduction of her alimony sum]. Mar Zutra said: she is forced. Such an incident once occurred, and Mar Zutra forced [the woman to remain married]. . . . This, however, was not [the proper course of action]. . . .[5]

---

2. Versus the principle of *pen yosif* (in excess) see below.

3. Shlomo Riskin, *Women and Jewish Divorce: The Rebellious Wife* (Hoboken, NJ: K'tav Publishing House, 1989), p. 30.

4. *Ibid.*, p. 32. Riskin here refers to rabbis in the Jerusalem Talmud.

5. B. Ket. 63b quoted by *Ibid.*, p. 167.

Riskin considers this passage, which is a record of the Talmud's account of the conflict between the woman's interest and society's interest in protecting the institution of marriage, as:

> a door for a liberal interpretation of the law, one which is concerned for the individual rights of a woman who cannot live with her husband. This interpretation would force the husband to divorce her and ensure that she receives her *ketubah*.[6]

There is an inherent problem with the idea that a husband can be "forced" to divorce his wife. Since the husband is often likened to a God, reigning supreme, at least in the fortress of his home, who can force him to do anything except his own will?

LIVING WITH SERPENTS IN BASKETS

The sages were not totally locked into the *shalom bayit* principle discussed in Chapter Five, and they devised a "saving" principle which stands in a state of tension to it. The principle is that *eyn adam dar im nachash be-kefifah achat* [nobody can be expected to dwell in a cage with a serpent]; that is, "no man or woman can be compelled to live with an obnoxious consort."[7] What this means is that it is impossible for a marriage to endure when the parties concerned are incompatible. The analogy of the snake is a good one. Not only is the snake a phallic symbol, but if one rooms with a snake, one must be always alert to potential attack. Similarly, a man (or a woman) who has to be careful about every word or action that might provoke hostility (or a physical assault) would find living in a marriage loaded with such tension to be an equally intolerable situation.

This principle serves as the paradigm for annulling and/or dissolving the marriage, since the root of the word *kefifah* (force) also means "bent."[8]

---

6. *Ibid.*, p. 42; however, this door is "tightly shut," as Riskin points out on p. 108, by Rabbenu Tam, who interpreted these passages differently and reversed this liberal direction, which might have granted the wife the right to initiate divorce through a stipulation in the marriage contract. (This will be discussed more in Chapter Ten of this book.)

7. Marcus Jastrow, *A Dictionary of the Targumim, the Talmud Bavli and Yerushalmi, and the Midrashic Literature*, vol. 1 (Berlin: Verlag Choreb, 1926), p. 659.

8. *Ibid.* Jastrow writes that it might also be a basket or a muzzle hung over the neck of a beast during the threshing of wheat.

This implies that one who is in such an intolerable situation is bent down, humbled, and humiliated, rather than erect and proud. A person who lives in such a situation has to distort his/her humanity to survive, which is what prisoners often do.[9] If applied on that level, this principle seems to be connected with the "partnership metaphor" of Genesis 1, rather than women as sources of evil in Genesis 3.

There are several cases where this principle is used. One case is discussed in the Talmud[10] about the marriage of a male or female imbecile, which should not have been legalized in the first place by the rabbis (unlike the marriage of a deaf person, which is allowed). There are other cases in the Tractate of Ketubot that refer to this principle. In the mishnah of Ketubot 72a it is written:

> These are to be divorced without receiving their *ketubah*: A wife who transgressed the law of Moses or who transgresses Jewish Practice. And what is regarded as a wife's transgression against the law of Moses? Feeding her husband with untithed food, having intercourse with him during the period of her menstruation, not setting apart her dough offering, or making vows and not fulfilling them.

When a wife makes vows without fulfilling them, it leaves the husband legally liable for their nonfulfillment. In such a case, where the husband might want to preserve his marriage and behave responsibly, he might want to demand that she makes vows only in his presence, so that he can later fulfill them when she neglects to, or so that he can nullify them. The rabbis, however, recognize that it is impossible for him to remain constantly vigilant about her vow-making, and thus suggest that he divorce her, because "no one can live with a serpent in the same basket."[11] They recognize that uneven responsibility can lead to unlivable tension.

A woman who does not put aside the required offering of dough [when she is making bread] causes her husband to sin if he eats from the bread. R. Judah said, "Any husband who knows that his wife does not properly set apart for him the dough offering should set it apart again after her"; but

---

9. See Judith Herman, *Trauma and Recovery: The Aftermath of Violence from Domestic Abuse to Political Terror* (New York: Basic Books, 1992), where she equates victims of wifebeating with prisoners of war and survivors of the Holocaust.

10. B. Yebamot 112b.

11. B. Ketubot 72a.

other commentators used the same quotation "no one can live with a serpent in the same basket"—implying that he could divorce her. The reason is that, in a marriage, a husband should not have to always be on guard, worried that his wife will undermine his religious needs.[12]

The third situation relates to the husband who refuses to support his wife. Rab stated:

> If a husband says, "I will neither maintain nor support [my wife]," he must divorce her and give her also her *ketubah*. R. Eleazar went and told this reported statement to Samuel [who] exclaimed, "Make Eleazar eat barley; rather than compel him to divorce her; let him be compelled to maintain her." And Rab [said]—No one can live with a serpent in the same basket.[13]

Although some might argue, as Samuel, that it is better to pay her mainte-nance, others, like Rab, said that incompatibility between man and wife has to be taken into account to the point where the husband will be considered a *mored* (rebellious husband) who will have to give extra payments to his wife in the divorce settlement.[14]

Although the "serpent" in the basket is the wife in the first two cases, it is the husband who is the "serpent" in the third case. What the rabbis are making clear in all three cases is that the principle of *shalom bayit* cannot always be applied. When it breaks down, and the mental anguish of one party is too great, the marriage can and should be dissolved at all cost. The third case, since it deals with the husband, has the potential to dissolve the marriage when the husband behaves cruelly and irresponsibly toward his wife or refuses to support her financially.

THE BRUTAL, BRUTISH HUSBAND: AMORAIC STRATA

There is another allusion to wife battering in the Talmud, (*cf.* Chapter Five),[15] which is couched in a discussion about the *am ha'aretz* (lit. native,

---

12. *Idem*.

13. B. Ketubot 77a.

14. See Tos. Ketubot 63a and the entry: "*Eyn Adam dar im nachash be-kefifa achat*," in the *Encyclopedia Talmudit*, vol. 1 (Jerusalem: Yad Harav Herzog, 1993), pp. 535–536 [Hebrew].

15. Although in a Tosafist note to Ketubot 66a, we find the following: "If a woman who has not renounced her maintenance refuses to perform her work, then the Tosafot urge 'Let him take a stick and beat her—he has the right to force her, according to Reish Lakish.'"

people of land). Although the passage is not sexist, it is certainly classist and reflects the animus of an elite rabbinate toward the uneducated ordinary man, perceived as irreligious by rabbinic standards. The animus in this passage is similar to the hyperbole we saw in the analogy of women as fish to be knocked around. Is it just hyperbole? The *am ha'aretz* is also considered a fish of no import—to be knocked around by his betters.

The context of the entire passage has to do with whom a scholar should marry. It is better to marry the daughter of another scholar because that will ensure that one's children become scholars. Under no circumstance should he marry the daughter of an *am ha'aretz*, for that is a repulsive and unacceptable thing.

The text goes on to proclaim in hyperbolic[16] manner that the *am ha'aretz* is

> detestable, their wives are vermin, and of their daughters it is said, 'Cursed be he that lieth with any manner of beast' (Deut. 27:21). . . . It is permitted to stab him [even] on the Day of Atonement which falls on the Sabbath. . . . One may tear an *am ha'aretz* like a fish . . . (B. Pesachim 49b).
>
> It was taught, R. Meir used to say: Whoever marries his daughter to an *am ha'aretz* is as though he bound and laid her before a lion: just as a lion tears [his prey] and devours it and has no shame, *so an am ha-aretz strikes [hits/beats] and cohabits and has no shame* (B. Pesachim 49b).

Who is an *am ha'aretz*?[17] The term *am ha'aretz* is used to refer to a common, uneducated person, and, in the Mishnah, it refers to a person who is not very careful about his observance of rabbinic law. In mishnaic times, there were restrictions governing relations between learned people and common people, but by Talmudic times they fell into disuse. The prejudice against the *am ha'aretz* remained, however, and this is evidenced even today in colloquial usage.

---

16. Isidore Epstein in *The Babylonian Talmud* (London: Soncino Press, 1935), Seder Moed, Pesachim, writes: "These and the following dicta show that a strong antipathy existed between the scholar and the *am ha'aretz*. Nevertheless, it is perfectly obvious that a statement like the present one is merely humorous and no more than a *jeu d'esprit*, and many others must be similarly understood" (pp. 236–37). In his notes, Epstein refers the reader to M. Lazarus, *Ethics of Judaism*.

17. For a full discussion on this topic, see Lee Levine, *The Status of the Sages in the Land of Israel in the Talmudic Era* (Jerusalem: Yad Ben Zvi, 1986) [Hebrew] and Aharon Oppenheimer, *The 'Am Ha-aretz* (Leiden: E.J. Brill, 1977).

R. Meir's answer is that "an *am ha'aretz* is one who hits [his wife] and takes possession [intercourse] and has no sense of shame."[18] What is the meaning of this proclamation? Is it to define what an *am ha'aretz* is? Does it mean an *am ha'aretz* is so primitive that this is what he always does? Or is Meir trying to say that one who has intercourse with his wife with no interval between beating her (i.e., right after), without apologizing or feeling a sense of shame, behaves in a manner befitting an *am ha'aretz*?

There is a difference in the reading of the passage. The intention of the first reading is to make clear that the *am ha'aretz* is not a human being, but rather a beast (like the lion) and an evil[19] person. The second reading is that anyone who beats his wife and then possesses her (without making up first) is not behaving properly, and is thus the same as an *am ha'aretz*.

If wifebeating is common only among the *am ha'aretz* (the majority of people, one should remember), it would explain why the rabbis, an elite minority, did not discuss wifebeating (typical of boorish behavior) in the Talmud except in this context.[20] However, a sensibility that assumes that it is only the out group which is guilty may serve to cover up the fact that wifebeating is prevalent in the elite group as well.

NON-TERRORIZATION OF ONE'S HOUSEHOLD

Although wifebeating is not directly mentioned except in the context we have seen in the above reaction by R. Meir, one can see that the rabbis were concerned that the husband's exclusive power could lead to abuse. On the one hand, it says in B. Megillah 12b that the woman has to respect her husband and that his fear and authority is over her. She has to do everything he demands as if he were a king: from acquiescing in his lustful desires (*ta'avat libo*) to distancing herself from anything he detests.[21]

On the other hand, the husband is told not to make her "too fearful"; that is, not to terrorize her, for if he does, it can have dire consequences, as in the case of the concubine at Gibeah.[22] Because the husband terrorized his

---

18. B. Pesachim 49b *makeh u-boel*.
19. Hebrew, *rasha*; this identification is common in rabbinic literature.
20. See Lee Levine, *Status of the Sages*, pp. 75–79.
21. See Maimonides, Ishut 5:20.
22. See Chapter Three on metaphors for the particulars of this case. Note too that a "little fear" is not considered bad!

wife, thousands of Israelites suffered as punishment. The rabbis say that whoever terrorizes (*eyma yetera*) his household, causes three sins to occur: incest or unchastity, bloodshed, and desecration of the Sabbath. Unchastity, because out of fear of his anger, she does not tell him she did not go to the *mikvah* (ritual bath) during the winter and unknowingly his terrorization of her causes him to sin when he has sexual intercourse with her. Bloodshed, because the members of his household run away from him and meet with fatal accidents. And finally, Sabbath violations because his wife lights the lamp after dark because he has not asked her to do so gently.[23]

Not to Excess

Although we have seen that in the early stages of rabbinic interpretation a wife was the husband's property, to do with as he pleased, rabbis were aware of the need to place limits on the arbitrary authority of a husband. Thus another principle was formulated, which was based on the following verse:

> When there is a dispute between men . . . the guilty one is to be flogged. . . . He may be given up to forty lashes, but not more, lest being flogged further, to excess [*pen yosif*], your brother [shall] be degraded before your eyes (Deut. 25: 1–3).

Although this particular verse has nothing to do directly with women, it is used later in rabbinic times, to explain why men shouldn't cause excessive suffering to their wives or slaves. A strict interpretation of the law would put the woman in man's power as his possession, but by using the authority of another verse, which points out that excessive punishment leads to humiliation, the husband's authority is curbed. The application of this principle views the woman as part of common humanity, despite her social status as quasi-property. Thus, whatever the motivation, the husband is obligated to care for his wife. This has resulted in certain specific obligations. The first has to do with the husband's duty to support his wife.

---

23. B. Gittin 6b-7a.

THE HUSBAND AS PROVIDER

There is an assumption that a husband is obligated to provide for his wife. In Exodus 21:9–11, in its discussion of marriage with a slave woman, the Bible states:

> he shall deal with her as is the practice with free maidens. If he marries another, he must not withhold from this one her food [she-era], her clothing [kesuta], or her conjugal rights [onata][24] If he fails her in these three ways, she shall go free, without payment.

One might ask is this obligation contingent on his wife's appropriate behavior? Or is it her intrinsic right (as opposed to his obligation)? The answer in the Bible seems to be that it is her unconditional right. And if he fails her, she is free and does not have to pay for this freedom.

Another question one might ask is does he provide generously? or grudgingly? Generously, because she is a person he cares about, or grudgingly, because she is akin to a beast of burden who has to be fed?

According to Wegner, women in the rabbinic period moved from "the status of near chattel . . . to a status *close* to that of full person. . . ."[25] The implication is that women were never fully reckoned as total persons. Clearly the roots lie in the fact that the husband, who rules his wife, is obli-

---

24. According to Rashbam and Kassuto, this may mean housing (*cf.* Hebrew *ma-ohn*). Shalom Paul in *Studies in the Book of the Covenant in the Light of Biblical and Cuneiform Law* (Leiden: Brill, 1970), pp. 56–61, dismisses the notion that *onata* means "her time" (*cf.* modern Hebrew, seasons). Paul found that, from 2,000–500 B.C.E., there was a triad of items that a master was obligated to provide to his dependent slaves; as was a husband to his wife. Most commentators are in agreement about the first two items: food and clothing. He brings evidence to show that *onah* means "ointments" or "cosmetics." (See note b to "conjugal rights," Exodus, 21:10, in *Tanakh* (Philadelphia: Jewish Publication Society, 1985), p. 117).

25. Judith Romney Wegner, "The Status of Women in Jewish and Islamic Marriage and Divorce Law," *Harvard Women's Law Journal* 5 (1982): 32.

gated not only to take care of her, but is expected to behave righteously toward her; that is, more generously than strictly defined by the law.[26]

One can, of course, infer from Exodus 21:9–11 that he must provide her with clothing, food, and shelter, and take care of her sexual needs. This obligation was extended by the rabbis. According to Maimonides there are a total of ten conjugal duties the husband must fulfill: he is obligated by the marriage contract to provide medical care for her; redeem her from captivity by paying the ransom money; pay for her burial; provide for her needs when she becomes a widow; take care of his daughters after his death; and see that the inheritance rights of her male heirs are honored.[27]

All these responsibilities are not clear cut. For example, although the husband has to take care of an ill wife, what happens if it is a drawn-out, lengthy illness and the husband will lose a lot of money in taking care of her? Maimonides says that it is legally permissible to divorce her and she will finance her illness from her marriage settlement. And this is allowed since a husband is not obliged to take care of his divorced wife. However, this is not recommended procedure. For although legally correct, one does not do it because of a sense of the correct way of doing things [derech eretz] and it is an ugly thing which the courts decry.[28] Unfortunately it is legal and is left to the husband's goodwill and the force of public opinion. These rules are not halakhic principles, but "quasi-halakhic" principles, general in nature, that *may* be used by a particular rabbi or rabbinic court as adjuncts to a halakhic decision. But they do not compel a rabbi to reach a specific decision.

What if there is no goodwill on the part of the husband?

---

26. Jewish sources include both laws that spell out obligation, and moral pronouncements that define righteous behavior. Some writers view the laws of obligations as implying legal rights (see e.g., Michael Graetz, "The Right to Medical Treatment in Jewish Law," *Et Laasot*, no 3 (1991): 80–89 [Hebrew] and its bibliography). The fact that these two elements are intertwined in rabbinic legal sources may be a unique feature of rabbinic law. In our case, the problem is the balance between these two elements. When the sense of righteousness vis-à-vis women is ambivalent, then the law needs to be much more affirmative to protect the woman's rights. On the other hand, laws in themselves cannot guarantee rights if society's attitude toward the minority is discriminatory to begin with; in other words, laws without real equality don't work either. Thus, a major consideration in Jewish law in general is that there should not be a strong contradiction between law and a sense of righteousness (goodwill), and specific points of tension and contradiction between the two is the chief focus of my thesis. In the end, the nonlegal dicta about women have to be purged of ambivalence and, instead, preach for real equality; on the other hand, the laws themselves have to be changed to reflect equal rights.

27. Maimonides, Ishut 5:1.

28. *Ibid.*, 14:17.

LOVE YOUR WIFE MORE THAN YOURSELF

The rabbis would like to assume that husbands will treat their wives better than themselves:

> Our Rabbis taught: Concerning a man who loves his wife as himself, who honors her more than himself . . . Scripture says, *And thou shalt know that thy tent is in peace.*[29]

One reason that he should always be especially careful to safeguard the honor of his wife is because the blessing in one's house is found only by the merit of one's wife: "A man should honor his wife more than himself and love her as himself . . . he should not unduly intimidate her, but should speak to her softly, not to cause her sadness or pain."[30] But the rabbis are also quick to point out many examples of wives who are involved in deliberate sabotage of food preparation.[31] This is another "quasi-halakhic" principle.

The rabbis advise a man to "be quick in buying land; [and] be deliberate in taking a wife. Come down a step in choosing your wife" so she won't put on airs, but "go up a step in selecting your best man."[32] It is interesting that the wife's status is supposed to go up with marriage. There is an interesting interpretation of the expression *beulat ba'al* (being possessed in marriage by the husband), which is that the wife's status should be connected with the rise (*ba'aliyato*) of the husband and not with his coming down. And why should she go up in status when she gets married? The rabbis answer: because she was given for life and not for sorrow [*le-chaim nitnah; ve-lo le-tza'ar nitnah*].[33]

Mingled in these tales that give advice to the husband about whom to marry, how to marry, and the benefits of marriage are stories of women who

---

29. B. Yebamot 62b.

30. A free translation of Maimonides; *Ibid.,* 15:19.

31. For an example of the bad wife who torments her husband by not preparing the food he likes, see B. Yebamot 63a: "*Rab* was constantly tormented by his wife. If he told her, 'Prepare me lentils,' she would prepare him small peas; [and if he asked for] small peas, she prepared him lentils."

32. *Idem.*

33. B. Ketubot 61a. A woman whose status is high does not have to breast feed. Since a woman's status is supposed to go up, not down, when she marries, if she marries someone from a class lower than hers, she is not obliged to breast feed.

should be divorced because they don't prepare food properly. Though the rabbis don't want the wife to be treated as a mere possession, they also consider a man who finds a good wife to be lucky: "Whoso findeth a wife findeth a great good; Find, because it is written, and I find more bitter than death the woman."[34]

Wegner has pointed out that the ambivalence of the rabbis toward women is connected with their attempts to categorize them: there were times when she was seen as a chattel, and times when she was an autonomous person. There were also times when she was good and times when she was bad. If she is a good wife, there is no end to her goodness; if she is a bad wife, there is no end to her badness. Here, too, the rabbis made distinctions that have bearing on our subject. "It is written in the book of Ben Sira (Ecclesiasticus): 'A good wife is a precious gift [to her good husband], she will be put in the bosom of the God-fearing man' (Ecclus. 26:3). A bad wife is a plague to her husband. What remedy has he? Let him give her a letter of divorce and be healed of his plague."[35]

We have seen that a husband is to treat his wife better than himself or a stranger. We are all familiar with the maxim ve-ahavta le-reyacha kamocha [you shall love your neighbor [friend] as yourself] (Lev. 19:18). Yet, in these sources, the husband is abjured to treat his wife *better* than himself. Why better? Is it because of the assumption of the wife's inferiority? Did the rabbis recognize that she has to be protected from the husband's instincts and legislated right to dominate? On the other hand, there is also the husband's legitimate fears of his wife's making his home life a misery, by pestering him with demands, putting on airs, burning his food, denying him sexual release. Perhaps the difficult burden of treating his wife—with whom he may have an ambivalent relationship—"better than himself" leads the husband to give up in frustration.

The "quasi-halakhic" principles suffer from the same problems as paternalism and chivalry; namely, that they can backfire when the object of chivalry is not the idealized version of a wife. In fact we will see that, despite the principle that a wife has to be treated better than himself or a stranger, Sar Shalom Gaon (9th century) felt that an assault on a woman by her husband was less severe than an assault on her by someone else, since the husband has authority over her.[36]

---

34. In B. Yebamot 63b, Rabba juxtaposes Proverbs 18:22 and Eccl. 7:26.

35. *Idem.*

36. From Otzar Geonim, Baba Kamma, p. 62, no. 198, as quoted by Samuel Morrell, "Independence of a Married Woman," *Jewish Social Studies* 44 (1982): 198.

We have seen halakhic principles that potentially support wifebeating: the wife as ward; the fact that the husband can beat his wife (but not someone else); the rule of the rebellious wife; and the principle of *shalom bayit*, which leads to control over the wife. We have also seen the principles that potentially oppose wifebeating, such as the marriage contract (*ketubah*), in which the husband takes on responsibility; the fact that one should not live with a "snake"; the fact that the wife was not given for sorrow; and that the husband must love his wife as himself, or even more than himself.[37]

These principles and themes are developed and applied in the vast halakhic literature of the codes and responsa after the Amoraic period. In this literature, we discern three major legal positions and configurations of these principles.

---

37. On the other hand, the purpose of the *ketubah* is to make it hard for the husband to divorce his wife; that is, to preserve the marriage. It is a double-edged sword for the woman who wants to get out of a marriage. See the discussion in Chapter Five on *shalom bayit*.

7

Rabbinic Acceptance of "Lawful" Wifebeating

OVERVIEW

We now turn to the later strata of *halakha*, where we find there is much more overt awareness and explicit relation to cases of wifebeating. What was implicit as a social phenomenon in the background of the early strata is dealt with openly in the later material. We will see that all of the metaphoric attitudes of patriarchal society, the aggadic exhortations, the quasi-halakhic statements, and the halakhic rules that we have discussed are in play in these sources.

It is possible to discern major trends or camps in *halakha* according to the particular configuration of all this material, which can be dealt with separately as standard patterns. I call the first pattern "acceptance," and it is the subject of this chapter. The other three patterns, or attitudes to wifebeating, that can be discerned in Jewish texts will be discussed in the following chapters.

Perhaps the most difficult thing for a modern Jew to face are texts that allow wifebeating. While there are sources in *halakha* that declare wifebeating unlawful, there are others that state otherwise. Gratuitous wifebeating, striking a wife without a reason, is unlawful and forbidden. Rabbinic sources are in general agreement about the beating of "good wives" who do not deserve beating. The attitude of rabbinic sources toward "bad wives" (who do not behave the way good women should) is ambivalent, and wifebeating

is occasionally sanctioned if it is for the purpose of chastisement or education. A bad wife is one who does not perform the duties required of her by
Jewish law, who behaves immodestly, or who curses her parents, husband,
or in-laws.

We have already studied the first part of the mishnah that defines a
wife's transgression against Jewish practice. Immodest behavior deemed worthy of punishment includes "going out with uncovered head, spinning wool
with uncovered arms in the street, conversing with every man." The list of
women deemed worthy of being divorced without receiving their *ketubah*
include the following cases as well:

> Abba Saul said: Also that of a wife who curses her husband's parents in
> his presence [and in his children's presence]. R. Tarfon said: also one
> who screams. And who is regarded a screamer? A woman whose voice
> can be heard by her neighbors when she speaks inside her house (B.
> Ketubot 72a).

Although beating is not allowed or even suggested in the case of the screamer,
the woman who curses is repeatedly used as an example where beating is seen
as a means to an end. The rabbis who justify beating see it as part of the overall
"duties" of a husband to chastise his wife for educational purposes. They see
battering as a way of obtaining *shalom bayit* (a stable household).[1]

Morrell writes that there is "a connection between the financial and the
personal aspects of the husband's authority over his wife, since his power in
the former may be used to exert his authority in the latter," and that a man is
responsible for his wife's proper behavior which might lead him to "apply
physical sanctions to her."[2] The most problematic pronouncements permit-

---

1. The rabbis' ideology is *shalom bayit*—the sanctity, primacy, and peace of the home.
Indeed, the Jewish home is seen in rabbinic rhetoric as the fundamental building block of the
Jewish people; its preservation and peace or wholeness is tantamount to being the wholeness
or peace of the entire Jewish nation. The word *shalem* comes from the same root (*slm*) as *shalom*. It means whole. Under the guise of this ultimate social value, the rabbis see nothing
wrong in returning women to homes in which they are battered. The rabbis who send such
women back to unhappy situations see the home in its entirety, as being more important than
the personal welfare of the individual woman, who is merely a part, an object, a means to an
end, and who is called upon to sacrifice herself for the sake of this ultimate social value. (See
Chapter Five in this book.)

2. Samuel Morrell, "An Equal or a Ward: How Independent Is a Married Woman
According to Rabbinic Law? *Jewish Social Studies* 44:3–4 (1982): 197.

ting wifebeating are made by highly prominent rabbis such as R. Yehudai Gaon,[3] Maimonides, R. Samuel ha-Nagid, Moses Isserles, among others. Morrell shows that rabbis such as Tsemach Gaon of Eretz Yisrael (884–915), Ibn Aderet (13th–14th century) and Maimonides (1135–1204) advise men to restrict their wives to the home and be responsible for educating them.

Thus Tsemach Gaon "calls upon a man to flog his wife if she is guilty of assault," and another Gaon assumes that "a husband may strike his wife if she curses his parents or hers." Ibn Aderet also justifies wifebeating when the wife curses her husband. Maimonides wants to ensure that the husband will prevent his wife from going out more than "once or twice a month, as the need may arise."[4]

S.D. Goitein[5] implies that these Jewish authorities in Islamic lands were influenced by the Koran which "permits, or perhaps recommends, beating the wife if she is inaccessible to milder forms of correction."[6] Thus he cites Yehudai Gaon, who counsels that his wife should remain silent even if her husband beats her, and Maimonides, who writes that a woman who does not do her work may be forced to do so with a stick. Goitein considers Maimonides to be a special case: "coming from the Muslim West with its stern mores . . . [H]e took a particularly hard stance—unwarranted by the law—with regard to a woman who refuses to do her household chores (which were mandatory)."[7]

Hayim Tikochinski refers to the "Gaon" who says she can be forced to do her work with a whip. He claims that Maimonides follows the lenient approach of the Geonim toward wifebeaters since he allows the husband to beat his wife.[8] He says that the meaning of this is that Maimonides saw no

---

3. For clarification of what a Gaon is, see section below in this chapter entitled, "The Geonic *Responsa*."

4. Morrell, *idem*.

5. In Vol. 3 of his monumental study, *A Mediterranean Society* (Los Angeles: University of California Press, 1978), S.D. Goitein uses Geniza sources to describe Jewish life in Egypt in medieval times. Section viii, C, 1 (pp. 184–189) of his book is on wifebeating. It begins by saying that husbands who beat and curse their wives present a "serious aspect of marital life [which] requires more than passing attention" (p. 184). He points out that, though wifebeating is very rarely mentioned in letters, the frequency of such references in legal documents cannot be easily dismissed.

6. *Ibid.*, p. 185.

7. *Idem*.

8. Tikochinski, *The Enactments (Takkanot) of the Gaonim*, (Jerusalem, Tel-Aviv: Sura Press, 1960), pp. 131–134 [Hebrew], has a short chapter on the husband who uses corporal punishment against his wife.

wrong in the husband's beating his wife if she did not do the work she was obligated to do. But Tikochinski thinks that Maimonides' view is an aberration—an exception to the rule which, in his opinion, is against wifebeating. Tikochinski, does not apologize for Maimonides; rather, he considers his opinion exceptional and misguided. "Even his teachers in Spain did not teach such a lesson; it fits the commandments of the Koran and is foreign to Judaism."[9] Tikochinski is denying the important precedent and the influence of a man of Maimonides' stature on future generations.

Grossman, however, recognizes that the repercussions of Yehudai's words could have reached beyond the confines of Babylon to the Mediterranean centers. He is aware that such pronouncements could have had a devastating effect on the status of women. Grossman believes that the famous Spanish courtier, R. Samuel ha-Nagid, was not merely expressing a personal viewpoint when, in his book *Ben Mishlei*, he advocated beating a shrewish wife (see below, "Moslem Spain"). He writes that it reflects the thinking of the Jewish courtiers in Moslem Spain of the 10th–11th centuries.[10]

After reviewing the Sephardi authorities, Morrell shows that the Ashkenazi authority R. Israel Isserlein permitted the chastising of wives in order that she not curse her parents. He discusses an interesting responsum of David b. Solomon Ibn Avi Zimra (Cairo, 16th century) who accepts the right of a husband to beat his wife "in theory only."[11] Ibn Zimra makes it clear that a husband has no right to beat his wife for interpersonal concerns, only if there are witnesses for her improper deeds.

Despite the fact that wifebeating was recognized as a legitimate form of chastisement, Morrell correctly points out that the rabbinic attitude toward its wrongful use was severe. Yet any pronouncements by an individual rabbi can be considered authoritative. Thus, it is especially problematic for all future generations that there are rabbis of stature who permit wifebeating for whatever purposes that seem important to the mores of their times.

---

9. *Ibid.*, p. 132.
10. See footnote 15, on Grossman.
11. Morrell, p. 198.

THE GEONIC *RESPONSA*

Many of the responsa that accept wifebeating date from the Geonic period. The Geonim flourished from the end of the 6th century through the middle of the 11th century in Babylon and Palestine. "The Gaon" (plural *Geonim*) was the formal title of the head of each of the academies of Sura and Pumbedita in Babylon (589–1058). Later this title was also used by the heads of academies in Palestine (844–1109). The Gaon was an officer appointed by the exilarch and his official duties were similar to those of the chief rabbis in Israel today. Thus, he was chosen for his knowledge of Judaic lore and for his administrative ability, although politics, as it does today, played a role in running the office.[12]

As noted by Freehof, Geonic responsa are generally brief and direct; in most, the question is not even preserved—only a phrase such as, "as for your question . . ." The answers themselves were not usually long, being concise responses to specific questions.[13] Yet, despite the brevity of the Geonic responsa, it is possible to discern a tolerant atmosphere to wifebeating in the particular documents.

Rabbi Yehudai Gaon (760s, Pumpedita), writes:

A wife's duty is to honor her husband, raise her children, and feed her husband (even from her own hand). She has to wash, cook, grind in accord with what the rabbis have decreed. And when her husband enters the house, she must rise and cannot sit down until he sits, and she should never raise her voice against her husband. Even if he hits her she has to remain silent, because that is how chaste women behave.[14]

Grossman considers this text to be the exception to the rule. He writes that in Geonic times, a husband is only allowed to beat his wife if "her behavior is improper" and the beating is for "educational" purposes. The above text is an aberration, according to Grossman, because it advises the wife to accept the beatings silently as her due. Not only is the allowance of violence unusual, but also the attitude that a women must stand up on her

---

12. For more details, see "Gaon," in the *Encyclopedia Judaica*, vol. 7, pp. 315–324.

13. Solomon B. Freehof, *The Responsa Literature* (Philadelphia: Jewish Publication Society, 1955), p. 27.

14. Grossman refers to Maimonides and Meir of Rotenberg to prove his claims that the *Gaonim* do not usually deal leniently with batterers; O.G. Ketubot, pp. 169–170.

feet when her husband enters the house. He tries to mitigate the negative impression of this source by trying to show that R. Yehudai could not have penned this opinion, that whoever wrote it was influenced by the Moslem environment, in which a husband regarded his wife as a subservient being.[15] However, even if, as Grossman argues, "the source belongs to the non-normative literature that flourished among the Jews in Muslim countries in the 7th to the 9th centuries,"[16] the quote was attributed to Yehudai Gaon and no one until the days of modern scholarship questioned its authenticity. Thus the source, normative or not, had the power to—and did—influence men's minds and countless halakhic decisions.[17]

There are other *Geonim* who, by virtue of a mild rebuke or minor punishment to the perpetrator, aid and abet husbands who batter their wives. A third (anonymous) Babylonian Gaon writes that, even if a husband batters his wife to the point where she has sores on her body, he cannot be forced to divorce his wife, but is merely fined.[18] Morrell cites Sar Shalom Gaon (ninth century) as

---

15. It is beyond the scope of this chapter to argue with Grossman's deductive scholarship concerning the doubtful attribution of these words to Yehudai Gaon. Avraham Grossman has written two articles "Medieval Rabbinic Views of Wifebeating (8th–13th Centuries)," in Division B, vol. 1, of the *Tenth World Congress of Jewish Studies* (1990), which has been subsequently translated in *Jewish History*, no 5: 53–62, 1991; and "Violence Against Women in Medieval Mediterranean Jewish Society," in *A View Into the Lives of Women in Jewish Societies: Collected Essays*, ed. Yael Azmon (Jerusalem: The Zalman Shazar Center for Jewish History, 1995), pp. 183–207 [Hebrew]. Although Grossman strengthened his argument against the probability that Yehudai actually wrote this responsum in the second essay, he admits that a great scholar such as Goitein accepted its authenticity. Were it to be true, he writes ("Violence Against Women," p. 188), the influence of his words would have reached beyond the confines of Babylon to the Mediterranean centers and been devastating to the status of the woman in her home (including the issue of family violence).

16. Grossman, "Medieval Rabbinic Views," p. 54.

17. Grossman selectively quotes from Yehudai Gaon of the eighth century, whom he uses as an example of how low the status of women was. He cuts off the quote after the following sentence, "She has no right to raise her voice at him, and even if he beats her, she should remain silent, as is the way of modest women." The end of the quotation is as follows: "They must beautify themselves before their husbands every hour/year and put kohl on their eyes, and sweeten their breath with all kinds of perfume so that their husbands hearts will desire them (*yehi libo gas bah*) so that they remain loved by them as on the day when their marriage was consecrated" (*Otzar Ha-Geonim Ketubot*, 428, pp. 169–70).

18. You ask: He who hits his wife and injures her. The law is: You fine him with money according to his ability to pay and according to his property, and he gives it to his wife and she does with it what she wants, providing she does not give it away without consulting him. You should have them compromise and you don't force him to give her a bill of divorce (*O.G. Ketubot*, p. 191).

saying that the husband can beat his wife, but not someone else. "The former case is less severe, since he enjoys a husband's authority over her."[19]

Tsemach Gaon (also of the ninth century) calls upon a man to flog his wife if she is guilty of assaulting others, "so that she not be in the habit of so doing."[20] This clearly falls under the rubric of character building; the husband is responsible for the actions of his wife and has to educate her to behave properly.

There is another anonymous Gaon about whom we know from R. Nissim Girondi (Barcelona, fourteenth century). This source contradicts Grossman's assertion about women's obligation to passively submit to beatings being an anomaly for which no other parallel has been found. Grossman himself quotes R. Nissim Girondi who "states in the name of 'the Gaon'" that a husband is permitted to beat her."[21]

> When she says, I won't do the required work, he would force her with a whip, or if she doesn't feed him. . . . Thus said the Gaon.[22]

R. Hananya (eighth century), another Babylonian Gaon, writes about fines to be paid by the man who pulls the hair out of his wife's head during a fight. He should be fined since he has no right to embarrass her or harm her. Yet Hananya points out that in some places a fine is paid, while, in others the ruling is that it is not paid—there is no real point in fining him, since the money will not be given to the wife anyway. But he feels that the husband should pacify (compensate) his wife and make up to her (*leratzotah*), and if he can afford it (*im yado maseget*), he should add something to her *ketubah* and should admonish himself not to habitually beat her. After doing this, he has fulfilled his duty (*yatza yeday hovato*), and she should then listen to him and forgive him (*timchol*) and make up (*titratzeh*) with him.[23]

The ideology of *shalom bayit*, though not mentioned here, is clear. If the husband expresses remorse, it makes up for his violence, and the wife, in turn, is instructed to submit to him, and even pacify him, for the good of

---

19. Morrell, "An Equal or a Ward," p. 198; *O.G. Baba Kamma*, p. 62, no. 198.

20. Morrell, "An Equal or a Ward," p. 197.

21. Grossman (1991), p. 55. Girondi quotes this Gaon to the effect that it is permitted to beat a wife in order that she do the household work required of all women.

22. Commentary on Ketubot 63b; source is Grossman, "Medieval Rabbinic Views" (1990), note 8.

23. Geonic responsa *Sha-arei Ztedek* Part 4, 13.

their marriage. We see in all of these sources how the social atmosphere reflects the metaphor and the application of many of the halakhic principles that we studied in support of wifebeating.

THE MOSLEM INFLUENCE

Grossman and Goitein pointed to the influence of the Moslem surroundings on the Geonim and later on during the Golden Period of Spanish Jewry in Moslem Spain. Talmudic academies flourished in Iraq, where Islamic jurisprudence developed in the eighth to ninth centuries. By the time of Mohammed (570–633), the redaction of the Talmud was near completion. Was later rabbinic thought influenced by Islam, or did Judaism influence the Moslem view of women? Both systems viewed women as enablers and in both societies women were supposed to stay at home.

In *The Koran*, a husband is encouraged to beat his wife if he thinks she is not acting modestly or is not obeying him:

(Verse 33) Men shall have the pre-eminence over women, because of those advantages wherein God hath caused the one of them to excel the other, and for that which they expend of their substance in maintaining their wives. The honest women are obedient, careful in the absence of their husbands, for that God preserveth them, by committing them to the care and protection of the men. But those whose perverseness ye shall be apprehensive of, rebuke; and remove them into separate apartments, and chastise them. But if they shall be obedient unto you, seek not an occasion of quarrel against them: for God is high and great.

(Verse 34) And if ye fear a breach between the husband and wife, send a judge out of his family, and a judge out of her family: if they shall desire a reconciliation, God will cause them to agree; for God is knowing and wise.[24]

On a passage in *The Koran*, "men shall have the pre-eminence," Sale, a commentator on *The Koran*, says the grounds for this "is said to be man's natural superiority over woman. Women are an inferior class of human

24. Chapter 4, Sipara V, verses 33-34 in *The Quran: Translation and Commentary by Rev. E.M. Wherry, Comprising Sale's Translation* vol. II (London: 1896, 1975), pp. 82–83.

beings."[25] Yet Yitzchak Abrabanel, who lived in Christian Spain in the fifteenth century, writes in a remarkably similar manner in his commentary on Genesis I. Only man is created in God's image; masculine man was the pinnacle of God's creation and woman was only meant to be a helpmeet and a vessel for man's use.[26]

Abdul Qadir, in his commentary on the passage, "Those whose perverseness," from *The Koran* quoted above, makes it clear that:

> Recreant wives are to be punished in three degrees: (1) They are to be rebuked, (2) if they remain rebellious, they are to be assigned separate apartments, and so be banished from bed; and (3) they are to be beaten, but not so as to cause any permanent injury.[27]

Thus the Moslems also made a distinction between the good and the bad wife, the latter to be punished if necessary.

Moslem Spain

R. Samuel ha-Nagid (936–1056), a Jewish Courtier, halakhic scholar, Hebrew philologist, philosopher, military leader, and poet, was one of the first sages to advise the husband to beat his dominating wife so that she stay in her place. In his halakhic work, *Hilkhot Gedolot*, he quotes frequently from the geonim, although he has no hesitation in disagreeing with them when he felt they were mistaken.[28] His attitude toward the domineering women is that she can be hit in order to educate her. He writes in his book *Ben Mishlei*:

---

25. *Ibid.* p. 82.

26. Abrabanel, commentary on Genesis I, p. 69.

27. Commentary on Sipara V, verse 33, p. 83.

28. Avraham Grossman, "Legislation and Responsa Literature," in *The Sephardi Legacy*, ed. Haim Beinart, vol. 1 (Jerusalem: Magnes Press, 1992), pp. 190–191.

Hit your wife without hesitation; if she attempts to dominate you like a man and raises her head (too high). Don't my son, don't you be your wife's wife, while your wife will be her husband's husband!"[29]

Underlying Samuel ha-Nagid's words is that a wife is as subservient to her husband as is a child to his father's authority. The ideal woman is one who listens and shuts up without argument, and the bad woman is one who is disputatious.

This is medieval poetry, not a halakhic work. Thus, one can argue that it is just metaphoric language. However, the motif appears too many times in this book to be ignored. Clearly, as Grossman writes, it reflects a *weltanschauung* and not just playful words. More important is the fact that R. Samuel ha-Nagid was one of the most admired figures of Spanish Jewry, and he influenced both his own and future generations.

Maimonides (1135-1204)

According to Grossman, Maimonides was "the greatest Jewish figure of the Middle Ages, and the greatest *posek* (codifier, one who makes rabbinic rul-

---

29. The first half is my translation of the S. Abramson edition (Tel Aviv: 1948), p. 117, siman 419; and the second half is thanks to H. Adelman, in his unpublished paper on "Wifebeating in Jewish History," (Toronto: Sinai Temple, May 8, 1992). The interested reader might want to compare R. Samuel ha-Nagid's poem with Andrew Marvell's "The Last Instructions to a Painter" (lines 373–389), which Natalie Davis quotes in her article, "The Reasons of Misrule," *Past and Present*, no 50 (1971): 57.

From Greenwich . . .
Comes News of pastime martial and old:
A Punishment invented first to awe
Masculine Wives, transgressing Natures Law,
Where, when the brawny Female disobeys,
And finds,
Nor partial Justice her Behavior binds,
But the just Street does the next House invade,
Mounting the Neighbor Couple of lean Jade;
The Distaffe knocks, the Grains from Kettle fly,
And boys and Girls in Troops run hooting by.
Prudent Antiquity, that knew by Shame,
Better than Law, domestick Crimes to tame,
And taught Youth by Spectacle innocent! (note 48, p. 57)

ings) of all time."[30] He was born in Spain and traveled widely in North Africa, Israel, and Egypt. Because of his compendious knowledge and senior status, his influence on his own and subsequent generations was very great. His creative output in the area of rabbinic writings was vast and included commentary on the Talmud and Mishneh, responsa, and letters. His greatest contribution was *Yad ha-Hazakah*, which he named *Mishneh Torah*. The purpose of the Mishneh Torah was to summarize all of the oral law. It was written in Hebrew and arranged logically by subject. His work was meant to be "user friendly" and was not meant to be confined to being read only by rabbis and their students. The impact of this work on succeeding generations was enormous.

Three of his sources impinge directly on the topic of wifebeating. In one responsum, Maimonides recognizes that, if a husband beats his wife and then blackmails her into paying for her divorce and there are witnesses, he is wrong and should not get away with it. This is in keeping with his commentary on the Mishnah, where he has written that the husband who causes physical harm to his wife (*hovel be-ishto*) must immediately pay her for damages, pain, and humiliation. The compensation money is all hers and she can do what she wants with her money and the husband must take care of her.[31] Allowing her total freedom to dispense her money as she pleases is a controversial decision, yet, as we have seen in Chapter Five, Maimonides allowed it.[32]

Grossman points out that we cannot determine whether he would have ruled this way for a wifebeater who did not cause physical harm to his wife. He feels that it is possible to use the verb *hovel* (causing physical harm) interchangeably with beating, yet is unwilling to do more than speculate.

---

30. Grossman, "Legislation," p. 195.
31. Maimonides, *Hilchot hovel U-Mazik* 4:16; see also Isshut 22:28.
32. *Question*: A. married a woman and began to pick on her, curse her and to beat her so much that she feared for her life with him. He told her, "if you want me to leave you in peace, give me your *meuchar* and I will divorce you." She agreed to his demand. Later he said she should remain with him and he would stop fighting with her, but she was afraid to go back. Does she have to leave him without her *meuchar*?

Answer: If she agreed to give up her rights before witnesses who realized she was forced [blackmailed] by him, she does not lose anything; but if there were no witnesses to his forcing her, she leaves without her *meuchar*. Thus wrote Moses [my translation of Maimonides' responsa #385; see the Bar-Ilan Responsa Project]. *Meuchar* might be a dowry, similar to *mohar* in Hebrew.

In another responsum on this issue, we have the case of Reuben who married Rachel. She "stood him for five years." During this time, he chased after her, maltreated her, beat her and verbally abused her (*zilzilah*). He said that, if she wanted out of the situation, she could redeem herself with her *meuchar* (dowry money) and then he would give her a divorce. After this he again began to beat her and terrorize her, and she finally left him for good. The question was, does she have to leave without her *meuchar* in this case, where she is able to bring evidence of her beatings and verbal abuse? Once again the answer is, if it is clear that she has witnesses to her innocence, then she will not have to give up her rights; but if she has no witnesses, she will have to give in to his demands (and leave without her *ketubah*).[33]

In the same vein, Maimonides says, a man should honor his wife more than his body and love her as his body.[34] He writes that "Woman is not captive. She should get a divorce if her husband is not pleasing to her." We have also seen in Chapter Four that he follows the Geonic responsum and says that the battering husband cannot use the money his wife is awarded for damages for misery and embarrassment unless she agrees to permit him to do so.[35]

Maimonides thus had much to say on the issue of wifebeating. Yet most telling, and the reason that I have included him in this chapter on acceptance, is that Maimonides also recommends in the *Mishneh Torah*—his authoritative code of Jewish law—that beating a "bad" wife, in order to force her to do the work she must do according to *halakha*, is an acceptable form of discipline. He writes:

> A wife who refuses to perform any kind of work that she is obligated to do, may be compelled to perform it, even by scourging her with a rod (Isshut 21:10).

---

33. This response appears following the first one, cited above, from the Bar-Ilan Responsa Project. In *Zera Anashim* (ed. D. Fraenkel, 1902), Maimonides' Responsa 19, there is only this response. In the Bar-Ilan Project version of this responsum, there is a reference to a commentary by Sha'arei Ztedek, which implies that if she gives up her *ketubah*, she cannot benefit from it.

34. *Isshut*, 15:19.

35. Maimonides, *Hilchot hovel U-Mazik* 4:16 ; Grossman (1990) in note No. 10, says the commentators were amazed that Maimonides ruled that the husband doesn't have access to the usufruct.

We saw above how Tikochinski denied the important precedent that this ruling of Maimonides set for future generations.[36] It was less easy for the commentators of his own time to whitewash Maimonides' words.

As we have noted, required work is generally understood to mean housework: grinding, baking, cleaning, cooking, breast feeding, preparing the husband's bed, and weaving wool.[37] If the wife refuses to do this work, then she "may be compelled." What does compel mean? Who compels her? Most commentators concur that Maimonides means that it is the "husband" who can force her. R. Vidal of Tolosa, the well-known fourteenth-century interpreter of Maimonides' *Mishneh Torah*, writes in the *Maggid Mishneh* that "Nahmanides wrote that we force her with a stick and it is also the view of Rabbenu [i.e., Maimonides] and the major rabbis (*ve-ikar*)." Some rabbis understand the referent to be the rabbinic court (*beit din*), since the word "force" (*kofin*) is in the plural, rather than the singular. Shem Tov Even Gaon (d. Safed, 1312), in his commentary *Migdal Oz* on Maimonides, understood it to mean the rabbinic court,[38] but he is clearly in a minority.

Finally, what is the possible motivation underlying Maimonides' pronouncement? Does it have to do with a faulty perception of woman's place, an earlier halakhic precedent that Maimonides knew of? Perhaps the motivation is as follows in Maimonides' own words:

> If the husband claims that she is not doing the work, while she claims that she has not refused to work, another woman or some neighbors should be asked to stay with them. This matter should be handled according to what the judge may consider feasible.[39]

The reason for this is that idleness leads to evil. Yet Maimonides has said earlier in his treatise on marriage[40] that if she brings enough servants with her to perform the work, she can sit at leisure at home.

---

36. Tikochinski, *The Enactments*, p. 132. He is probably referring to R. Abraham b. David of Posquieres (Rabad), who wrote in his notes on the *Mishneh Torah* that he had never heard of such a precedent.

37. See Maimonides, *Mishneh Torah*, "Isshut," 21:3, where there is a list of required duties; see 21:5 and 21:7 as well.

38. If it is the *beit din*, then we have community-sanctioned wifebeating, which to the modern sensibility may be even worse than finding it acceptable for a husband to do so! Yosef David Kapah, in a commentary on the *Mishneh Torah*, concurs that it is the court, since it is inconceivable to him that the sages allowed husbands to beat their wives, a custom of the gentiles!

39. Continuation of Isshut, 21:10.

40. Isshut, 21:6.

Therefore it may be impossible to understand why Maimonides wrote what he did. In addition to speculating about the Moslem environment of the times, Grossman speculates about a hypothetical source dating back to the Geonim. He also raises a more interesting question: What was the influence of this pronouncement on the status of Jewish women in both the Moslem world and outside? For those rabbis who understood Maimonides to mean that the husband had the right to discipline his wife with a beating, a dangerous precedent was set. Violent husbands could claim that their action was justified by the great Maimonides himself.[41]

Two rabbis who understood that Maimonides' words justified beating one's wife for "good" cause were R. Solomon B. Abraham Aderet, who lived in Barcelona, and R. Jonah ben Abraham of Gerona, two major figures in Spanish Jewry, whose influence extends into our own times.

Rabbi Jonah ben Abraham of Gerona (Gerondi) [D. 1263]

Rabbi Jonah ben Abraham of Gerona, was related to, and influenced by, the great medievalist scholar Nahmanides (1194–1270). Nahmanides gained some of his knowledge of the French tosafists (see Chapter Eight) from his relative, R. Jonah, who played an important role in transmitting the ethical values of German and French rabbis to Spanish scholars. His literary work was diverse and his halakhic monographs and ethical works were the main source of his fame. Although he did not always agree with Maimonides, it appears that he accepted the idea that a husband may beat his wife if she transgresses. The normal course of events is that the husband should not beat anyone and certainly not his wife:

> A man must not beat his neighbor. . . . The man who beats his neighbor transgresses two negative precepts. . . . And so it is with the man who beats his wife. He transgresses two negative precepts, *if he did not hit her in order to reprove her for some transgression.* The man who raises his hand

---

41. As a testimony to the fact that this knowledge is in the common domain, see Chapter 28 of Naomi Ragen's bestselling novel, *Jephte's Daughter* (New York: Warner, 1989). Her heroine complains that her husband, a wifebeater and a learned rabbi, quoted Maimonides as saying that a man is allowed to beat his wife in order to get her to obey him.

against his neighbor is called wicked from the time of lifting his hand, as it is said "why would you smite" and not "why did you smite."[42]

Despite the fact that a man transgresses two negative precepts if he beats his wife, R. Jonah still allows the use of a beating "if justified" for the sake of "reproving her" for some transgression.[43]

R. Solomon B. Abraham Aderet (Rashba) [1235–1310]

Rashba was also of an important family, and like his mentors, R. Jonah and Nahmanides, he attacked detractors of Jews and Judaism. According to Grossman he was "the greatest Spanish Jewish scholar of his generation,"[44] and exerted great influence on the students who came to his yeshiva from many countries. Rashba was a product of Moslem Spanish teachings, and his learning was in turn transmitted to Western European Jewry by his students. He was one of the most important and prolific writers of responsa. Questions were addressed to him from all parts of the world, as well as from Spanish communities. His "ten thousand" responsa are considered to be one of the highest achievements in this literary genre.[45] According to Grossman, "his decisions were of a general, fundamental nature, his responsa became a cornerstone of Jewish law."[46] Because many of his responsa were inserted in the *Tur*, and then incorporated by Caro in his *Shulhan Arukh*, they have continued to play a considerable role in the development of *halakha*.

---

42. Jonah Girondi, *Iggeret Ha-Teshuvah* [Letter of Repentance], (Cracow, 1586) and (Prague, 1596), p.11 [Hebrew]. This book is available in the manuscript room of the Jewish Theological Seminary.

43. A.T. Shrock, in his book *Rabbi Jonah ben Abraham of Gerona* (London: Edward Goldston, 1948) admits that, "in spite of the exemplary home life that must have been an outstanding feature among Jewish families at that time, cases of wifebeating were not unknown." He then refers to Girondi's two works, *Sha'are Teshubah* and *Iggeret Ha-Teshubah* and, in an apologetic mode, adds, "We are, however, inclined to the view that such cases were not very frequent (p. 162)." For a similar view cf. Finkelstein, *Jewish Self-Government*, p. 70.

44. Grossman, "Legislation," p. 202.

45. See Isidore Epstein, "Chapter on Matrimony" in *The "Responsa" of Rabbi Solomon Ben Adreth of Barcelona* (1235–1310) *as a Source of the History of Spain* (London: Kegan Paul, Trench, Trubner, 1925) and notes to this chapter. See also Grossman's article "Legislation," pp. 199–204.

46. Grossman, "Legislation," p. 203.

Rashba writes a response to the following question:

> Question: What is the sentence for a husband who regularly beats his wife, so that she has to leave his home and return to her father's home?
> Answer: The husband should not beat his wife. She was given to him for life, not for sorrow. He should honor her more than his own body. The rabbinic court investigates to find who is responsible. If he beats her and torments her, *not according to the law* and she runs away, the law is with her, for a person does not have to live with a snake [reminiscent of Hagar's situation with Sarah]. But if she is the cause of the beating—i.e., if she curses him for no reason—the law is with him, for the woman who curses her husband in front of him, leaves without her *ketubah*. At any rate, in cases where it is not clear who is at fault, or even in cases where it is clear, I don't see that the rabbinic court can make him swear not to beat her. It can only tell him in strong words not to beat her and warn him that if he beats her, *not according to law*, he will have to divorce her and give her her *ketubah*.[47]

In this source we see the confluence of almost all of the halakhic rules and quasi-rules that we have met up to this point. The ambiguity and tension implicit in these rules are also obvious here. The bottom line, however, is that one is permitted to beat his wife when "the law is with him." Maimonides has given one instance of when one is allowed to beat his wife. One wonders under what other conditions "the law" is "with him."

When does Jewish law deem it proper to beat wives? Clearly, when she curses him. The issue of cursing is complicated. We have seen in several sources that cursing the husband, the husband's parents, the wife's parents, and possibly even his/her ancestors, can have serious consequences for the wife. Already in the Talmud, there are sources that indicate that a woman

---

47. Rashba Responsa, part seven, p. 32: #477. But see also another version of Responsum #102 on p. 93. I wish to thank David Golinkin for bringing this second responsum to my attention. In this one, the court seems to be more sympathetic to the woman, and there are elements that are not in the version above. It would seem that our responsum is an abridged version of the longer one; it is also often attributed (erroneously) to Nahmanides (see *Maggid Mishnah*, above, or Caro in *Beit Yosef*, below). On the various editions of Rashba, see Kasher, M. (1979). *Sarei ha-Elef*, vol. 2 (Jerusalem, 1979), pp. 361–362. To the best of my knowledge, Nahmanides did not write any responsa on wifebeating; I could find only the one in the volume attributed to him.

who curses her husband's parents is behaving in a manner not consonant with the Jewish religion. The logic is that, since she does not behave properly, the husband has the right to reprove her, since she is in his care and he is responsible to the community for her actions. Thus, if she violates Jewish law, it is in fact the husband's *obligation* to reprove her. There is even a biblical injunction to back him up: "reprove your kinsman, and [but?] incur no guilt because of him" (Lev. 19:17). If the husband does not reprove her—if he remains silent when he hears her cursing him, her parents, or his parents—he himself incurs guilt.

In the Talmud there is nothing about beating a wife to educate her; her ultimate punishment is that she can be divorced by the husband and must leave without the monetary settlement due her in the marriage contract.[48] At some point in history, however, a wife's cursing becomes a just cause for the husband to beat his wife, for "educational purposes," even to the point of death (see below).

R. David B. Solomon Ibn Avi Zimra (Radbaz) [1479–1573]

Another example of a scholar who was influenced by Maimonides is R. David B. Solomon Ibn (Avi) Zimra (Radbaz), one of the pillars of Jewish life in Egypt and in Palestine during the latter part of the fifteenth and sixteenth centuries.[49] Radbaz traveled to Safed, leaving Spain in 1492 with other Spanish exiles. From Safed he went to Egypt, where he headed both a yeshiva training rabbinical scholars and the rabbinic court. Later he returned to Safed, where he lived out the remainder of his long life. His library was world renowned and his responsa (c. 2,400–10,000)[50] are considered to be important both historically and *halakhically*. He was certainly aware of Maimonides' *Mishneh Torah*, since his was one of the classic commentaries on it.

In a responsum, he strongly objected to the ruling by R. Simhah (see Chapter Eight), who allowed civil authorities to force a man to divorce his wife if he beat her. In general, Radbaz did not like the rabbis of the German

---

48. B. Ketubot 72a-b; see also Jer. Ketubot, Chapter 7, pp. 31a and b, *halakha* #6.
49. Israel M. Goldman, *The Life and Times of Rabbi David Ibn Avi Zimra* (New York: Jewish Theological Seminary of America, 1970), p. 1.
50. Source for 10,000 is the *Bar-Ilan Responsa Project* capsule biography.

school, with the exception of R. Israel Isserlein.[51] In the Sephardi *minhag* [custom], polygamy was still the rule, and Radbaz upheld the primacy of *minhag*, writing that it often superseded the law.[52] Radbaz ruled that, if a forced divorce were allowed, the children who would be the issue of a possible remarriage would be considered illegitimate (*mamzerim*).[53]

Radbaz's reasoning here is that, since it is against *halakha* (as interpreted by many) to force a man to divorce his wife, if a wife gains a forced divorce and then remarries, her remarriage is an adulterous one, since the forced divorce is not valid; that is, according to *halakha*, she is still married to her first husband. Again we encounter the double standards which are at the base of *halakha*. One double standard is that adultery applies only to a married woman since a man—who is allowed more than one wife—cannot be considered to be engaging in adulterous behavior.[54]

Another application of a double standard is that only the man can obtain or grant divorce by his "will." So a married man may sleep with an unmarried woman, but a married woman can sleep with no one but her husband—and husband he remains if she has not been "legally" divorced. The woman cannot initiate divorce or marriage. This double standard puts the woman at the man's mercy, for if he refuses to divorce her there is not much she can do even if he beats her.

Radbaz, also accepts Maimonides' notion that a man may beat his wife for a reason and adds: "if she does improper or immoral things, according to our teachings, he has a right to chastise her and beat her and bring her back to the good path, since she is under his aegis (*be-reshuto*)."[55] However, he qualifies this general permission with more specific limitations (see Chapter Ten).

Thus we can see that Maimonides' statement that one can beat one's wife if she has not performed her duties, albeit a minority opinion, has served as a precedent.

---

51. Goldman, *Life and Times*, pp. 41–42. Is it a coincidence that Isserlein's position on the battered woman was harsh and a throwback to Geonic times? See later in this chapter, where I quote Isserlein, the author of *Terumat Hadeshen*, in response to a query about whether a man can hit his wife in order to keep her from cursing his parents. "Anyone who is responsible for educating someone under him, and sees that person transgressing, can beat that person to prevent the transgression" (Responsa #218).

52. Goldman, *op.cit.*, pp. 44–46.

53. Radbaz Responsa, part 4: 157.

54. Unless, of course, the woman "belongs" to another man! See the discussion in Chapter Two about the *sotah* for a fuller description of the adulterous man and woman.

55. Radbaz Responsa, part 3: 447, *Bar-Ilan Responsa Project*.

GENIZA SOURCES

Many extant responsa were found in the lumber room of the Great Synagogue in Cairo. This Geniza, the "burial" room and hiding place of sacred texts written in Hebrew, was uncovered in the second half of the nineteenth century.[56] It is a window onto the social reality of the period in Palestine and North Africa.

Goitein states that wife-battering was very common, especially among the lower classes. According to him, it had to do with economic difficulties and the young marriage age during the eleventh through thirteenth centuries. Often the husbands were much older than their wives and acted toward their child-brides as if they were children who had to be educated. The young wife often had to leave her mother and become part of her husband's family, where she might be seen more as an intruder or a "dog's body." In such cases, the husband had to serve as a buffer between his family and his wife.

The frightening picture of one young wife is revealed in a complaint to a judge. She relates that her husband maltreats her and curses her, the sister hits her with her shoe, the father calls her names. As if that were not enough, her husband implies that she is guilty of adultery and that she has to be examined by a midwife to see if she is pure. The woman cries for help to the judge![57] There is not much else she can do, for, as one uncle writes to his niece, "A wife has no one in the world except her husband." Goitein also mentions that the Yemenite women have a saying, "Hell with my husband is better than Paradise with my family,"[58] to illustrate this point.[59] All of this explains very well the social setting in which wifebeating is tolerated.

The types of complaints in the Geniza sources vary; some reflect deep discord between the spouses, very often about property and possessions. Often, however, the reason has to do with the wife's general unhappiness with a husband who isn't willing to provide for her needs.[60]

---

56. Solomon Freehof, *The Responsa Literature* (Philadelphia: Jewish Publication Society, 1959), p. 195. Freehof writes that it was discovered by Solomon Schechter.

57. Goitein, *A Mediterranean Society*, p. 175.

58. *Ibid.*, p. 179.

59. We have already encountered this theme in Isaiah 4:1 and with Resh Lakish, the tannaitic rabbi of the mid-second century, "It is better to live [an unhappy life] in a married state than to live [a happy life] in solitude" (B. Yebamot 118b). The original statement is without the words in brackets; many are those who understand this saying in the expanded manner.

60. See the case of Matsliah ha-Kohen, in Goitein, *A Mediterranean Society*, p. 186.

It would seem that in those countries that were influenced by Moslem thought, the attitude toward wifebeating (for a "good" cause) was more lenient. One reason was that, as already noted, girls were often wed in their teens, or even as children. Many skills and duties these young wives were expected to know would have to be learned in their husbands' households. Thus the attitude of the court, the father, and the husband was that the education of the wife was only proper. Another reason lay in the fact that, in Islamic countries, polygamy was never banned as it was in the European countries. Thus, the attitude that the wife is property was re-enforced. Finally, we can not ignore the direct and indirect influence of the surrounding culture of Islam which may have predisposed husbands to regard their wives first as chattel and only then (perhaps) as persons.

Goitein's opinion is that the position of Jewish women was still better than that of the Moslem women in Moslem countries, where, according to him, wifebeating was rampant. He also believes that the negative attitude in Judaism toward women is a result of Moslem influence.[61]

However, Salo Baron came to the opposite conclusion, writing, "wifebeating, particularly in imitation of their German neighbors, seems to have spread among the Jews of medieval Germany to a sufficient extent to constitute a problem, and Meir of Rotenberg proposed the Draconian penalty of cutting off the guilty husband's hand."[62]

Assis establishes that Spanish Jewry was exposed to influences from both Christian and Muslim influences at the same time that it was part of the medieval Jewish world.[63] He describes the uphill battle that the rabbis had to counter these influences. He says that the price that had to be paid for being integrated into the general society was that the Jew was influenced for the worse.[64]

---

61. Goitein, pp. 171–189. See also Judith Romney Wegner, "The Status of Women in Jewish and Islamic Marriage and Divorce Law," *Harvard Women's Law Journal*, no 5 (1982): 1–33.

62. Salo Baron, *The Jewish Community*, vol. 2 (Philadelphia: Jewish Publication Society, 1942), p. 318.

63. Yom Tov Assis, "Sexual Behavior in Mediaeval Hispano-Jewish Society," in *Jewish History: Essays in Honor of Chimen Abramsky*, ed. Ada Rapoport-Olpert and Steven J. Zipperstein (London: 1988).

64. It resulted in sexual laxity, doubt, apostasy, converts, and traitors. He blames the activities of rapists, criminals, forgers, and thieves on the openness of Spanish society (pp. 239–241); Yom Tov Assis, "Crime and Violence among the Jews of Spain (thirteenth–fourteenth centuries)," in *Zion Jubilee Volume*, 50 (1986): 221–240 [Hebrew].

The verdict is not yet in, and we should not uncritically accept judgments about whose influence caused wifebeating to be tolerated or even advocated when circumstances were deemed to warrant it. Not enough research has been done to judge whether there was mutual influence between the cultures on this point. Even if the influence was one way, it does not let the Jewish tradition "off the hook," since, in many areas of religious practice, Jews were not under the influence of their neighbors (see Chapter Nine).

CHRISTIAN EUROPE

In Christian Europe, unlike in Christian Spain, the economic status of women was relatively high in the late Middle Ages. Many women lent money and appeared in public in connection with their business roles. It is possible that women's high status was resented by men[65] and led to a backlash. Evidence for this is that, in the fifteenth century, the status of women started to go down. Coincidentally (or not) during this time period, wifebeating is dealt with less stringently in the responsa literature than it was when women's status was higher.

ISRAEL ISSERLEIN (MAHARI)

This less stringent approach to wifebeating is illustrated in a book called *Sefer Terumat ha-Deshen*, which is the collected responsa of Israel Isserlein. According to Shlomo Eidelberg, Isserlein (c. 1390–1460) "was the last famous rabbinical scholar of medieval Austria. He was a disciple of the old Franco-German school of the preceding centuries."[66] *Terumat ha-Deshen* con-

---

65. Aviva Cantor, in *Jewish Women, Jewish Men* (San Francisco: Harper, 1995), suggests that the Beruriah libel introduced by Rashi was part of this backlash. In the twelfth century, certain rabbis encouraged their daughters to wear *tefillin*, *tzitzit*, be part of the *minyan*, etc. "Some scholars, seeing this trend emerge . . . created a misogynist libel about how a learned woman came to grief as a warning to the men who were allowing women to participate in such rituals." However, since Rashi himself was one of those rabbis, encouraging his daughters to wear *tefillin*, etc., there is a certain contradiction in Cantor's suggestion (p. 108).

66. Shlomo Eidelberg, *Jewish Life in Austria in the XVth Century: As Reflected in the Legal Writings of Rabbi Israel Isserlein and His Contemporaries* (Philadelphia: Dropsie College, 1962), p. 38.

tains 354 responsa, all corresponding to the three Hebrew consonants *daled*, *shin*, and *nun* (of the word *Deshen*), which follow the order and arrangement of Jacob ben Asher's work, *Arba'ah Turim*. It is not clear whether the questions are genuine, or if Isserlein fabricated them so that he could respond.[67] Jacob Weil, who was an older contemporary of Isserlein, refers to Isserlein's decisions with such respect that he wrote that they could not be changed. Isserlein, he wrote, was considered a Gaon, a prince of his generation. His writings were popular among both Ashkenazi and Sephardi scholars. Solomon Luria said of him, "Do not deviate from his works because he was great and eminent."[68] R. Joseph Caro refers to him as an important codifier, although he also criticizes him. He was well thought of by R. Moses Isserles, who cites him constantly.[69]

Isserlein was a man of independent thought and wide learning. According to Freehof, he was a bridge between East and West.[70] Isserlein mentions the Spanish scholars like Alfasi and Maimonides, but believed "in the German rabbinic tradition that the Law had to be interpreted according to the Ashkenazic *Rishonim*, or classicists. . . . When he found a contradiction between the decisions of the Spanish and the German scholars, he followed the German tradition."[71]

Despite this general tendency, he occasionally contradicted Rashi, Maimonides, and Mordecai b. Hillel (1240–1298), disciple of R. Meir of Rotenberg, and others when it suited him. This we can see in the following responsum.

Question: Can a man, who hears his wife cursing and saying bad things about her mother and father, reprove her for this several times? If this does not work, can he then beat her in order to ensure that she does not do this any more?

Answer: Even though Mordecai [b. Hillel] and R. Simhah wrote that he who beats his wife transgresses the negative precept "not to excess" (*pen yosif*) [Deut. 25:3, see Chapter Six], and is dealt with very harshly, I disagree with this strict interpretation.

---

67. *Ibid.*, p. 51.
68. Solomon Freehof, *The Responsa Literature*, p. 76.
69. Eidelberg, *Jewish Life in Austria*, pp. 58–59. See *Beit Joseph*, "Gittin vekiddushin," No. 9.
70. Freehof, *The Responsa Literature*, p. 76.
71. Eidelberg, *Jewish Life in Austria*, p. 55.

I base my interpretation on R. Nahman, writing in the name of R. Isaac, who wrote that it was permissible to beat a Canaanite slave woman, in one's possession, in order to prevent her from transgressing. He of course should not overdo it or else she would be freed.

Anyone who is responsible for educating someone under him, and sees that person transgressing, can beat that person to prevent the transgression. He does not have to be brought to court.[72]

The implication of this responsum is that a wife's status is similar to a slave. Both are "under" the husband/master's jurisdiction. He is responsible for both. Thus, he is permitted to strike her in order to educate her and prevent her from sinning, since, if she transgresses, he is responsible for her action. It is clear that a man can hit his wife in order to preempt a transgression.[73] Isserlein's responsum is not a one-time interpretation, since it is later quoted by other rabbis.

SOLOMON LURIA (c. 1510–1574)

One rabbi who refers to this responsum is R. Solomon ben Jechiel Luria (Maharshal) in his work, *Yam Shel Shelomo*, (on Baba Kama) a commentary on the Talmud. Luria founded his own yeshiva in Lublin, Poland, and wrote *novellae* on the Talmud as well as responsa. Luria addresses the specific issue of the slave/master relationship and cites both Isserlein's responsum #218 in *Terumat ha-Deshen*, and Maimonides to justify the master's beating his slave. But Luria goes much further than Isserlein does in punishing the wife, for he writes:

A man may hit his wife when she curses her father and mother, because she transgresses the law. . . . There is no need to bring her to the court, as is so in the case of the Jewish slave. And he can beat her for other reasons as well—whenever she transgresses the laws of the Torah. He can beat

---

72. My paraphrase of *Terumat ha-Deshen*, Responsum #218.

73. It is interesting that Isserles (see next paragraph), in a gloss to the *Shulhan Arukh* (Hoshen Mispat 421:13), quotes the last words exactly: "And so it is for someone under his jurisdiction. If he sees him transgressing, he may hit him and reprove him in order that he no longer transgress and there is no need to bring him to the court." This is not the place to judge whether there is a common source to which both Isserlein and Isserles refer.

her until she dies [until her soul departs—*ad she-tetzeh nafsha*], even for transgressing a minor negative prohibition. Of course, he shouldn't hasten to beat her. He should warn her first. He can only beat her if she doesn't heed his warning.[74]

Luria writes that this can be applied in other situations as well. We have seen above that any Israelite can strike another person to prevent him [or her] from violating the law (Lev. 19:17).

Luria is aware of the anarchic potential if this application is carried to an extreme. Yet he considers every Israelite responsible for the observance of divine law by others, and is also aware of the gravity of allowing the wife to get away with cursing and not being reproved for it. A wife who curses her husband, her parents, or his parents is going against the hierarchical order. If the husband is considered to be *in loco parentis* (and guardian of God's law), to allow cursing of authority figures is like allowing cursing of God. We can sense this when he cites, not only Isserlein, but Maimonides and Moses of Coucy, the thirteenth author of *Sefer Mitzvot Gadol (Semag)*:

> Maimonides and Semag ruled like Abba Shaul, "strike only the one who curses her husband's father in the husband's presence" . . . because the father-in law is like the father . . . and I found in a responsum of Nahmanides[75] that even if she curses him [her husband?] to his face, he can beat her. . . .

Thus Luria has given extensive powers to the husband. Luria is empowering him to beat his wife (even until she dies) for the serious infractions of cursing her parents, her husband's father, and perhaps even the husband. This is because the husband is responsible for his wife's actions and has to educate

74. Luria, *Yam shel Shelomo*, Baba Kama, third chapter, 20b #9. One might argue that "until her soul departs" does not mean until she dies. The intent might be to break her will and spirit, in order to get her to toe the line.

75. Julie Ringold Spitzer, in "Spousal Abuse in the Rabbinic and Contemporary Judaism," (Unpublished Thesis in partial fulfillment of the requirements for Ordination at Hebrew Union College-Jewish Institute of Religion, 1985), has written a literal translation of the entire section as part of her thesis, pp. 39–42. Although she writes Maimonides instead of Nahmanides, it would appear that it is neither one; this is the responsum of Rashba, which was wrongly attributed to Nahmanides, and which is being referred to (see above, note 47).

her to behave properly. But it is also to preserve order and hierarchy in Jewish society.[76]

MOSES ISSERLES (1520–1572)

R. Moses ben Israel Isserles (Rema) is best known for his extensive glosses, or appended notes (*hagahot*) to R. Joseph Caro's *Shulhan Arukh*. He was an outstanding halakhic authority who served as head of the rabbinic court in Cracow, Poland. He corresponded with rabbinic scholars in Germany, Poland, and northern Italy, and his responsa and glosses reflect Ashkenazi halakhic practice. His (Ashkenazi) glosses on Caro's work (supposedly reflecting Sephardi practices) are one of the main reasons why the *Shulhan Arukh* is still so widely accepted as a halakhic authority today.

Isserles rules that, although unwarranted wifebeating justifies compelling a husband to divorce his wife, there are extenuating circumstances when one does not have to force the husband. He writes about wifebeating in *Darkei Moshe*, his commentary on the *Tur* and in two different glosses on the *Shulhan Arukh*.

In *Darkei Moshe* he writes that:

> A man who beats his wife commits a sin, as though he has beaten his neighbor, and if he persists in this conduct the court may castigate him and place him under oath to discontinue this conduct; if he refuses to obey the order of the court, they will compel him to divorce his wife at once (and pay her the *ketubah*), because it is not customary or proper for Jews to beat their wives. Only let the court warn him first once or twice [not to persist]. But *if she is the cause of it*, for example, if she curses him or denigrates his father and mother and he scolds her calmly first and it does not help, then it is obvious that *he is permitted to beat her* and castigate her. And if it is not known who is the cause, the husband is not con-

---

76. There are two other sources in which Luria discusses wifebeating. One is a continuation of his commentary on Baba Kama, and the other is a very long rambling responsum. In the continuation (#21), he takes an adamant stand against wifebeating in the case of a husband injuring his wife during intercourse and quotes R. Simhah and R. Meir of Rotenburg (see Chapter Eight) to back him up. In his responsum #69, he opposes forcing the husband who beats his wife to give her a divorce, yet is clearly aware of the problem of women who go to the civil authorities to get a divorce, thus increasing the chances of illegitimate issue (*mamzerim*).

sidered a reliable source when he says that she is the cause and portrays her as a harlot, for all women are presumed to be law-abiding.[77]

Thus far we have seen in Israel Isserlein's responsum and the commentaries of Solomon Luria and Moses Isserles that there is an Ashkenazi precedent for allowing *lawful* wifebeating if the wife is the cause of the argument, or if she curses, and has to be castigated to prevent further occurrence.

In the two glosses to Caro's *Shulhan Arukh*, (EH 80:15 and EH 154:3), Isserles relates to whether wifebeating is ever justified as a form of punishment. In *EH* 154:3, which is a discussion of whether one can force a recalcitrant husband (who also beats his wife) to give her a divorce, Isserles returns again to the issue of the wife as cause of the beating:

> . . . if she curses him without reason, or puts down his father or mother and he reproves her with words, and she does not listen to him, some say that it is permissible to beat her. Some say that it is forbidden even to beat a bad wife, but the first opinion is the correct one.

What this means is that, although Isserles has two choices, he chooses to follow the first opinion, that it is permissible to beat a "bad" wife. Further on in this gloss, Isserles writes that "if she curses him with no reason, he divorces her without paying her the money stipulated in the marriage contract."

On the other hand, in the same gloss, Isserles mentions the option that if the husband is the source of the provocation, and a frequent wifebeater, the court can force him to divorce her, since the man who strikes his wife commits a sin. All this, he is careful to say, is after first warning the husband once or twice not to beat her. Thus, even though in *Darkei Moshe* Isserles writes that "the husband is not considered a reliable source when he says that she is the cause and portrays her as a harlot . . .," it is still necessary to warn the husband. What this means, from the wife's perspective, is that she continues to be under the power of a wifebeater until the court makes up its mind.

In EH 80:15, Isserles comments on Caro's interpretation of Maimonides' statement about beating one's wife with a whip if she does not perform her required wifely duties. Again, he gives divergent views about forcing one's wife to do her duties.

---

77. Moses Isserles, *Darkei Moshe, Tur, Even Ha-Ezer,* 154:15.

According to Judith Hauptman, this gloss is a departure from Caro's exact words in EH 80:15, which does not use the words "even with a whip." She feels that Isserles "on his own, not mandated by the code he was glossing, raises the possibility of beating a wife who angers her husband. . . ." Her opinion is that, by considering the possibility of wifebeating as a means of discipline, Isserles is making a break with the Franco-German tradition.[78]

Although there is clearly a diversity of halakhic opinion on the subject, it is worthwhile quoting Spitzer's words:

> Men should not beat their wives. But, if the wife may be prevented from committing a transgression, beating is sometimes considered understandable. If a man is habitually abusive, his punishment is most severe, yet the woman is also liable for punishment if the guilt is found to be hers.[79]

Thus, there are two kinds of wifebeating: one a form of aggression and the other a form of punishment or education. It is to Isserles's credit that he considers women to be innocent unless proven guilty—and this is because he recognizes that the husband can easily be omnipotent in the home and that the wife therefore must be protected from his wrath. Yet he also accepts as a given that a husband is permitted to beat his wife in certain cases.

We must keep in mind that those rabbis who allowed wifebeating in specific situations were among the most central and influential of all rabbinic authorities. The works of Yehudai Gaon, Maimonides, Radbaz, Rashba, Isserlein, Luria, and Isserles are in the front line of halakhic precedents. Fortunately, however, they were also in a minority. Most rabbis reject this position. The majority attitude, like Rabbi Jacob Weil's, is that "He who beats his wife is in greater fault than he who beats his neighbor." Weil implicitly criticizes Isserles, referring to the classic texts in the Talmud (B. Ketubot 60a and 61a) that stress that a husband has to honor his wife more than himself. Weil's approach constitutes "unconditional rejection," the second approach to wifebeating, which will be discussed in the next chapter.

---

78. Judith Hauptman, "Traditional Jewish Texts, Wifebeating, and the Patriarchal Construction of Jewish Marriage," (unpublished paper, 22 May 1995 version): 12.

79. Spitzer, "Spousal Abuse," p. 13.

8

Rejection: There Is No Excuse for Wifebeating*

In this chapter, I will focus on the pattern I call rejection, which is the attitude of the group of rabbis who rejects wifebeating. There are two types of rejection: unqualified and qualified. Rabbis who hold the former attitude state that battering is considered sufficient grounds for divorce. Rabbis holding the qualified attitude, however, view battering as a terrible thing that should not be done, yet take an evasive attitude, which will be discussed fully in Chapter Ten.

Unqualified rejection is an attitude that does not allow compromise. It looks injustice squarely in the eye and will not tolerate what is wrong. In order to repair the state of injustice, it will not perpetuate the root of the injustice, it will not permit the perpetuation of the *status quo*, which is the root of the injustice—in our case, having the wife remain married to a violent husband.

"Rejection" first of all confronts the problem of wifebeating; it does not deny it, accept it, or excuse it. Rejection clearly states that wifebeating

* Parts of this chapter have appeared in *Gender and Judaism: The Transformation of Tradition*, ed. T. M. Rudavsky, pp. 13–24. New York: New York University Press, 1995 and *Proceedings of the Eleventh World Congress of Jewish Studies*, Division B, vol. 1, pp. 143–150. Jerusalem: World Union of Jewish Studies, 1994.

is wrong and demands some kind of redress or release of the victim from her suffering.

Unconditional rejection is the approach of those rabbis who face up to the fact that there is a problem and condemn it. Some of them relate creatively to *halakha* by use of *takkanot* (pl. of *takkanah*) or creative legislation to change what they perceive to be an unjust law.

A *takkanah* is a halakhic amendment that changes an existing law. It usually redresses an existing social problem whose source is in the law as practiced. It is an agreed-upon procedure, often announced publicly, by a group of rabbis constituting a rabbinic court. Often it is a decision attributed to a charismatic leader. Its legitimization comes from the community, which seeks change and guidance from its local rabbis.[1]

Takkanot became necessary very early in Jewish history; some rabbis have suggested that they were enacted even before Moses.[2] One of the earliest is the *prosbul* of Hillel the elder, which is a legal fiction canceling debts in the Sabbatical year.[3] One of the better known examples of a *takkanah* dealing with women's issues is that of R. Gershom (960-1028), which banned polygyny (a man's being married simultaneously to two or more women) for those who lived in Christian Europe.[4] A *takkanah* overrides and abrogates accepted halakhic rules that precede it. Thus it is a radical revision of an existing practice.

During the thirteenth century, cases of maltreatment of wives by husbands that came before the Ashkenazi rabbis were not taken very seriously; consequently during this time, a *takkanah* was proposed that dealt with the subject of wifebeating.

---

1. Simcha Goldin, "The Role and Function of the *Herem* and the *Takanah* in the Medieval Ashkenazic Community," *Proceedings of The Eleventh World Congress of Jewish Studies*, Division B, vol. 1 (Jerusalem: World Union of Jewish Studies, 1994), pp. 105–112 [Hebrew]. See also Chapter Five and the Appendix for more on *takkanot*.

2. Mayer Gruber, "The Mishna as Oral Torah," *The Motherhood of God and Other Studies* (Atlanta, GA: Scholar's Press, 1992).

3. M. Shevi'it 10:3 *ff.*

4. The way this *takkanah* works is as follows: It excommunicates the person who violates the *takkanah*. The authority behind the *takkanah* are the community and its leading rabbis, since the punishment is *not* prescribed by the Bible, Mishnah, or Talmud; see Rachel Biale, *Women and Jewish Law* (New York: Schocken Books, 1984), pp. 50–51. Since the Bible itself is ambiguous on this issue, the Karaites, who adhered literally to the Bible, insisted that the Bible proscribed monogamy.

Not too much is known about this *takkanah*. Its author was R. Perez b. Elijah of Corbeil, who died toward the end of the thirteenth century.[5] It is not known whether the rabbis to whom it was sent approved it. According to Louis Finkelstein, who first reproduced and translated it, it consists of two sections, "the first providing that any man might be compelled to undertake by a *herem* or oath that he would not strike his wife again. He might be compelled to do so on the complaint of either the wife or one of her near relatives."[6]

When the *takkanah* is supported by a *herem*, it is a very strong enactment. A *herem* is a sanction. It can be in the form of an oath or of excommunication. It is a last-resort measure, since one does not want to expel Jews from the community, nor is oath-taking encouraged. The strength of the *herem* lies in its power to curse or exclude those who deviate from Jewish law.[7] According to Finkelstein, "The second part of Perez's *takkanah* states that if the husband refused to undertake such a *herem*, the Court should assign the wife alimony as if the husband were away."[8]

The *takkanah* begins with the shrill cry of a sympathetic rabbi:

(1) The cry of the daughters of our people has been heard concerning the sons of Israel who raise their hands to strike their wives. Yet who has given a husband the authority to beat his wife? Is he not rather forbidden to strike any person in Israel? Moreover R. I(saac) has written in a responsum that he has it on the authority of three great Sages, namely R. Samuel, R. Jacob Tam and R. I(saac), the sons of R. Meir, that one who beats his wife is in the same category as one who beats a stranger. Nevertheless we have heard of cases where Jewish women complained regarding their treatment before the Communities and no action was taken on their behalf.

We have therefore decreed that any Jew may be compelled on application of his wife or one of her near relatives to undertake by a *herem* not to beat his wife in anger or cruelty so as to disgrace her, for that is against Jewish practice.

---

5. According to Louis Finkelstein, *Jewish Self Government in the Middle Ages* (New York: Jewish Theological Seminary of America, 1924), the text of this proposed *takkanah* was taken by Guedemann from a Halberstam manuscript.

6. Finklestein, *Jewish Self Government*, Ch. VI, p. 216.

7. Goldin, "The Role and Function of the *Herem*."

8. Finklestein, *idem*.

(2) If anyone will stubbornly refuse to obey our words, the Court of the place to which the wife or her relatives will bring complaint, shall assign her maintenance according to her station and according to the custom of the place where she dwells. They shall fix her alimony as though her husband were away on a distant journey.

If they, our masters, the great sages of the land agree to this ordinance it shall be established.

Perez b. Elijah[9]

Although Finkelstein, who reproduced Perez's *takkanah* in *Jewish Self-Government in the Middle Ages*, hypothesizes that the reason the takkanah never became normative is because the "crime was one that rarely, if ever, gave trouble to Jews of the Middle Ages,"[10] one can read the text at its face value: if a rabbi needs to make such a *crie de coeur* it reflects a widespread problem. It is also clear from the wording of the *takkanah* that abused wives were not receiving satisfactory answers from their communities or the rabbis, who either ignored their complaints, did not take them seriously, or did not consider these complaints as grounds for compelling a divorce.

In the preamble of this *takkanah*, Perez makes clear whose side he is on. Just as no man may hit "any person in Israel" so a husband may not hit his wife who is also a person in Israel. Yet despite the injustice of this, no one is acting to make it clear that the husband does not "have the authority to beat his wife"; that is, that his authority over her does not include beating. Therefore, to redress this social problem, Perez has proposed a *takkanah*, which he hopes will have teeth. Perez is suggesting that the community intervene in the family's intimate affairs and makes it clear that wifebeating is not a private, but a communal, affair.

The *takkanah* of R. Perez b. Elijah of Corbeil was unusual. It changes many of the basic principles of *halakha* and heads in a new direction: the guilty husband is to be forced to take a solemn oath not to beat his wife; further only the word of the wife or one of her near relatives is sufficient to bring the husband to book. It is not clear from this *takkanah* if the husband

---

9. *Ibid.*, p. 217: Finkelstein's translation.

10. *Ibid.*, pp. 70–71. Finkelstein writes that "there may have been some temporary cause that moved R. Perez to urge the adoption of the *takkanah*. . . . We never hear of the *Takkanah* elsewhere, and it probably failed to gain the support of R. Perez's colleagues because the rarity of the offense made the revolutionary measure seem unnecessary."

is allowed under any circumstance to beat her. If the husband stubbornly refuses to repent, the woman will be allowed to live with relatives, separate from him, without being divorced, and he will have to support her as if she were still at home. To allow the wife of a husband guilty of beating her to get alimony from her husband's property and to live separately from him without divorce was a revolutionary measure. Presumably that is why the *takkanah* failed to gain widespread support.

Finkelstein attributes the *takkanah* to the high economic status enjoyed by the women of Ashkenaz. "There can be no doubt that the movement toward 'women's rights' . . . had its origin and compelling force largely in the fact that women began to occupy a prominent position in the economic world."[11] R. Perez attempted to establish legal separation without divorce, for it did not occur to him to change the divorce laws to allow the wife to divorce her husband.[12]

THE RESPONSA OF THE TOSAFISTS

Most of the responsa that unconditionally reject wifebeating date from the twelfth and thirteenth-century tosafists, who lived among the Jews of Ashkenaz in Germany and France. The English designation for tosafists derives from the fact that their glosses on the Talmud are called in Hebrew *tosafot*.[13]

Among the tosafists who wrote responsa, we find clear instances of unqualified rejection of wifebeating. Besides the French tosafist Perez of Cor-

---

11. There does appear to be a relationship between women's general status and rabbinic attitudes to wifebeating. As we have seen, in the fifteenth century, the status of women started to decline, and wifebeating was dealt with less stringently by the rabbis than it had been when women's status was high. Some examples of this higher status was women being admitted as witnesses, being counted as members of the quorum to recite the Grace, being permitted to be called up to the Torah. (*Ibid.*, pp. 378–379).

12. Phillip Sigal sees this as negative. However, I have included Perez in this chapter, rather than in Chapter Ten, which deals with evasion, because it is clear whose side Perez is on and that he is doing everything that he thinks he can to provide for the wife's welfare. See "Elements of Male Chauvinism in Classical *Halakha*," *Judaism* 24:2 (1975): 231.

13. According to Marcus, their "methods developed in rabbinic circles in Germany and northern France as an extension of the ancient Talmud's own method of questions and answers" [in Ivan Marcus, "Jewish Learning in the Middle Ages," *The Melton Journal* (Autumn 1992): 24].

beil, there are two other notable examples of such rabbinic authorities: Simhah b. Samuel of Speyer and Rabbi Meir of Rotenberg.

These two European rabbis of the German tosafist school were very strict with wife batterers. They prescribed harsh punishment to the wifebeater and refused to allow husbands to force their wives to do their required housework or to beat them for "their own good." Both rabbis considered battering as grounds for compelling a man to issue a divorce.[14]

R. Meir of Rotenberg (c. 1220 to 1293)

Rabbi Meir of Rotenberg, whose acronym is Maharam, was one of the great German tosafists of this period.[15] Although he composed original work and edited earlier material, his responsa and legal decisions were his best-known compositions. He was one of the first tosafists to preserve his own responsa and to collect those of earlier Ashkenazi authorities. R. Meir wrote several responsa about wife-battering, two of which Agus has translated and abridged into English. The first one (#297) states:

> Question. "A" often strikes his wife. "A's" aunt, who lives at his home, is usually the cause of their arguments, and adds to the vexation and annoyance of his wife.

> Answer. A Jew must honor his wife more than he honors himself. If one strikes one's wife, one should be punished more severely than for striking another person. For one is enjoined to honor one's wife but is not enjoined to honor the other person. Therefore, "A" must force his aunt to leave his house, and must promise to treat his wife honorably. If he persists in striking her, he should be excommunicated, lashed, and suffer the severest punishments, even to the extent of amputating his arm. If his wife is willing to accept a divorce, he must divorce her and pay her the ketubah.[16]

---

14. Grossman Avraham. "Medieval Rabbinic Views of Wife Beating: (eighth–thirteenth Centuries)," *Proceedings of Tenth World Congress of Jewish Studies*, Division B, vol. 1 (Jerusalem: World Union of Jewish Studies, 1990), p. 121 [Hebrew].

15. Irving Agus, in *Rabbi Meir of Rotenberg,* has written extensively about R. Meir's life and works as sources for the religious, legal, and social history of the Jews of Germany in the thirteenth century. This subject is the subtitle of his book.

16. *Eben ha-Ezer* #297, as translated and cited by Irving Agus in *Rabbi Meir of Rotenberg,* vol. 1 (Philadelphia: Jewish Publication Society, 1947), p. 326.

In the second responsum that Agus has translated and abridged (#298), R. Meir reiterates that "one deserves greater punishment for striking his wife than for striking another person, for he is enjoined to respect her." He then adds:

> Far be it from a Jew to do such a thing. Had a similar case come before us we should hasten to excommunicate him. Thus, R. Paltoi Gaon [842–857, Pumbeditah, Iraq] rules that a husband who constantly quarrels with his wife must remove the causes of such quarrels, if possible, or divorce her and pay her the *ketubah*; how much more must a husband be punished, who not only quarrels but actually beats his wife.[17]

R. Meir says that a woman who is hit by her husband is entitled to an immediate divorce and to receive the money owed her in her marriage settlement. This is significant since a woman who leaves the marriage does not always receive this money. Although R. Meir's responsum relies on the precedent of a much earlier responsum by Paltoi Gaon to make this point, it opposes an earlier responsum by the ninth century Gaon of Sura, Sar Shalom, who distinguishes between an assault on a woman by her husband and an assault on her by a stranger. The Gaon of Sura's opinion, you will recall,[18] was that the husband's assault on his wife was less severe, since the husband has authority over his wife.[19]

In the unabridged responsum on which Agus based his translation, R. Meir expresses himself very forcefully against wifebeaters. Responsa #81 is reproduced below:

> Every son of the covenant must honor his wife more than his own body, she rises with him and does not go down with him in the act of marriage [*be-ulat ba'al*]. She was given to him for life, not for sorrow and we can learn from her *ketubah* that he has to take care of her, cherish her and support her [*aflach ve-okir ve-eezun*]. It seems to me in the case of a husband who beats his wife, we have to act more stringently than with the person who beats his friend, for he does not have to honor his friend, but he does have to honor his wife. It is the way of the nations (*derech ha-*

---

17. Cited in Responsum #298, *Eben ha'Ezer*, in Agus, pp. 326–327.
18. See Chapter Seven.
19. Otzar Geonim, Baba Kamma, p. 62, no. 198, as cited by Samuel Morrell, "An Equal or a Ward: How Independent Is a Married Woman According to Rabbinic Law?" *Jewish Social Studies* 44 (1982): 198.

goyim) to act thusly—but God forbid that sons of the covenant should act in like manner.[20]

Although Klein,[21] in his commentary on Maimonides, and other apologists for the Jewish tradition[22] have quoted the last sentence out of context to show that Jews do not beat their wives, R. Meir himself makes clear that Jews of his time did hit, beat, and batter their wives, and that he considered that to be wrong. In the continuation of his responsum, he says that the perpetrator should be punished by putting him into *herem*, separating him from the community, beating him, and punishing him with all kinds of torture. If he is a habitual beater, they can even cut off his hand:

> As we saw in B. San. 58b, R. Huna [recommended] cutting off [the perpetrator's] hand [of one who habitually beats his friend]. Even in Babylon, where we do not fine him, we punish them, so that they do not [beat their wives] too easily. And *if she wants to leave*, let her leave and give her the *ketubah*. . . . In [another] case the husband has to remove her from there to live in another house—and if not, he has to give her the *ketubah*, for it is said she was given for life, not for sorrow.[23]

R. Meir's advice to cut off the hand of a habitual beater of his fellow, echoes the law in Deut. 25:11–12, where the unusual punishment of cutting off a hand is applied to a woman who tries to save her husband in a way that shames the beater.[24] He is also concerned with the mental distress of the wife, specifically from psychological abuse directed at the wife by in-laws such as aunts, sisters, and mothers-in-law.

---

20. My translation of the *Bar-Ilan* responsa of the Maharam of Rotenberg, part 4 (Prague edition), p. 81. At the top of this responsa, the anonymous Gaon is identified with R. Paltoi. The *responsa* is found in the commentary of *shiltei giborim* on Mordecai, in the chapter about *na-arah* (Cremona 291).

21. Isaac Klein, trans., *The Code of Maimonides*, book 4, The Book of Women, Yale Judaica Series, vol. 19 (New Haven, CT: Yale University Press, 1972), p. xxxv.

22. See Chapter Nine on apologetics and denial.

23. See note 20, above.

24. I quote the reference in full for those who find it cryptic: "If two men get into a fight with each other, and the wife of one comes up to save her husband from his antagonist and puts out her hand and seizes him by his genitals, you shall cut off her hand; show no pity" (Deut. 25: 11–12).

In the next responsum, which refers back to that just cited, R. Meir develops the theme of shame and dishonor more clearly. In Responsum #927, R. Meir writes about a son-in-law who regularly beats his wife

and shames her by exposing her hair in public [*priyat rosha*]—not according to the Jewish law [for she was given for life, not for sorrow— and if a female Hebrew slave who is purchased is to be treated well, it follows that so should one's wife.] For every beating he gives her, he violates the principle of not to excess [*pen yosif*][25] and his punishment should be greater than one who beats his friend, because she [is at his mercy]. . . . If his words are true, he should be fined with both corporal and financial punishment.

[But] one should try to establish peace between them (if possible) by positioning witnesses in their homes and on the basis of that they should be judged.

His verdict is startling:

If the husband does not observe the peace, and continues to beat her and verbally abuse her, we agree that he should be excommunicated by the upper and lower courts and be forced by the non-Jews to issue a divorce [a *get*].[26]

It is rare that rabbis countenance forcing a man to divorce his wife and it is even rarer that they countenance involving the non-Jewish community in their internal affairs. To justify his opinion, Meir uses biblical and talmudic material to legitimatize his views. At the end of this responsum he discusses the legal precedents for this decision in the Talmud (B. Gittin 88b). Thus he concludes that "even in the case where she was willing to accept (occasional beatings), she cannot accept beatings without an end in sight." He points to the fact that a fist has the potential to kill and that if peace is impossible, the rabbis should try to convince him to divorce her of "his own free will," but if that proves impossible, force him to divorce her [as is allowed by law—(*ka-torah*)].

This responsum is found in a collection of R. Meir's responsa and is his copy of a responsum by R. Simhah b. Samuel of Speyer. By freely using this responsum, R. Meir endorses R. Simhah's opinions.

---

25. See Chapter Six for a discussion of "not to excess" (Deut. 25: 1–3).
26. *Bar-Ilan Responsa Project*, part 4, #927.

Rabbi Simhah of Speyer (D. 1225–1230)[27]

The next rabbi we look at who unconditionally rejects wifebeating is Simhah b. Samuel of Speyer, who may have been R. Meir's teacher for a short period of time, since the latter's father, R. Baruch, had studied with R. Simhah.[28] It is clear from the above responsum, which Meir copied in its entirety from Simhah, that Meir respected him and was influenced by his views. Simhah was a leading member of the Rabbinical Synod of the Rhine Provinces held in 1223. His responsum was reported by Mordecai ben Hillel Ha-Cohen (1240?–1298), another tosafist, who was one of R. Meir's disciples.

In addition to the responsum cited above (attributed to R. Meir), Joseph Caro also quotes Simhah, whose responsum concerning the man who beats his wife he found:

> It is an accepted view that we have to treat (a man who beats his wife) more severely than we treat a man who beats a fellowman, since he is not obligated to honor him, but is obligated to honor his wife more than himself. . . . *If he wants to divorce her*[29] let him divorce her and give her the *ketubah* payment . . . if the husband . . . continues to beat her and denigrate her, we agree that he should be excommunicated and forced by Gentile authorities to grant her a divorce (in accordance with) what Israel (authorities) tell you to do.[30]

---

27. The date of his death is calculated according to the citations of his name by his pupil R. Isaac b. Moses of Wurzburg (Vienna) in the *Or Zarua*. (Agus, *Rabbi Meir*, p. 10, fn. 34); the *Germania Judaica* puts Simhah's death at 1225–30. I thank Howard Adelman for bringing this to my attention.

28. *Idem.*; also Ephraim Kanarfogel, "Preservation, Creativity, and Courage: The Life and Works of R. Meir of Rotenberg," *Jewish Book Annual*, no 50 (1992): 249.

29. Compare the underlined passage here of Simhah (if he wants to divorce her, let him divorce her and give her the *ketubah* payment) with Meir's, above (if she wants to go away, he should divorce her and give her the *ketubah*). Howard Adelman, in his comparison of the Simhah and Meir responsa, points out that Meir "allows the woman's feeling toward the marriage to determine its future (#81). However, in another responsum, Meir argues that a man who beats his wife cannot be forced to divorce her, nor can she be forced to live with him." Unpublished paper, "Wifebeating in Jewish History," Toronto: Sinai Temple (8 May 1992): 19.

30. Joseph Caro, *Bet Yosef, Eben ha-Ezer*, Hilchot Gittin, 154:15. Much of this is translated by Biale, *Women and Jewish Law*, p. 94. She identifies R. Simhah as being Rabbenu Simhah ben Shmuel of Vitri (author of the *Vitri Mahzor*); because of the popularity and high quality of her book, this error has been perpetuated in other people's writing.

Simhah, using an aggadic approach, wrote that a man has to honor his wife *more* than himself and that is why his wife—and not his fellow man—should be his greater concern. Simhah stresses her status as wife rather than simply as another individual. His argument is that, like Eve, "the mother of all living" (Gen. 3:20), she was given for living, not for suffering. She trusts him and thus it is worse if he hits her than if he hits a stranger.

Simhah lists all the possible sanctions. If these are of no avail, he takes the daring leap and not only allows a compelled divorce, but allows one that is forced on the husband by gentile authorities. He is one of the few rabbis who authorized a compelled divorce as a sanction.[31]

Why was R. Simhah so forceful? It is difficult to know what accounted for his sympathetic attitude to women. Perhaps it was simple moral outrage. Perhaps it had to do with a view of marriage that goes beyond the halakhic injunction to "serve and honor and feed and maintain" his wife.[32] Unfortunately his opinions were overturned by most rabbis in later generations.[33]

Rabbi Jonah ben Abraham of Gerona (D. 1263)

In the previous chapter we saw that R. Jonah, in *Iggeret ha-Teshuvah* [Letter of Repentance], allows the husband to beat his wife if it is to reprove her for some transgression. However, in his monograph *The Gates of Repentance,* he implies that the perpetrator should have his hand cut off if he beats his wife:

---

31. Howard Adelman, in "Wife-Beating Among Early Modern Italian Jews, 1400–1700," *Proceedings of The Eleventh World Congress of Jewish Studies,* Division B, vol. 1 (Jerusalem: World Union of Jewish Studies, 1994), pp. 134–142, disagrees that Simhah's responsum is clearly in favor of forced divorce. "Simhah's responsum does not seem as clearly in favor of forced divorce as Or Zarua and many later rabbis thought. He allowed only reluctantly that force could be applied to Jewish men by gentiles, but not by Jews, without specifying if constraints on Jewish use of force were internal or external." [Adelman's footnote no. 3 is Menahem Recanati, Piskei Halakhot (Bologna, 1538; Sedlkov, 1836), no. 511.]

32. See any standard copy of the *ketubah,* the Jewish marriage contract.

33. The Radbaz, R. David b. Solomon Ibn Avi Zimra (1479–1573), was one of the first to question R. Simhah's *responsum* (see Chapter Seven). He said that Simhah "exaggerated on the measures to be taken when writing that (the wifebeater) should be forced by non-Jews (*akum*) to divorce his wife . . . because (if she remarries) this could result in the offspring (of the illegal marriage according to Radbaz) being declared illegitimate (*mamzer*)." *Responsa of Radbaz,* part 4, p. 157, The Bar-Ilan Responsa Project.

There are exhortations, such as those against injuring or striking, which are unobserved in essence by part of the populace. . . . Many transgress these negative commandments in the striking of their wives. Our Sages of blessed memory have said, "Anyone who raises his hand against his neighbor, though he does not strike him, is called "wicked," as it is said, 'Wherefore would you smite thy fellow?' [Exod. 2:13]. . . . Our Sages of blessed memory have said, "R. Huna ordered that *the hand of one who was given to striking his neighbors, be cut off*. He said, 'And the high arm is broken' (*ibid.*, 38:15)" (B. Sanhedrin 58b).[34]

R. Jonah reveals to us that wifebeating was a widespread problem. His argument has important ramifications for the wifebeater. Threatening to beat is almost as bad as the beating itself. The raising of the hand causes the victim to cringe in anticipation and gives the perpetrator control and a sense of power.[35]

R. Israel of Krems

R. Israel of Krems, who lived in the fourteenth and fifteenth centuries in Austria, quotes R. Simhah in his notes on R. Asher b. Yehiel's commentary on the Talmud (B. Baba Kama 32a):

A man is forbidden to beat his wife, and is moreover liable for any injuries caused by him. If he is in the habit of beating her or continually insulting her in public, he should be forced to divorce her and pay her *ketubah* money. And R. Simhah of blessed memory responded that he could be forced (to issue a divorce) by the gentiles to 'do what Israel tells you to do.'[36]

This note is interesting because it is an unsolicited opinion in answer to what should be done to a husband who injures his wife during the act of intercourse. What is interesting is that, while Simhah's opinions are quoted by

---

34. *Sha'are Teshubah*, III, 77, in Yonah b. Avraham of Gerona, trans. by Shraga Silverstein in his *The Gates of Repentance* (Jerusalem: Feldheim, 1976), p. 197.

35. For more information about R. Jonah, see A.T. Shrock, *Rabbi Jonah ben Abraham of Gerona* (London: Edward Goldston, 1948).

36. See Klein, *The Code of Maimonides*, p. xxxvi; Chapter 3, Baba Kamma, Rabbenu Asher, Hameniach, *Haggahot Asheri*, p. 250.

Ashkenazi authorities with approval during the same time period, they are rejected by another authority such as Israel Isserlein (1390–1460).[37]

R. Simon B. Tzemach Duran (1361–1444)

R. Simon b. Tzemach Duran (Rashbetz), was the author of the *Tashbetz*, a collection of his responsa. He was born on the Island of Majorca and died in Algiers. Like so many of the great Sephardi rabbis, he was a physician. He had to flee during the anti-Jewish riots of 1391 and ended up as a *dayan* (a rabbinic judge) in Algiers, where he wrote responsa. In particular, he specialized in writing *takkanot* dealing with the Jewish marriage contract (*ketubah*), which were accepted by many Jewish communities. He fathered a rabbinic dynasty which was most influential on North Africa for many generations.[38]

R. Simon b. Tzemach Duran responds to a question about a long-suffering wife, whose husband is a difficult person whom she cannot stand. He has deprived her of food until she hates the thought of living. She is afraid to come to the rabbinic court because her husband has so intimidated her that she believes she will forfeit her rights if she goes in search of legal help. Duran responds as follows:

> You can certainly write that he should divorce her and give her the *ketubah*, as it is written she is given for life, not for sorrow. . . . She should get her *ketubah* because one does not have to live in close quarters with a snake. . . .
>
> Even though the Alfasi wrote that even if the husband says I will not provide for her, he does not have to divorce her and give the *ketubah* to her (I think otherwise).

R. Simon b. Tzemach Duran is willing to extend himself halakhically by disagreeing with R. Isaac Alfasi, a rabbi who was held in great esteem. He shows that one can interpret the husband's unwillingness to provide for her as grounds for forcing a divorce and shows that it is better to live in a house where there is love than one in which there is hate. He comments, "What good is there for a woman whose husband causes her sorrow by daily fights."

---

37. See Chapter Seven on acceptance.
38. Source of biography, *Bar-Ilan Responsa Project*.

And he goes on to show that there are precedents which allow us to force the husband to divorce her and, if he starves her, obviously this should be the case. He writes that the difference between forcing him to divorce her and advising him to divorce her is not that great. If he agrees to divorce her of his own free will, so be it. But if he does not, we force him.

Rashbetz justifies his interpretation by the following radical claim:

> Even though in the responsa of some great later rabbis, may their memory be for a blessing, there are opinions that you never force divorce, we are not second class rabbis (workers who cut reeds in the pools). In a matter which is dependent on judicial discretion [s'varah], the judge has to proceed on his understanding of the evidence before him. It could be that the later rabbis would not say this about a case like this in which so much suffering is involved, and surely not if he starves her. And if they had that example of suffering before them, they would not have judged in such a manner. Rashba z"l wrote in his responsum [that you can force the husband] as we do.

If this responsa were not remarkable in itself, Rashbetz goes on to use midrashic metaphors to justify his moral stance—something which is not very usual in responsa literature. Thus he refers to Jacob who was unsympathetic to Rachel when she was trying hard to get pregnant [Gen. 30:2]; to the case of King Ahab who not only killed, but inherited [I Kings 21:19], and finally to the lion, who not only tramples on his prey but also devours it. He says that these are Moslem practices and we should not behave in like manner. And "that the rabbinic judge who forces a women who rebelled to go back to her (abusive) husband is following the law of the Ishmaelites and should be excommunicated. . . ."[39]

Rashbetz uses these stern words to justify what is right, having made clear that his halakhic stance rests not only on legal literature, but also on midrashic literature. We have seen this creative use of *midrash* with R. Simhah and will see more of it in the responsum of Binyamin Ze'ev.

---

39. Simeon bar Tzemach, *Sefer Ha-Tashbetz*, Part 2, p. 8 (Lemberg, Tarna, 1891).

Binyamin Ze'ev B. Mattathias of Arta (16th century, Greece)

A major source of medieval responsa that reject wifebeating unconditionally is Binyamin Ze'ev b. Mattathias of Arta, whose views display great sensitivity to injustice. Binyamin Ze'ev, who lived in the first half of the sixteenth century in Greece and Turkey, wrote a long review of the literature known to him in response to a question of whether a habitual wifebeater can be forced to grant his wife a divorce (if it is proved that he is to blame and not her). He quotes the entire responsum of R. Simhah (attributed above as being R. Meir's) to support his own point of view. Thus, he is in favor of a forced divorce even if forced by non-Jews, using the argument that the external (non-Jewish) authorities force him to issue the divorce by telling him to do what the Jewish law demands.

Binyamin Ze'ev recognizes that the perpetrator agrees in the end to divorce her "of his own free will" (*ad she-yomar rotzeh ani*) as a result of the force of the court. But he interprets this to mean that, by his saying "It is my will," his free consent is assumed at that point.

Binyamin Ze'ev quotes several sages (Rabbenu Samuel, Eliahu and Meshullam) who were in favor of denying all the privileges of the community to the perpetrator who refused to give his wife a divorce. This would include denying his right to circumcise and educate his son and even the right to be interred (in a Jewish cemetery). Binyamin Ze'ev does not view these extraordinary means as coercion—they are to be considered as aids to help the husband to do what is right.

He goes on to quote biblical and talmudic sources showing how important it is for a man to honor his wife. He considers the story of the Concubine of Gibeah and the story of Hagar as cases of battered women and says about the Concubine that, because of her husband's maltreatment of her, thousands of Israelites were subsequently killed.[40]

He also was in favor of the *herem* suggested by Perez (see above) and quotes his entire *takkanah*. Binyamin Ze'ev's views are considered to be controversial and certainly unusual for the sixteenth century. Most rabbis base themselves on the *mishnah*, which says that when a woman knows *prior* to her marriage that something is wrong with her husband, she is more or less stuck in the situation. Binyamin Ze'ev, however, writes:

---

40. He allowed her to be raped by the men of a whole town and may have murdered her—see above, Chapter Two.

If we cannot find another solution for the situation, we compel him to divorce her and give her the marriage settlement payment even if she had accepted the situation knowingly.[41]

Although it makes for an unwieldy long responsum, he reviews those rabbis who opposed forcing the husband to grant the wife a divorce. It is usual to cite all sides in responsa literature. It is clear from his explicit last words that he views the wifebeater as being no better than any other common criminal who violates the rulings of the sages.

R. Shlomo B. Abraham HaCohen (1520–1601)

R. Shlomo b. Abraham HaCohen (Maharshach), the sixteenth-century rabbi who lived in Yugoslavia and Greece, wrote two interesting responsa. They both concerned the case of Reuben HaCohen who habitually beat and denigrated his wife Dinah bat Yakov. He was warned by the court not to lift a hand against her and they imposed a *herem* on him as a preventative measure. The case was fairly complicated since a lot of property was involved, and the husband felt that he had been pressured into a subsequent divorce by the local authorities with whom his wife's father had connections.[42] The condition was that, if he violated the *herem*, they could force him to release her with a coerced decree (*kofim ve-onsim...get me-u-seh*) and the divorce would be valid. This decree included a clause that was common to divorce decrees of non-Cohanim—that the man could remarry his divorced wife if she did not marry again in the interim (Deut. 24:1–4). Accordingly, in responsum #129, Maharshach, declared this divorce decree invalid.

A Cohen cannot take back his divorced wife, because a Cohen is not allowed to marry any divorcee (Lev. 21:7). Therefore, Maharshach declared the first divorce invalid, so that the woman would not be a divorced woman and would therefore remain married to her husband the Cohen.

In his second responsum (#130) to a revised version of the question concerning the same case, Maharshach recanted and decided to take a new

---

41. Responsa #88.

42. See Howard Adelman's discussion of the first responsum (but not the second) in his unpublished article "A Disgrace for All Jewish Men: Methodological Considerations in the Study of Wifebeating in Jewish History," which he graciously shared with me.

look at earlier authorities, in particular at the comments of Maimonides,[43] that a bill of divorce that has scribal errors is valid if no one notices the errors at the time of the delivery of the divorce document. Moreover, even if the husband protests in order to invalidate the divorce on the basis of the errors, his wife cannot be allowed to go back to him and he must issue another valid bill of divorce which will allow her to remarry.[44] If not, the woman would be in limbo, for she could not go back to her husband because the validity of the divorce was not contested at the time of divorce.

Referring to Maimonides enables Maharshach to deal with the same case about Reuben and Dinah from another halakhic angle. He does this so that she will not be an *agunah*, a woman who is figuratively "anchored" to her husband—in a state of limbo, unable to remarry. A woman whose husband deserts her or who disappears (with no witnesses to his death) can be declared an *agunah*. A woman whose husband refuses to divorce her also falls into this category. Maharshach's second responsum shows a sensitivity to a woman's plight in this situation. Normally the concern is that an invalid divorce decree can result in a woman inadvertently remarrying illegally and having a child who would be a *mamzer* (illegitimate issue). Here the focus is on her plight as well—the fact that she should not be left hanging in a situation that prevents her from getting on with her life.

Hayim Palaggi (1788–1869)

As we come closer to our century we find that there are many more responsa dealing with cases of wife abuse. It is not the goal of this book to determine if there are more cases of abuse in modern times or if there are fewer attempts to deny its existence. Hayim Palaggi, a rabbi who lived in Ismar and Smyrna (Turkey), wrote a review of the literature known to him in his work, *Sefer Hayim Veshalom*.[45] "There are many people," Palaggi writes, "who beat their wives and do not know how great a sin it is."[46]

---

43. *Hilchot Gerushim* 84.

44. *Bar-Ilan Responsa Project, Responsa of Maharshach*, Part 2, #130.

45. A two-volume work published in 1857–1872.

46. Hayyim Palaggi, *Sefer Hayim VeShalom*, vol. 2, *Eben ha-Ezer* #31, (Izmir: 1857–72) [reprinted 1979, Hebrew].

What we see in the responsa literature is an awareness of the earlier debates and an increased interest in issues of money and property. Palaggi, in another work, *Sefer Ruach Hayim*, a partial commentary on the *Shulhan Arukh*, writes about wifebeating, but his main interest is with vows. Vows were looked upon very seriously. Therefore the question arose as to whether a man who beats his wife is to be permitted to vow not to do it again, or if he should be forced to divorce her right away. The long discussion assumes that it is wrong to beat his wife and that it is possible to force him to divorce her on these grounds, and to excommunicate him after warning him. However, it is seen as wrong to allow him to take an oath not to beat his wife. Palaggi reaches this decision in the usual way, by depending on previous responsa literature. Thus, wifebeating serves as background to the discussion of taking oaths, which takes up the center stage in this particular responsum.[47]

In the next century, R. Aaron b. Simon (see below) refers back to Palaggi as "a great wise man from our generation—a model and example for us . . . who in his book *Tochechat Hayim* expressed surprise at Moses Isserles (see Chapter Seven), and said that, in our times, it is not permissible to beat one's wife at all." Thus, Palaggi's message was clear, since R. Aaron understood Palaggi to be saying that today's husbands might try to use Isserles to justify beating their wives. R. Aaron quotes Palaggi as attacking Isserles's approach, which he feels might condone wifebeating.

Avraham Yaakov Paperna (1840–1919)

In 1867, Avraham Yaakov Paperna, wrote a polemic against the rabbis of the town of Radom, in the Kielce province of Poland. Paperna was part of the Haskalah (Enlightenment) Movement and had rabbinic ordination, yet did not serve as a rabbi. His work combines rabbinic learning with willingness to confront problems from a modern perspective. His article shows the widespread phenomenon of wifebeating in the Jewish community.

His polemic is in the form of a review of the literature concerning questions asked of rabbis in his country and their responses, and he accuses them of insensitivity and hard-heartedness toward the plight of women in general and battered women in particular. The tone of his article drips with sarcastic

---

47. Hayim Palaggi, *Sefer Ruach Hayyim*, Part 2, *Eben ha-Ezer* #74. (Izmir: 1876–77) [reprinted 1977, Hebrew].

comments against the rabbis of his day, whom he feels, are clearly biased against women. Rather than help them, he says, the rabbis put obstacles in their way. He opposes the rabbinical decision to overlook Maimonides' ruling forcing a man to divorce his wife. He quotes Maimonides in full, referring to the favorable decisions in the *Tur* and Isserles, and says that the Radomite rabbi (R. Abraham Tzvi Perlmutter)[48] rejected all of these learned opinions and directed the rabbinic court not to force the husband who beats his wife to divorce her.

Paperna writes:

> These are our mothers, our sisters, our daughters, our flesh and blood. We must be concerned for their welfare and not let them be ridiculed and downtrodden by men of greed, who treat them like dust to trample on and allow decisions to be made against them. This failure is your fault, rabbis of Israel! Instead of getting on a soapbox to curse the Zionists, instead of debating in the "palace" business deals of the Colonial bank, instead of forbidding the new methods (of study), you should be sifting through the terrible confusion of rabbinic literature and working on ways to make halakhic decisions (to help). . . .[49]

Paperna rejects without any qualifications those rabbis who have decided against women such as these and who thereby have created more *agunot* (pl. of *agunah*, the chained, anchored woman) by not using the *halakha* creatively to force abusive husbands to divorce their wives.

Eliezer Papu (D. 1824)

Eliezer Papu, a Bulgarian rabbi in Sarajevo, wrote a guide to morality in alphabetical order. In part one of this work, *Pele Yoetz*, he writes about the education of children. Included in his discussion of whether one is permit-

---

48. Perlmutter (?1844–1926) served as a rabbi in Poland. He was the rabbi in Radom from 1886 and was awarded a silver medal by Czar Nicholas II in 1894. He represented Agudat Israel for the Warsaw district in 1919 in the first Polish parliament, and was active both in communal activities and in world conventions even in his eighties. ("Perlmutter, Abraham Zevi" *Encyclopedia Judaica*, p. 297).

49. Avraham Yakov Paperna, *Complete Works* (Vilna: 1867), pp. 429–430 [Hebrew]. I would like to thank Iris Porush for bringing this source to my attention.

ted to beat children for educational purposes are a few lines about wifebeating. His conclusion is that, although one can occasionally beat one's children to educate them (rabbis and teachers can do so), excessive use of force directed toward anyone should be avoided because of the principle of "not to excess" (see earlier).

All the leaders of the cities should see to it that men of might are punished, in particular those worthless men who beat their wives with cruel beatings—may their spirit be destroyed—who treat daughters of Israel as servants and stamp on them and beat them and ravish them sexually without shame. Whoever has the authority to stop them should do so; and if they can be told to divorce their wives to get them out from under their rule—if the wives wish this—it should be done because a wife should not live with a snake. It is a great mitzvah to save a slave from being overpowered by one stronger than he. It is even wrong to beat little children, unless it is a father to his sons or a rabbi to his pupils. And even these should do so with moderation. . . .[50]

However, there is a recognition that a man's temper might get out of hand, and so the author advises the husband, "if he must hit her," not to hit her too hard and to avoid a cruel, murderous blow to the womb area or the eyes or any other place where he can cause injury that might be life-threatening. "He should calmly rap her on the feet without anger, for it is good for a man to behave in a measured manner." It is clear from the context of this section that this is considered a last resort, not a model of behavior.

Raphael Aaron Ben Simeon (1848–1928)

Raphael Aaron Ben Simeon, the author of *U-Mitzur Devash*, was the Chief Rabbi of Cairo in the nineteenth century.[51] He received a query from a rabbi in Haifa about a drawn-out battle between a husband and wife. She was

---

50. Eliezer Papu, *Pele Yoetz*, Part One, The Letter "heh" (Vienna: 1876), pp. 100–101. There seems to be a reference to the Talmud here [*makeh u-boel*], in that the husband who would indulge in this behavior is similar to the *am-ha'aretz*, the low-life we have seen in Chapter Five.

51. Raphael Aaron b. Simeon, *Sefer U-Mitzur Devash: Responsa on all Four Parts of the Shulhan Arukh*, printed in Jerusalem, 5672.

beaten cruelly and had witnesses to the "bruises and marks black as a raven's" on her body. Her husband had torn her *ketubah* to pieces and denied beating her, despite the witnesses. They tried to make peace between the couple, but after six months the wife again came to complain that he abused and cursed her and gave her cruel beatings. The rabbi was too busy to deal with the problem and sent her to other rabbis to take care of the issue. She was sent from rabbi to rabbi and "like the dove, did not find a perch to rest on" (Gen. 8:9) and so the rabbi from Haifa was stuck with the case.

To complicate matters, the husband claimed that she cursed him. Moreover, there were financial problems stemming from the fact that since her *ketubah* was torn, she theoretically had no rights and protection as a married woman. Moreover, the husband wanted to marry again and the question was, could the first wife live in peace with a second wife ("*tzarah*," referred to as "her sorrow" (I Sam. 1:6)), and if not, could he be coerced to divorce his first wife in order to marry someone else.

The author of *U-Mitzur Devash* writes that he has read the case of the "man who beats his wife unlawfully, so that his wife agrees to submit to his demands (to give up some of her *ketubah* rights)." He agrees that her forced acceptance of his demands can be canceled and are invalidated. This is so for two reasons: first, it is coercion. Second the issue of the torn *ketubah* is not clear cut. There is a misunderstanding concerning the wife's lack of rights when the husband has willfully destroyed the *ketubah*. In other words in this case the *halakha* is that her rights do not depend on the written document! The author discusses a *takkanah* instituted in western countries that protects the wife and gives her—and her heirs—a third of the *ketubah's* value.

As to the husband's desire to remarry, the author discusses a case of remarriage when the first wife is infertile or has not given birth to a male child after more than 14 years. If the husband can guarantee equal provisions for both, he can remarry and not have to divorce his first wife, if she is willing to put up with bringing a *tzarah* (a second wife; lit. one who causes sorrow) to her house.

Is this case, when the husband was known to beat her cruelly and has not cohabited with her for six months, further complicated by her cursing her husband? Isn't he allowed to beat her "for cursing him for no good reason" (as cited by Moses Isserles in Chapter Seven)?

The author of our responsum comes down very hard on those who say it is permitted to beat such a wife. He quotes and favors those sources that say that it is forbidden to beat *even a bad woman*. We have seen above that he uses Palaggi to show that "it is not permissible to beat one's wife at all."

He ends his responsum by making it clear that this same husband (who beats his wife and wishes to marry another) should be spoken to softly. If he refuses to provide equally for both wives, they should persuade him with "sweet words and gentle tones" to divorce her "of his own good free will." He should also be responsible for restoring the original *ketubah* to his first wife and provide for her.[52] However, there is no guarantee that the husband will do this and the use of a conciliatory tone might convey the wrong message to him that he does not have to take the rabbis advice seriously.

David Pipano (1851–1925)

The author of *Nosei Ha-Ephod*, David Pipano (known as *Avnei Ha-Ephod*) was a rabbi and public speaker in Salonika, Greece, and Sofia, Bulgaria. Although much of his writings were lost in the conflagration in Sofia in 1915, many of his extant responsa divulge much about the Bulgarian Jewish community. In the following responsum #32, written in 1925, we have the case of a husband who viciously beat his wife, frequented whorehouses, was an alcoholic who had not supported his wife for 8 years, and had threatened her several times with a gun. He claimed that this was done in a joking manner, but she said there was no way in which she could continue to live with him—even for a minute—because she feared for her life. He admitted the truth of her words, but said he would change his ways. He refused to divorce her, asking her father for a great sum of money as a condition for giving her a divorce.

The responsum has twenty-four parts, most of which deal with how to force the husband to divorce his wife. In the fifteenth section he returns to the issue of her fear of living with him. (He had once threatened her with a gun; she waited until he was asleep and removed the bullets from the gun.) There are sources which would say that a man who acts as if he is crazy is not a threat—even if he threatens his own life, but Pipano feels that a woman who fears for her life if her husband is self-destructive and unstable has valid grounds for a forced divorce.

The sixteenth section begins a discussion centered on the issue of wifebeating and the grounds for a forced divorce. The author introduces the

---

52. See pp. 121b–123a. The heading of this responsum attributes it to his father.

responsum of Simhah of Speyer and others who favor a forced divorce even when forced by gentiles. In the seventeenth and eighteenth sections, the discussion centers on the use of beatings with whips to force the husband to divorce his wife. Pipano discusses both the views opposed to force and those favoring it, and pronounces himself in favor of forced divorce, especially in this case, where the husband has been clearly warned and has refused to heed the court's decision.

The nineteenth and twentieth sections focus on the husband's habit of frequenting prostitutes, and the author makes it clear that this habit of his threatening her with a gun, and his refusal to provide for her basic needs as he is obligated to by the Torah, makes him a prime candidate for a forced divorce.

In the last four sections (twenty-one through twenty-four) Pipano raises the issue of the validity of a forced divorce. He is well aware of its being a controversial issue and questions those rabbis from Ashkenaz who fear that forced divorce leads to the divorce decree being considered invalid. He expresses surprise that these objections to forced divorce received such prominence and that later authorities seemed to forget that there was "tremendous controversy between codifiers" on the issue.

Pipano goes overboard in being intellectually honest—citing all sources and then applying them to his case. He makes clear that in the end, the husband who refuses to give his wife a divorce, even if he lives in another town, can be forced to do so even by outside authorities—that he is in fact obliged to accept their ruling. Unfortunately, as we shall see in Chapter Ten, Pipano's verdict did not serve as a model for most twentieth century rabbis who followed him.[53]

R. Isaac Herzog (1888–1959)

R. Isaac Herzog was an Ashkenazi Chief Rabbi of Israel, and had previously served as a rabbi in Belfast and Dublin. In *Heichal Yitzchak*, which is the collection of his responsa, Herzog discusses the validity of a divorce decree obtained by coercion of the husband. Herzog leans very heavily on Maimonides, who said that we assume a bill of divorce is valid because *we*

---

53. I suggest that the interested reader try and get the entire responsum, which is full of sources and much lengthier than my paraphrase. The source was from the *Bar-Ilan Responsa Project*, *Nosei Haephod*, #32.

assume that every Jewish man wants to observe the Torah—and so, even if a wrongfully constituted rabbinic court forced the man to issue a bill of divorce, we uphold it. If it was done by a Jewish court, that reasoning would hold, but if the coercion of the husband was done by non-Jews, then the ruling is problematic. Because such a divorce by the civil court is Jewishly problematic, it would cause the children of the women's subsequent marriage to be considered *mamzerim* (illegitimate issue).

Maimonides' argument is: Since a man wants to observe Jewish law, and since it is the Jewish rabbinic court which is forcing him to observe Jewish law by divorcing his wife, therefore the Jewish man has "willingly" issued the divorce. The argument, says Herzog, is based on the primary assumption that the man wants to observe Jewish law, but in the case of a civil decree, we cannot assume that a man wants to abide by *non-Jewish* law of his own free will. Therefore we have the situation that such a divorce might be considered as not given willingly and thus has no validity.

Herzog introduces the Hatam Sofer's (see Chapter Ten) opposition to Maimonides, who allowed a divorce decree to stand even if there were questions about its being coerced. Herzog disagrees with the Hatam Sofer, writing that, when there is a doubt, the *halakha* should follow Maimonides, whose stature is so great that his opinion should override the objection raised by the Hatam Sofer and others like him.

Herzog's understanding of the real meaning of Maimonides' answer is not that Jewish force is more valid, but that once anyone has forced a man to issue a bill of divorce, at the moment he says "it is of my will" and issues it, it is valid and binding. It is not the intention of a non-Jewish court autonomously to force a Jewish divorce. They are merely enforcing the "intention" of the Jewish court.[54]

There is great willingness on the part of Herzog to take a less stringent stance about recognizing a coerced bill of divorce; that is, about allowing the non-Jewish civil authorities to force the battering husband (or any husband) to divorce his wife, even to the point of overriding the Hatam Sofer. However, we shall see in Chapter Ten that the Hatam Sofer's ruling is still the major opinion followed in today's Israeli rabbinical courts. In fact, since the Hatam Sofer was completely against a coerced divorce, most authorities continue to comply with his understanding of the *halakha* and not with Maimonides' and Herzog's.

---

54. *Heichal Yitzchak*, Eben ha-Ezer, 1:3.

She'ar Yashuv Cohen (B. 1927)

In October 1991 the Israeli media excitedly referred to an "unprecedented breakthrough halakhic ruling"[55] by She'ar Yashuv Cohen, Chief Rabbi of Haifa. This ruling was that one could force a husband to divorce his wife if he habitually beat her. What the press neglected to point out was that She'ar Yashuv Cohen was leaning heavily on preceding responsa and on Herzog in particular.

The problem under question had to do with a woman whose case had been under review for eight years while the rabbinical court tried to "make peace" between husband and wife. The husband had refused to abide by the court's decision that he give her the marriage contract money and support her. Thus the court, convening in an emergency session, decided to force the husband based on the saying "a person should not have to live in the same quarters with a snake." The husband still refused to honor the rabbinical court and the case was referred back to the civil authorities who decided he was to be arrested and imprisoned until he said "I want to (divorce her)."

The excitement on the part of the media had to do with the emphasis on wifebeating as a primary cause for forcing the divorce. In an article published in *Techumim*, She'ar Yashuv Cohen listed the halakhic precedents for a coerced divorce in our time and discussed the case referred to above. In part seven of his article entitled "A Practical Suggestion and a Model Ruling," he wrote:[56]

> I therefore suggest: If a rabbinic court ruled that a husband must divorce his wife, and he refused, and stands firm in his refusal for several years, and anchors his wife in order to squeeze money out of her, or to torture her or to take revenge on her, the rabbinic court should rule to coerce him.

The case, which lasted ten years, involved the lower and higher rabbinic court, and the Israeli Supreme Court, as well as the local civil court.

The woman was beaten again and again and feared for her life. She had been misled about his mental health prior to their marriage. After the husband refused to be persuaded by the court to issue a bill of divorce, the wife

---

55. Ruth Rasnic, director of the Herzliyah battered women's shelter, as quoted in *Ha'Aretz*, October 27, 1991.

56. She'ar Yashuv Cohen, "A Forced Divorce in These Days," *Techumim* 11 (1990): 195–202. I would like to thank the author for sending me a copy of this article.

raised the issue of her *ketubah* money. Because of the recurrent beatings, the court ordered that the husband give her the *ketubah* money and also the additional (*tosefet*) money written into the marriage contract. She'ar Yashuv Cohen cited *Beit Yosef*, Isserles, Binyamin Ze'ev, Simhah, and Herzog as precedents, and wrote that "All that is left is to force him to issue a divorce. . . . One of the means we can use to force him . . . is to force him to provide for her . . . for as long as she is prevented from remarrying due to his holding her back."

When this failed, She'ar Yashuv Cohen felt he "had no choice" and agreed to the woman's request that the court force the husband to divorce her. He wrote that we "pray that we do not actually have to force him," because otherwise it would be halakhically problematic.

When interviewed on television, She'ar Yashuv Cohen made this clear, and also pointed out that the problem was not "finally" solved, as the press and activists implied. For if one forced the husband to divorce his wife, he could still recant—and then the divorce could be declared invalid at some future date.

R. Eliezer Waldenburg (B. 1917)

Another similar reading of the *halakha* is a case to which R. Eliezer Waldenburg wrote a *responsum*, which appears in his collection of responsa, *Tzitz Eliezer*, about a husband who battered a woman for years outside Israel. While the rabbinic court was trying to help the couple and influence the woman to go back and live with her husband on a trial basis, he tried to kill her and her brother with a weapon, and succeeded in seriously wounding his wife. The husband was given five years imprisonment by the local court, and she demanded that he issue a bill of divorce, since she was afraid to live with him.

Waldenburg suggests two reasons why the husband should be forced to issue a bill of divorce. The first has to do with the fact that he will be in prison for 5 years and *will be unable to support her*. Waldenburg quotes Hayim Palaggi (1788–1869) of Turkey, who says the main reason to use force is because the husband cannot provide for her. He also quotes Moses Trani, author of the Mabit and a sixteenth century rabbi in Safed, who said it was permissible to force a husband to divorce his wife if he deserts her (by wandering from town to town), since he is *de facto* not supporting her.

The second reason is that we should not permit a *permanent situation in which a woman has to live with a cruel husband.* Here we are referred to early sources in the Mishnah, which state that a woman cannot be forced to live with a husband whose breath she cannot stand. And if this is so, surely she does not have to be forced to live with someone who beats her. He quotes Rabbi Simhah, that if a man habitually beats his wife and abuses her in front of others, he can be forced to issue the divorce bill and restore her marriage contract, even if the civil court has to pressure him to do it in accordance with what the rabbinical court decrees. Thus, we have two totally different reasons for compelling a divorce.

What would happen if we forced the husband's family to provide for her? Waldenburg argues that, even if we can take her support from the husband's estate, the argument rests on her saying, "I cannot live in a situation in which I am at the mercy of getting beatings that have no end in sight."[57]

It appears that where there is a will there is a way. Waldenburg quotes Simhah and the Mabit, who are willing to interpret *halakha* in a way that will help women.

SUPREME RABBINICAL COURT OF ISRAEL'S CHIEF RABBINATE DECISIONS (1953–1979)

We will now take a quick look at some examples found in the collection of responsa of the religious court system of the State of Israel. One case has to do with a man who was diagnosed as insane after being married and who threatened his wife's life. The questions raised are familiar: Did she know about it before they got married? Because if she did, she might be unable to get a divorce according to the *halakha.* However, in this particular case since her husband tried to kill her, the rabbis actually ruled against the majority opinion in the *halakha.* They did so by basing themselves on an opinion found in the *tosafot*, which says that, when there is a matter of danger, we do not have to follow the majority opinion, but can follow the minority opinion that a husband has to divorce his wife even if she knew in advance of his mental illness.[58]

---

57. Free translation of Eliezer Waldenberg, *Responsa of Ztitz Eliezer,* 2nd ed. (Jerusalem, 1985) Part Six: p. 42, Ch. 3, p. 267.

58. *Piskei Din Rabaniyim,* part 8, p. 216, *Piskah,* pp. 50–51.

Often there is a reversal of a lower rabbinical court's decision when the lower court found in favor of the husband. In such cases, the Supreme Rabbinical Court upheld the woman's request that the husband be forced to grant a divorce. A typical example of such a case, dated 1979, overturned a lower court opinion that did not force the husband to issue a bill of divorce. The higher court followed an *a fortiori* argument based on a responsum attributed to Nahmanides (1194–1270). In this responsum, Nahmanides says that a woman has grounds for divorce if her husband stops her from spending time with her friends, or from visiting her parents. He has to let her go and give her the *ketubah*. The supreme religious court argued that if that was so, then certainly when he hits and injures her, he has to grant a divorce.[59]

R. Moses Feinstein (1895–1986)

The last modern responsa we will look at are those of Rabbi Moses Feinstein, the leading 20th-century halakhic authority of American Jewry, whose responsa were widely circulated and considered authoritative. Feinstein writes careful and detailed "lenient" responsa in order to educate and set boundaries, providing the individual who petitions does not intend to violate the sacred law.[60]

We see examples of this "leniency" in three responsa that tangentially relate to the plight of battered women. All three are in his collection of responsa *Igrot Moshe* (Eben ha-Ezer). Two of them relate to an insane man who, among other things, beat his wife (1:80 and 3:46). In both cases, in answer to rabbinic queries from Moscow and Baltimore, Feinstein suggested invalidating, or annulling (*hafkaat kiddushin*), the marriage, since it was clear that the wife did not know the husband was insane when she married him, and thus the marriage was performed under false circumstances. Even if she did know about the insanity—and was willing to take this burden initially, thinking that it is better to be married to anyone, rather than to remain single—R. Feinstein wrote that one should treat this marriage as a mistake—as a marriage that was no marriage at all. This marriage should therefore be annulled; that is, invalidated.

---

59. See note 57 in Chapter Seven. *Piskei Din Rabaniyim*, part 11, p. 327, 1979.

60. Norma Baumel Joseph, "Mehitzah: Halakhic Decisions and Political Consequences," in *Daughters of the King: Women and the Synagogue*, ed. Susan Grossman and Rivka Haut (Philadelphia: Jewish Publication Society, 1992), p. 126.

We see his painstaking care in his responsum (3:44) to a rabbi who writes from Sidney, Australia, about a husband who cruelly beat his wife several times and then made a settlement in the secular courts. The husband was told that he had to divorce her in accordance with Jewish law of his own free will and he was interrogated to see if this was the case. He said "I consent to issue a bill of divorce to my wife without any compulsion or conditions." Despite this statement, it was questionable if it was of his own free will, and most of Feinstein's discussion relates to this point. His bottom line is that there is room to consider even a possibly coerced divorce as valid, which is in opposition to the Hatam Sofer (see earlier).

It appears that Feinstein is willing to stretch the law in order that women not have to be anchored to insane husbands for fourteen years.

CONCLUSION

In this chapter we have been looking at some responsa of rabbis who viewed the plight of the battered wife as an inherent injustice and who were thus willing to interpret the *halakha* in order that she be able to get on with her life. We have seen examples of disagreement with those authorities who opposed a forced divorce and authorities who allowed women to live separately from their husbands and yet be maintained by them. We have seen extreme suggestions, such as cutting off perpetrators' hands and excommunicating them.

Yet despite these precedents, we know there are many women who are running the gauntlet of today's rabbinical court system, unable to get a divorce from their husbands. Depending on who is counting, between 8,000 and 20,000 women are left in limbo in the State of Israel, many of whom are battered wives.[61] Part of the problem is denial on the part of some rabbis; that is,

---

61. Danielle Valensi, founder of the Israel-based Organization for Agunot and Wives of Get-Refusers, estimates that these are the numbers (*The Jerusalem Post Magazine*, 12 March 1993, p. 8). Not all *agunot* are the result of rabbinic refusal to force a divorce. There was a case of a woman whose husband was allegedly killed during a gang shooting and no witnesses came forward. The Beer-Sheva Chief Rabbi even offered the witnesses to the murder "confidentiality" if they would come forward to help the *agunah*. Unfortunately, no one took him up on his offer and the woman is still an *agunah*. This was reported at a conference I chaired in Beer-Sheva on the plight of the *agunah* in January 1994. Na'amat recently gave the numbers as 20,000! In an editorial, "Predictable Acts of Murder," *Ha'aretz Daily Newspaper* (11 September 1997), depicting the death of Irma Yizraeli, whose husband stabbed her to death in the presence of police officers, "it is estimated that some 40,000 women in (Israel) live under the shadow of constant threats," although only 19,000 complaints are actually filed with the police. The discrepancy is because in Israel the law does not require that every act of violence be reported, unlike the mandatory reporting of child abuse.

the unwillingness of rabbis to face the fact that there is a real problem. Then too, many rabbis are busy "defending the faith," justifying it and apologizing for it. Rabbis are disinclined to interpret the *halakha* in such a way that men's rights over their wives are diminished, so that a husband who habitually batters his wife would be forced to give his wife a divorce. The prevailing attitude today among the majority of rabbis, despite the precedents shown in this chapter, is one of conditional rejection, or evasion of responsibility. These rabbis at least recognize that the *halakha* treats women unjustly, but they also claim they "cannot," by law, force the wifebeater to divorce his wife.

I will address these and other modern-day problems in the next two chapters, in which we will first discuss denial and apologetics, and then evasion of responsibility.

9

Modern Attitudes Toward Wifebeating: Denial and Apologetics*

We have seen that the metaphor of marriage influences reality and lays down what is acceptable behavior to those who accept the norms. But what happens when the normativity of the metaphor is abruptly questioned or becomes unacceptable? This may occur when we try to defend our normative metaphor to outsiders or to an outgroup within Jewish society. Suddenly the metaphor has to be justified, explained, and rationalized—and a polemic is thus created. As Jewish society opens up to assimilation outside of Jewish ghettos, the group loses "control" over individuals. The "hostile world" becomes a part of Jewish consciousness, and Jews become integrated into the "outside" society. Large groups of Jews adjust to the notions and metaphors of the outside world, causing stress within Jewish society. Gradually there develops a need to defend traditional behavior, because the Jewish outgroup has a different perception of what constitutes normative behavior.

However, polemical arguments themselves, like metaphor, become building blocks for our perceptions of reality, and they influence us. They

---

* Parts of this chapter were presented at the 1996 Rabbinical Assembly Convention and is available in an audio-cassette format.

serve, as does metaphor, to pit one group's view of morality against another: "Our group is moral, the other group is not." As with metaphor, we have an emotional investment in preserving our polemical arguments; they become entrenched attitudes and develop a status as a kind of metaphor themselves. The attitudes toward wifebeating of denial, apologetics, and evasion are particularly prevalent in modern times; these attitudes can be conceptualized as "polemical metaphors."

The first attitude, denial, is based on a metaphor of Jewish society in a "hostile world," and assumes that the former is relatively more moral than the latter. The second attitude, apologetics, shows some of the qualities of the first, but also pits an older "traditional" morality against the "inferior" modern one. The third, evasion, is an internal polemic attempting to uphold traditional laws and values by assuming their inviolability as "sacred norms" and claiming that the reality is not desperate enough to justify tampering with those norms. While these attitudes are not legal principles, they inform the legal texts as background and are part of that crucial part of legal precedent known as "the mindset of the judge" or "the spirit of the law."

DENIAL

Denial is the technical term for a common human reaction to pain or "bad news," such as a death. In that context, Richard Momeyer wrote:

> Denial . . . is less an action than an attitude, a way of coping with information that is disconcerting and threatening. It is a way of considering (or not considering) what we would rather not have to face, a way to protect ourseves from the danger of loss of self-esteem, or of an important relationship, or of anything of value. At its extreme it requires extensive self-deception, a kind of lying to oneself which, paradoxically, involves simultaneously knowing something to be so and not believing it.[1]

The person who denies that a problem exists does not have to deal with it. The way to avoid painful self-examination is to say, "It is the gentiles who

---

1. Richard W. Momeyer, "Death Mystiques: Denial, Acceptance, Rebellion," *Mosaic,* XV:1 (1982): no 2; see also Avery Weisman, *On Dying and Denying: A Psychiatric Study of Terminality* (New York: Behavioral Publications, 1972).

beat their wives." This refrain allows the Jew to retain his sense of superiority: We are not like the barbarian who selects his wife by stunning her by a blow, carrying her back to his camp, and pronouncing her his property.[2] We are not like "those" people whose "women hold the lowest position in human society."[3]

If the person who denies is forced to confront the problem, he may cling to denial by saying the problem is new; it is a modern phenomenon caused by too much freedom and the erosion of the strong Jewish family. This form of denial implies the opposite: in strongly traditional Jewish families, husbands don't beat their wives.

Howard Eilberg-Schwartz, demonstrates that this kind of denial corresponds to the artificial distinction that academia makes between departments of anthropology (which include primitive religions) and departments of religion (which include Judaism and Christianity). This distinction, he points out, is a form of denial on the part of those in academia who refuse to recognize the savage in the origins of "civilized" religions. But by "marginalizing" the primitive or savage in modern discourses on Judaism, they have unwittingly furthered the cause of "savagery."[4]

Similarly, Jewish scholars who deny often reflect the opinions of the community at large. Rabbenu Tam (1100–71), perhaps the most important rabbi of the French *tosafist* school, which flourished in the twelfth century, made the claim that "wifebeating is unheard of among the children of Israel."[5] Since we saw in Chapter Eight that, as one of the signatories to R. Perez's *takkanah*, he was well aware that there was a problem in the Jewish community of his time, was this disclaimer actually one of denial? His disbelief may have been genuine, since his family included learned women who were respected, positive role models for him. Thus his reaction that "it just was not done" may have been based on an idealization of life as it should be—a generalization from his own life which he extended to society in general.

---

2. Nahida Remy's *The Jewish Woman*, authorized translation by Louise Mannheimer, with a preface by Prof. Dr. Lazarus, Fourth Edition (copyright, Cincinnati, OH: 1895, by Louise Mannheimer; 1915 by Bloch) (New York: Bloch, 1923), p. 17.

3. Remy refers to the Indians and Chinese to make her point; *ibid.*, p. 19.

4. Howard Eilberg-Schwartz, *The Savage in Judaism: An Anthropology of Israelite Religion and Ancient Judaism* (Bloomington, IN: Indiana University Press, 1990), p. 50.

5. Isaac Klein, trans., *The Code of Maimonides*, Book 4; The Book of Women, Yale Judaica Series, vol. 19 (New Haven, CT: Yale University Press, 1972), pp. xxxv–xxxvi.

Jumping from Rabbenu Tam to the present, what about the case of a modern Conservative rabbi who reported at a Rabbinical Assembly convention "I have been in the rabbinate X number of years, and I have never had a case of wifebeating," despite the fact that at the time he made this statement, three of his congregants were in a domestic violence support group run by Rabbi Naomi Levy. To say "not in my congregation" is to echo the denial-promoting, defensive message of past generations.[6]

When a great modern scholar such as Louis Finkelstein[7]—who had the evidence of Rabbi Perez of Corbeil's *crie de coeur* (see Chapter Eight) in front of him saying that the women of Israel are crying out for relief from their husbands—decided that wifebeating wasn't a real problem among Jews, surely he could be accused of having his blinders on! Is it that modern Jewish scholars don't and didn't want to directly confront the less beautiful parts of Jewish existence?[8]

What about the modern day rabbi in a Chassidic community who refuses to believe that a prominent (i.e., a learned and wealthy member of his community [*talmid hacham*]) is beating his wife or sexually abusing his little daughter? Is it not further denial when he quotes Maimonides—who said that there is nothing wrong with a father sleeping in the same room with his daughter, and in the same bed, if both are fully clothed—in order to help us "contextualize" this act? The rabbi uses Maimonides to assert that "it's not going on."[9]

As late as 1990, Robert Gordis wrote in his book *The Dynamics of Judaism*:

> . . . women were physically weaker than men and legally subordinate to them, but they were far from helpless. As the Talmud sagely observes, "A

---

6. Debra Orenstein (with Jay Stein), "Domestic Violence and Jewish Responsibility," *Women's League Outlook* (Fall 1995): 23–24. It is possible that the women didn't want to go to a rabbi with such an attitude.

7. Louis Finkelstein, *Jewish Self-Government in the Middle Ages* (New York: Jewish Theological Seminary of America, 1924).

8. Compare this with Rabinowitz, *Social Life of the Jews of Northern France*, who writes that this "long" *takkanah* shows the "prevalence of the custom of wifebeating" and that "the prohibition may have been the result of an addiction to the habit" (p. 152), as cited in Howard Adelman's "Wifebeating in Jewish History," a paper presented to Sinai Temple in Toronto (May 8, 1992, p. 21).

9. This was a personal communication from Ari Hahn, a social worker in the Lubavitch community in Brooklyn.

woman carries her weapons in her own person" [B. Baba Batra 115a; B. Avodah Zarah 25b]. As for the physical abuse of women, centuries later the medieval work *Sepher Hasidim*[10] declared as a matter of fact, "We Jews do not beat our wives, as do the gentiles."[11]

This is another example of self-imposed "ignorance" inherent in apologetics. Mimi Scarf, despite her citations of hearsay evidence of a Yiddishist colleague, which implied that Jewish men beat their wives in Warsaw, court cases in the post-Holocaust period, and Abraham Cahan's *Bintel Brief* column, concludes:

> It seems that, historically, as much wife-abuse did not exist, as might be expected. Unless more evidence is unearthed, it may be safe to say that Jewish wifebeating is, after all, primarily a modern problem.[12]

Obviously I, and others, do not agree with this. Scarf has been overly generous in her reading of the medieval sources in order to conclude the following:

> Further, the modern response to a Jewish woman who seeks redress from a court because she is being beaten by her husband, "Go home and work it out," is a far cry from the response to her ancient or medieval ancestress who was promised a divorce, payment on five counts, and the assurance that, if her husband beat her again, he would be lashed, excommunicated, or have his arm amputated.[13]

She overlooks the preponderance of responsa that decide for *shalom bayit* [peace, or harmony, in the home], starting from talmudic times.[14]

An important first-person source of the inequities in Jewish Divorce law *vis-à-vis* women is Leah Ain Globe's pamphlet, *The Dead End: Divorce Proceedings in Israel*.[15] In it she writes movingly of many women who have

---

10. No source is cited for this. The interested reader is directed to *Sefer Hasidim*, by Yehuda Hehasid (Jerusalem: Rav Kook Institute, 1957).

11. (Bloomington, IN: Indiana University Press), pp. 146-147.

12. Mimi Scarf, *Battered Jewish Wives: Case Studies in the Response to Rage* (Lewiston, Queenston: The Edwin Mellen Press), pp. 55-56.

13. *Ibid.*, p. 56. [no source cited]

14. See article from *Encyclopedia Talmudit* on Shalom Bayit and Ba'al [husband].

15. Published in 1983. This can be obtained from: B.A.L. Mass Communication Ltd., P.O.B. 8324, Jerusalem.

suffered at the hands of the modern rabbinate in Israel. Writing from the perspective of an Orthodox woman, her thesis is that modern-day rabbis have perverted the ancient Jewish tradition where women were protected by the Torah, when women were not considered inferior.

Her method is to present case studies of women who have been physically or mentally abused by their husbands. These women apply for justice in the rabbinical courts and are sent back to their homes (which she shows are anything but sanctuaries) for the sake of *shalom bayit* [peace in the home]. After each case study and its unhappy conclusion, she quotes from the halakhic or midrashic sources to demonstrate by juxtaposition the perversion of justice in present-day rabbinical courts.

She uses sources that imply that all was well in the Jewish past and that today's rabbis are not basing their decisions on past precedents. Her selective use of quotations leaves out those scholars who did justify wifebeating and who are serving as authorities for present day rabbis to deal leniently with wifebeaters. Thus she writes after describing a horrendous case of wife abuse and the rabbinical courts' ineffective handling of the case:

> The crime of wifebeating, which has been denounced by our Sages in the harshest of terms, is being disregarded in modern Israel. Ignoring brutality is tantamount to encouraging it.[16]

While she attacks the abuse of justice by today's rabbis, she idealizes the sages of the past. If she were less romantic about the past, and would admit that the opinions of sages were not monolithic about whether wifebeating constituted grounds for divorce, her argument would be stronger.

Romanticizing Jewish law, both past and present, gives Jews who "care" about tradition the possibility to ignore a "battering culture." Beverly Horsburgh decries the legal scholarship of Jewish professions who

> often uncritically praise the Jewish tradition, omitting its sexism and condonation of woman-abuse. . . . In creating various idealistic myths about Jewish law, these academics cause great harm to Jewish battered women who require the legal community to face the reality of their problems. Just like the romance of the Jewish family, the romanticization of *halakha* increases the difficulties of Jewish women to receive the help they so des-

---

16. *Ibid.*, p. 37.

perately need. The hesitation of legal scholars to criticize Jewish law in effect amounts to a condonation of the status quo.[17]

It is difficult to know whether it is ignorance, or refusal to see the possible roots of misogyny in the past, that lead Jewish professionals to imply, by omission, that Jewish sources are monolithic about wifebeating. The implications of this omission is not only connected with scholarly dishonesty; it affects one's world view. Romanticizing is a form of apologetics and has its dangers.

APOLOGETICS

"Apologetics" in Judaism is defined as "that literature which endeavors to defend Jews, their religion, and their culture in reply to adverse criticism."[18] Apologetics was prevalent whenever Jews felt threatened by the surrounding culture. It was used consciously as a tool by Jewish historians of the late nineteenth and early twentieth century. Today, perhaps it is a form of conscious suppression or unconscious denial.

Saul Berman, in his article on the status of women in halakhic Judaism, calls for a "moratorium on apologetics," recognizing that "it is dishonest and dysfunctional to attempt through homiletics and scholasticism to . . . reinterpret discrimination to be beneficial."[19] On one hand, he recognizes that the "*distinguishing* line between apologetics and explanation is exceedingly thin."[20] On the other hand, he falls into the apologetic trap himself due to his inability to see sexist and even misogynist tendencies (unconscious denial perhaps) among rabbinical authorities: "It is difficult to conceive of these same jurists setting out with malice aforethought to subject their own mothers, wives and daughters to the most blatant forms of injustice and

---

17. Beverly Horsburgh, "Lifting the Veil of Secrecy: Domestic Violence in the Jewish Community," *Harvard Women's Law Journal* (Spring 1995): 211–212.

18. *Encyclopedia Judaica*, vol. 3, p. 189. In the context of Christianity "its function is both to fortify the believer against his personal doubts and to remove the intellectual stumbling blocks that inhibit the conversion of unbelievers" (*Encyclopedia Britannica*, p. 486).

19. Saul Berman, "The Status of Women in Halakhic Judaism," in *The Jewish Woman*, ed. L. Koltun (New York: Schocken Books, 1976), p. 116.

20. *Ibid.*, p. 117.

inequity."[21] He falls into apologetics rather than plead guilty to plain sexism. Confronting possible misogyny is avoided by use of apologetics.

Blu Greenberg restates the need for modern apologetics in an article she wrote that appeared in a journal of ecumenical studies. She admits that "much of Jewish literature, law, and language surrounding marriage and divorce reflects hierarchy and sexism," yet feels constrained to be apologetic when writing to people of other religions "who would not naturally feel the love and appreciation [for Judaism] an insider feels and who would, therefore, come away with a one-sided view. . . ."[22] She then makes a statement in the apologetic mode:

> I ask you to bear in mind these general truths: that the tradition was sexist more in theory than in practice, more in certain cultures than in others, more in the past than in the present, more in legal formulation than in actual relationships, more in ancient law than in scriptural narrative.[23]

By suggesting that theory has no bearing on practice, that tradition has no bearing on the present,[24] the reader, taking her words out of context, could be lead to overlook the dangers of sexism in the Jewish tradition.

The use of apologetics is connected with anti-Semitism. Jews perceived the world as hostile (and it is naive to think otherwise), so they wanted to look good—both to themselves and to others—in order to defend against outside hostility. When used as a defense, apologetics minimized negative elements in Judaism, apparently on the assumption that Judaism was too fragile to admit them.

But Judaism is not a fragile institution. Questioning certain of its aspects does not constitute a threat to its integrity. Judaism is not and has never been a monolithic institution; it thrives on controversy and multiplicity of opinions. Unfortunately, apology, which starts out by whitewashing, ends up obfuscating the roots of abuse and thus in the end perpetuates it.

---

21. *Idem.*

22. Blu Greenberg, "Marriage in the Jewish Tradition," *Journal of Ecumenical Studies* 22:1 (1985): 4.

23. *Ibid.*, p. 4.

24. As Greenberg indicates in her footnotes, she has approached sexism in the sources differently in her own work, *On Women and Judaism* (Philadelphia: Jewish Publication Society, 1982).

Another danger of apologetics is that it stifles self-criticism. According to Judith Plaskow,

> . . . [C]riticism is an ongoing and essential part of the Jewish feminist project. Not only is criticism a precondition for imaging a transformed Judaism, without a clear critique of Judaism that precedes and accompanies reconstruction, the process of reconstruction easily can be misconstrued as a form of apologetics.[25]

Worse perhaps is that Judaism is denigrated by the explanations and rationalizations made in order to "guard the law from humiliation."[26] The net result of apologetics is that contemporary Jews, for whom an important frame of reference is western modernity, are led to question the validity of halakhic analysis for themselves.

How do apologists for Judaism and Jews relate to the problem of wifebeating? One reaction, as we have seen, is to *deny* its existence: Jews don't do it. And if they do, it is among the "lower classes."[27]

I will confine my use of "apologetics" to other reactions that are less than total denial. When apologists are forced to acknowledge that wifebeating is a phenomenon they cannot ignore, they then *marginalize* and state that those Jews who do engage in wifebeating do so less frequently and less violently than do non-Jewish batterers. They will try to *justify* it by claiming that those Jews who actually engage in such behavior don't really hurt their wives, and if they do, perhaps it's for a good reason. Finally, they will *displace* the blame, by shifting it to others: It is not our fault; if Jewish men batter, it is only because of environmental influences.

Apologists usually *romanticize* Judaism, by depicting a rosy picture of the traditional Jewish family. Jews often quote from those apologists who perpetuate the myth of the happy Jewish family in order to reconfirm their own positive self-image. The following sections will review chronologically selected apologists whose writings, despite their stated intentions, have been harmful to women.

---

25. Judith Plaskow, *Standing Again at Sinai* (San Francisco: Harper and Row, 1990), p. 2.

26. Chaim Seidler-Feller, "Female Rabbis, Male Fears," *Judaism*, no 33 (1984): 81.

27. Horsburgh writes that the tragic story of Hedda Nussbaum prompted little public interest. "In commenting on the death of Lisa Steinberg, one writer criticized the Jewish community for its psychological denial of domestic violence among upper and middle-class Jews that allows perpetrators with money and influence to minimize their responsibility and rationalize their behavior" ("Lifting the Veil," note 4, p. 177).

Nineteenth-Century Apologetics

In 1895, Louise Mannheimer translated *The Jewish Woman*, a book written by the philo-Semite Nahida Remy in 1891.[28] Remy's book is a very sympathetic accounting of the history and status of Jewish women, starting from biblical times until the end of the nineteenth century. It is apologetics at its best. After two chapters detailing the barbaric attitudes of men to women in ancient times and the attitude of Christianity to women, she argues in hyperbolic terms the superiority of Jewish tradition vis-à-vis the fate and status of Jewish women as compared with non-Jewish women.[29]

Levenson writes that "Remy's Jewish apologetic crowds out her feminism and we are left with an essentially conservative prescription for the modern Jewish woman; to wit, 'the only way to an honored and prominent position is the practice of the virtues of their foremothers.'"[30] The sanctification of life finds its truest expression in family life. The woman had the main responsibility for the sanctification of the home. This was her duty:

> The Jewish view of marriage is loftier than that of any other nation. The main quest is not submission and blind obedience on the part of the wife; what is required of her are morals and morality. There is no question of a gloomy, silent subjection, but of a loving alliance; of a union of purpose and aspirations. The wife is not the slave of her husband, but, as God himself calls her, his "helpmate."[31]

Most Rabbinic commentators are uncomfortable with the case of the *sotah*, Numbers 5:12–31 (see Chapter Two). Remy, however, considers this chapter a case where "Jewish law was very merciful"[32] to the unfaithful wife.

---

28. Nahida Remy's *Das Judische Weib* (1891) went through at least four editions in German between 1891 and 1922. By 1923, when the Bloch Publishing Company released the book in the United States, it was in its fourth edition. In the preface to this popular book, Remy's mentor, Moritz Lazarus (later to become her second husband), wrote that he hoped Jewish women would learn from this non-Jewish woman (she later converted) to respect the heritage that they often neglected.

29. Nahida Remy, *The Jewish Woman*, p. 43.

30. Alan T. Levenson, "An Adventure in Otherness: Nahida Remy-Ruth Lazarus (1849–1928)," in *Gender and Judaism*, ed. T.M. Rudavsky (New York: New York University Press, 1995), p. 100.

31. Remy, p. 51.

32. *Ibid.*, p. 47.

A further example of her rosy depiction of Jewish tradition, which serves as a form of denial, are her comments on incest and child abuse: "I can safely assert that no Jewish mother would be guilty of such unnatural conduct.[33]

Because of her philo-Semitism, Remy consistently subordinates the interests of women to the higher consideration of the interest of Judaism.[34] But in doing so, she ends up revictimizing the victim—all in the name of a higher good. The assumption that the Jewish tradition is beyond reproach often serves to sweep away suspicions about abuse.

Thus, in a recent article on child abuse that brings that problem out of the Jewish closet, Rabbi Irving Greenberg cannot resist asserting (parenthetically of course) that when Jews follow tradition, they don't practice child abuse:

> Resistance to admitting that this problem exists in the Jewish community apparently grows out of some mistaken claim, that morally speaking, Jews are intrinsically different, and better—our generation's version of the claim that Jews do not drink and Jews do not beat their wives. Just as those claims have proved false—*with the erosion of Jewish culture, drinking and wifebeating made their inevitable appearance among us*—so will any claim that incest is not a Jewish problem.[35] [emphasis added]

Greenberg criticizes those who practice denial of the facts, yet in explaining the facts away with the simplistic notion of abandoning tradition, he is practicing apologetics by implying that wifebeating appears only with the erosion of tradition.[36]

To say that the erosion of tradition is responsible for social ills leads one to believe that there is a cause and effect relationship: if the tradition is kept, there is no battering. From this one can be led to erroneously believe that the more observant and traditional the family, the safer the woman. This assertion was made and advanced by Remy and other nineteenth-century writers.

Paula Hyman described the nineteenth-century Jewish intellectuals who regarded the Jewish family with pride. Their answer to anti-Semitism

---

33. *Ibid.*, p. 160.

34. *Ibid.*, p. 100.

35. Irving Greenberg, "Abuse in Jewish Families: Rabbis Can Help by Speaking Out," *Moment* (April 1990): 49.

36. Although he speaks openly about the problem, he does not highlight the fact that in the comprehensive list of forbidden incestual relations in Leviticus 18 there is a glaring omission: there is no mention of an incestuous relationship between father and daughter. That it is forbidden is part of later rabbinic interpretation.

was "to point to traditional Jewish family life as a model of noble domestic behavior" that could "rehabilitate both Judaism and the Jews."

> "Nowhere is family sentiment more profound than among the Jews," claimed the *Archives Israelites* in 1846: ". . . One never hears of a depraved father, of a mother who has antipathy for her children, of a son who refuses assistance to his elderly parents." . . . Or, again, in 1875, the *Jewish Chronicle* noted smugly: "The papers have again lately reported several cases of *wifebeating*. This iniquity, we are happy to see, is *very rare in the Jewish community*."[37] [emphasis added]

Besides the *Archives Israelites*, other writers of the apologetic mode on the continent, such as Morris Gudemann (1835–1918), implied that there was a direct correspondence between the observance of laws of morality and modesty among Jews and the success of love and marriage.

Gudemann includes in his apologetics polemics against Christianity, thus attempting to show that Jews are better than the gentiles. He writes that one of the few positive things Jews learned from their non-Jewish neighbors was to display the value of their women by dressing them suitably,[38] and, since it is the duty of the Jewish husband to spend money on his wife, it is ridiculous to even think that he might torture her like one of the maids. Clearly, Gudemann assumes that wife-battering was limited to the lower class since he writes that if a woman (non-Jewish and Jewish) is dressed as befits her station she is no doubt honored by her husband.[39]

---

37. Paula Hyman, "The Modern Jewish Family: Image and Reality," in *The Jewish Family: Metaphor and Memory*, ed. David Kraemer (New York: Oxford University Press, 1989), pp. 186-187.

38. Morris Guedmann, *Geschichte des Erziehungswesens und der Cultur der abendlandischen Juden wahrend des Mittelalters*. Translated into Hebrew (Warsaw: Ahiasaf, 1897). Reprinted in Jerusalem, 1932, p. 195.

39. Apologists among the late nineteenth- and early twentieth-century writers were reacting to those who accused Jews of being "oriental" in their approach to life. Apologists claimed the superiority of the Jewish way of life over others. Samson Raphael Hirsch (mid- to late-nineteenth century), who eschewed the apologetic mode, wrote a laudatory chapter about the Jewish woman to argue against those who distort and disregard the testimony of the Bible and tradition. See Samson Raphael Hirsch, "The Jewish Woman," *Judaism Eternal*, vol. 2 (London: Soncino Press, 1956). For a more detailed discussion of this topic, see Mordecai Breuer, "Apologetics," *Jewish Orthodoxy in the German Reich: 1871–1918* (Jerusalem: Zalman Shazar Center, 1990), p. 182.

Early Twentieth-Century Apologetics

Israel Abrahams (1858–1924) wrote in his study of the medieval period that "Jews were clear of the more hideous vices which eat at the root of social life in civilized states."[40] He echoes Gudemann, whose work he knew.

> The Jew who indulged in the physical ill-usage of his wife was regarded as a monstrosity. The wifebeater was not altogether an unknown figure in Jewish life, but the attitude of public opinion towards him is very instructive.[41] [emphasis added]

Abrahams substantiates his view that wifebeating was frowned upon by referring to the twelfth century Rabbenu Tam, who, although he "forced the wifebeater to provide his wife with separate maintenance,"[42] yet says about wifebeating, "This is a thing not done in Israel." He quotes Rabbi Meir of Rotenberg to show that "Jews are not addicted to the prevalent habit of ill-treating wives."

Rabbi J. H. Hertz (early twentieth century) of England, comparing the status of Jewish women with Christian women, used wifebeating as his litmus test.

> The respect and reverence which womanhood enjoyed in Judaism are not limited to noble and beautiful *sayings*. That respect and reverence were translated into life. . . . [O]ne test alone is sufficient to show the abyss in actual life, between Jewish and non-Jewish chivalry down to modern times. That test is wifebeating.[43]

Hertz quotes Coulton and Trevelyan to show that, among non-Jews, chastising one's wife by beating her was not only customary, but was even formally permitted by Canon Law. In Trevelyan's words: "wifebeating was a recognized right of man, and was practiced without shame by high as well as low."[44] But not by Jews! Christian men beat their wives; Jewish men don't.

---

40. Israel Abrahams, *Jewish Life in the Middle Ages* (1896) (Philadelphia: Jewish Publication Society, 1961), p. 86.

41. *Ibid.*, pp. 87–88.

42. *Ibid.*, p. 88.

43. Rabbi J. H. Hertz of England, his commentary on the Book of Deuteronomy in *The Pentateuch and Haftorahs*, 2nd ed. (London: Soncino Press, 1936, 1962, 1971), p. 935.

44. *Idem.*

Like Abrahams, Hertz quotes Rabbenu Tam, to show that "This is a thing not done in Israel" and the *Shulhan Arukh,* which "prescribe[s] it as the Beth Din's duty to punish a wifebeater, to excommunicate him, and—if this be of no avail—to compel him to divorce his wife with all the rights she is entitled to in her *ketubah,* her wedding contract (Even ha-Ezer, CLIV, 3)."

If we compare Hertz's selective quotation from the *Shulhan Arukh* with the text we have seen that includes Isserles's notes, it is clear that Hertz chooses to refer only to those rabbis in the *Shulhan Arukh* who consider wife-beating as grounds for divorce, while ignoring the majority who do not! (see Chapter Ten). As we have seen above, one of the major distortions upon which an apologetic stance is based is that Jewish tradition is monolithic.

We have seen that apologists are other-blaming. We saw that Gudemann reaffirmed a major assumption that the socially advanced and stable classes do not beat their wives.[45] We have seen instances of modern Jewish thinkers who have recognized the dangers of apologetics, yet have, themselves, felt the need for its use.

Ruth Nadelhaft, analyzes this type of thinking in her discussion of domestic violence in short stories. She makes clear that when women deny a grim reality, what starts out as self-protection often ends in self-destruction. What she writes can serve as a commentary on those who delude themselves into thinking that it is the "other" who beats his wife:

It is tempting for those women who are securely registered in the middle class to perceive domestic violence as a problem of class, or color, or "culture" which confines it and promises immunity to those outside its mysterious boundaries . . . [Attitudes such as these] lay bare the self-serving and in the end self-destructive thinking which perpetuates the problem of domestic abuse within a social network. What will the neighbors say? Whose neighbors?[46]

---

45. Goitein assumes this as well in his volume on the Jewish family during the Geniza period, despite the fact that he faithfully records instances of wifebeating. He mitigates its harsh effect, both for himself and the reader, by using the apologetic mode: it's mostly "them" not "us": "it mostly concerns couples from the lower and lowest strata of society." S. D. Goitein, *A Mediterranean Society,* vol. 3 The Family (Berkeley, CA: University Press of California, 1978), pp. 171-189.

46. Ruth Nadelhaft, "Domestic Violence in Literature: A Preliminary Study," *Mosaic* XVII:2 (1984): 249.

To imply that wifebeating exists only in the lower strata is to leave the Jewish middle-class readers off the hook, allowing them to breathe a sigh of relief. To precisely define the scope of a phenomenon salves the conscience. Defining an issue also gives the false impression that it is under control. If I am not in the "high-risk" group, I can give up worrying about it.

In an otherwise positive review of Goitein's book, M.A. Friedman criticizes his assumption that wife-battering was a lower-class phenomenon.

> Due to the nature of Geniza materials, the information concerning disruptions of harmonious life is more abundant than that attesting to peaceful family existence. It is frequently not clear how representative these data are. Thus many documents concerning the wifebeating and cursing syndrome emanate from the lower strata of society. *Instances of wifebeating may have existed in other segments of the society but went unreported.*[47] [emphasis added]

We saw that Louis Finkelstein (earlier) denied the evidence in front of him when he concluded that wifebeating was not a problem. Theodore Friedman and Eliezer Berkovits are two additional modern scholars who are guilty of apologetics. Both of them ascribe the source of misogyny to "Greek" and/or "Moslem" influence.

Friedman apologizes for the "lapses" in Kohelet (Ecclesiastes):

> Koheleth's misogynic view of women is readily explained by the consensus of Biblical scholars that the book is to be dated somewhere in the Hellenistic period and that it *clearly betrays strong Greek influence.*[48] [emphasis added]

After summing up the social situation of women in the Talmudic period by describing a woman "swathed like a mourner— a reference to the covering of her face and hair by a veil—isolated from people and shut up in prison,"[49] Friedman draws the following conclusion from his evidence.

---

47. M.A. Friedman, *JAOS* 100:2 (1980): 130.
48. Theodore Friedman, "The Shifting Role of Women, From the Bible to Talmud," *Judaism* 36 (1987): 481.
49. *Ibid.*, quoting from B. *Eruvin* 100b, p. 483.

Virtually every one of the features of the picture that we have drawn of the seclusion of women in the Talmudic period *finds its analog in ancient Athenian society* in the post-Homeric age.[50] [emphasis added]

In his conclusion Friedman writes that

one would search rabbinic literature in vain for anything approaching such acidulous statements [about women]. *Compared with the dominant strain of anti-feminism that runs through classical Greek literature . . . rabbinic statements on the subject are sweetness and light.* The Midrash that describes a woman as a tattler, gadabout, etc. *is really a ribbing* and hardly breathes the misogyny of the Greeks. On the contrary, the Sages advise a man to be zealous in honoring his wife because it is through her that blessing is found in his home.[51] [emphasis added]

Friedman's conclusion, that, in comparison, "rabbinic statements are sweetness and light," is to let the Jewish sources off too lightly. His final argument—that the discriminatory life of Jewish women in Talmudic times "was not a home-grown produce, but rather, a foreign import"[52]—is laudable only in that he wants to show that it is not intrinsic to Judaism and thus cannot be justified today. However, in his love for Jewish tradition, he is willing to overlook the fact that some Jewish sources are intrinsically misogynist and that Jewish sexism cannot be blamed totally on foreign influences.

In a recent apologetic book, Eliezer Berkovits[53] quotes the same sources as Friedman and arrives at a similar conclusion:

In attempting to understand this strange phenomenon in Jewish life, we must realize that *many of the negative opinions about women and their place in society are not authentically Jewish.* For instance, a study of the practices in classical Greece reveals many similarities and parallels between the two societies. For example, the established principle was "that men are born to rule and women to obey."[54] [emphasis added]

---

50. *Ibid.*, p. 484.

51. *Ibid.*, p. 486.

52. *Ibid.*, p. 487.

53. Eliezer Berkovits, *Jewish Women in Time and Torah* (Hoboken, NJ: K'tav, 1990). For a different and more complimentary opinion of his book, see the short review in the *Israel Women's Network Bulletin* of April 1992.

54. Berkovits, *Jewish Women*, p. 25

Further on, in the opening sentence of his section "Torah-Tolerated, Not Torah-Taught," he writes:

> Undoubtedly, the basic views and values that originally determined the status of women in Jewish society *were not derived from the Torah*, even though many of them were later given midrashic justification. They were Torah-tolerated because they could not be abolished with an act of Torah legislation. They had to be tolerated, but certain changes and differences were present which indicated that an entirely different system of values and teachings also existed.[55] emphasis added]

In his foreword to his book, Berkovits explains just what he means by "Torah Tolerated." First of all, it is NOT

> Torah-established or Torah-taught. It derived from the mores, conditions, and circumstances of an early age, and was not essentially different from what we find in other societies in the same stage of development.[56]

In other words, although the *midrash* may have justified a misogynist approach to women, that was not the intent of the Torah. The Torah simply tolerated (and thereby recorded) what were the norms of its time. Had the Torah deviated from the norms of its time, it might not have "spoken to" its intended audience. Women as nonpersons was so established in Biblical times that for the Torah to have deviated from this understanding would have diluted and endangered its essential message. Berkovits's argument is ingenious apologetics, and; in essence, not very different from Nahida Remy's, who subordinated women's specific interests to the greater needs of an endangered Judaism. However, Berkovits, in recognizing the misogynist tendencies of the Bible and Talmud, suggests that we not continue in the same path.

Robert Gordis, the former editor of *Judaism*, and a modern scholar (d. 1992), argues that:

> apologetics designed to explain, or explain away, the male centered character of biblical and rabbinic law are no service to the truth or the tradition.

---

55. *Ibid.*, p. 33.
56. *Ibid.*, p. 1.

On the other hand, attacking the classical tradition on the score of its being male-centered is a flagrant anachronism; it means demanding of an ancient society the egalitarian ideals that are barely emerging in the twentieth century.[57] [emphasis added]

Abrahams, Gudemann, Hirsch, Hertz, Gordis, Berkovits, Friedman, and others cannot face up to the fact that sexism and misogyny were rampant and prevailed in all human history, including Jewish history. Why is it necessary for them to apologize for the practice of misogyny? Do they feel by confronting misogyny they will be forced to admit they are not different from the non-Jews, the very same people whom they are trying to influence. It is easier not to face the truth, not to see the evidence.[58]

In the end, apologetics uses denial and marginalization and justifies immoral practices. It leads to accepting assertions, such as, "sex-role differences and sexual distraction are intrinsic factors"[59] in Judaism, and to favor the nurturance of "gender-based distinctions by prescribing domestic roles for women . . . [such as] the creation and preservation of *shalom bayit* [household harmony]. . . ."[60] It can be sanguine about the tradition's assumption that women are frivolous, a source of temptation—in short, sex objects with no intrinsic worth. And then it can argue that, under certain circumstances, immoral means, such as women's "benevolent subordination," can be used to justify "more important" goals of stable marriage and society.

---

57. Robert Gordis, *The Dynamics of Judaism* (Bloomington, IN: Indiana University Press, 1990), pp. 148-149.

58. Howard Eilberg-Schwartz, in his book *The Savage in Judaism*, speaks of four types of defensive strategies that have been used to cope with the unpleasant, primitive aspects of Judaism that most people prefer not to have to deal with. He calls them "denial, marginalization, excision, and temporization." These are included in the categories I have proposed. The strategy of denial involved claiming that the similarities between the religions of Jews and heathens were superficial and the result of a misunderstanding. Such commonalties dissolved if one truly understood the character of Judaism. While the strategy of marginalization acknowledged the presence of savage elements in Judaism, it defused their potentially damaging implications by denying that those elements were part of Judaism's essence. Rather, he claimed, *such practices and beliefs were regarded as necessary evils that enabled true Judaism to survive in its pagan environment* (p. 50).

59. Phillip Sigal, quoting David Feldman's, "Women's Role and Jewish Law," *Conservative Judaism* 26: 4 in his article "Elements of Male Chauvinism in Classical *Halakhah*," *Judaism* 24:2 (1975): 226.

60. Judith R. Baskin, "Feminism Within Orthodoxy," *Reconstructionist* (Winter 1991/ 92): 29.

Apologetics often leads to a kind of justification of the fact of wifebeating under the guise of relativist morality, and thus perpetuates acquiescence of the majority to the fact. To face the basic problem of women's marginalization in society, Jewish leaders need to outgrow the use of apologetics and develop a rhetoric of "plain-talking," so that they may deal creatively with the truth about the past.

The practice of apologetics and denial demeans the Torah, which stands for, and teaches unpopular ideas of freedom and justice. To imply that the Torah is incapable of rising above the standards of surrounding societies is to obfuscate the truth. When it wanted to, the Torah could and did rise above its surroundings: when it chose to, it had a proud history of being uninfluenced (or influenced for the better) by those who would practice idolatry, infanticide, and so on.[61]

Judaism is not pure and untainted by other influences. The Torah's *weltanschauung* includes the nonpersonhood of woman as a given. Until feminism, there was a general callousness toward women's needs and feelings and an assumption by all societies that these concerns could be legislated by men only from their own perspective and understanding. Sometimes the Torah text "chooses" to be better than its neighbors on this issue and sometimes it does not. "It both rejected and absorbed elements from neighboring traditions. Moreover, even when an element was absorbed it was often recast in distinctive ways."[62] Thus, if the Torah text does not meet the highest standards of *our* morality, it can legitimately be questioned. We should not accept the premise that what is in the Torah is automatically moral, if our own moral sensibility is repelled by it. Since the Torah purports to be a book with eternal relevance, its shortcomings should be faced squarely, not justified. The Torah is strong enough to face criticism. To do otherwise—to be satisfied with the "benevolent subordination"[63] of women in ancient and medieval times—belittles the Torah, mocks our intelligence, and perpetuates injustice.

---

61. See Maimonides, *Guide to the Perplexed*, on Sacrifice. However, we should gird ourselves for the findings of some future historian, anthropologist, archaeologist, and so on, who will one day uncover evidence that Jews did practice infanticide. See Meir Bar-Ilan's, "Infant Mortality in the Land of Israel in Late Antiquity," in S. Fishbane and J. N. Lightstone (eds.), *Essays in the Social Scientific Study of Judaism and Jewish Society*, (Montreal: Concordia University, 1990) pp. 3–25.

62. Howard Eilberg-Schwartz, *The Savage in Judaism*, p. 89.

63. Gordis, *The Dynamics of Judaism*, p. 148.

Another form of injustice is recognizing the shortcomings of our tradition, yet doing nothing about it. This leads to the practice of what I call "evasion of responsibility," an attitude that will be dealt with in the next chapter.

10

Evasion of Responsibility:
The Problem with Jewish Divorce Laws

We have seen different approaches to wifebeating in halakhic literature, yet, in modern times, the prevailing approach when it concerns actual cases—when the facts can neither be denied nor apologized nor "explained," is an approach I call "evasion."

What characterizes the evasive approach is that all of the halakhic rules that offer relief to women are "evaded," overlooked, conveniently forgotten when the principle of the husband's sole control of divorce is at stake. This patriarchal principle is connected to the halakhic principles and lore that imply that the woman is acquired (*kinyan*) by her husband who is her owner (*ba'al*) (see Chapters Four and Five). The husband's control of divorce is also allied with the double standard of adultery. One act of betrayal by the woman can result in her husband's divorcing her, but similar acts of betrayal by the husband are not considered just cause for her to sue for divorce. The principle being upheld can be traced back to the metaphors of God/husband as possessor.

The principles being evaded by the husband and the rabbinic courts are those that treat woman as person, not as chattel or possession. These include such principles as: a husband should not terrorize his household (B. Gittin

6b); a husband should provide his wife more than the required minimum; a husband should honor his wife more than himself; a husband should view his wife as being given to him "for life, not for sorrow" (see Chapter Six).

The evasion of these principles by the courts results in nondecisions that keep battered wives in their abusive marriages. Wifebeating does not occur in a vacuum; it is inseparable from woman's status in marriage, which is overwhelmingly dependent on the husband's desire whether to maintain the marriage.

We have seen that most rabbinic authorities, both past and present, do not sanction wifebeating, yet, for most of them, wifebeating is not perceived as sufficient cause for forcing a husband to give his wife a *get* [a Jewish bill of divorce]. The primary reason for not considering wifebeating as grounds for forcing a divorce is that this would require a major reshuffling of the husband's role in *halakha* as the one who "controls" the very status of marriage.

Yet, even if the idea is entertained that wifebeating constitutes grounds for divorce, objections are immediately raised to a forced divorce. The absurdity of the situation is that the violent husband, who by his actions proves his desire to rule over his wife, is the only one in the end who can free her.

Thus, despite the fact that most rabbis view battering as a terrible thing that shouldn't be done and reject the notion that husbands should be allowed to beat their wives with impunity, they qualify their rejection by taking an evasive attitude. They do so because they do not want to diminish the husband's status in *halakha* or change the wife's status from passive agent to active controller of her own status. The attitude is called "evasion" because it is typified by an evasion of responsibility and a fear of change. We can also refer to it as the "wringing hands syndrome": "Isn't it terrible! But what can we do?"

What underlies the evasive attitude of rejection is, first, the paramount importance of the sacred institution of marriage in Judaism—the preservation of marriage is more important than a solution to the problem of a wife's individual suffering. For this reason, battering by itself is not sufficient grounds for divorce. Second, the person who has an evasive attitude is not willing to tamper with the primacy of the male in Judaism. Thus, although the rights of women in family law have increased since biblical times, there is still widespread acceptance among many Jews of the inviolate nature of the rule that only a man can give to his wife a divorce.[1] In modern times these two reasons are seen as totally linked.

---

1. In the case of a recalcitrant husband, his power reigns supreme and he can hold her up for blackmail-type payments, which is conveniently overlooked by many rabbis.

Both of these attitudes converge with a fearful reluctance to change Jewish law in general and the parts of *halakha* that fortify these two attitudes in particular. Phillip Sigal, a conservative rabbi, says that the "evasion move" is played out essentially in the way *halakha* has been used by the rabbis to deal with divorce.

> *Evasion* marks the reluctance of the Rabbis to confront the male chauvinism inherent in the divorce legislation dating back over two millennia and still incorporated into the functioning *halakha*. The challenge that belies our cherished claim of liberalism is the rule that only a man can execute a Jewish religious divorce, except in some very unusual circumstances.[2]

Sigal points out that, although R. Perez b. Elijah is an excellent example of a rabbi in the thirteenth century who suggested that wifebeating should be grounds for legal separation and support, because of the strictures of *halakha* "it did not occur to R. Perez to allow the wife to divorce her cruel husband."[3]

Evasive positions vis-à-vis relief for a beaten wife are part of *halakha* and rest on the husband's dominant position in marriage. As early as the eighth century, R. Hananya, a Babylonian Gaon, writes that, although the husband should not beat his wife, the monetary compensation due to his wife belongs to him, so there is no real point of giving her compensation. The husband vows not to habitually beat her and in doing this, has fulfilled his duty (*yatza yeday hovato*). She, in turn, should listen to him, forgive him, pacify him and make peace with him.[4]

In the responsum of R. Solomon B. Abraham Aderet (Rashba) (1235-1310), who lived in Barcelona, what was then part of Christian Spain, we have a typical decision of evasion.[5] He writes that it is wrong to beat one's wife, but the court can do no more than issue a strong warning to the husband:

---

2. Phillip Sigal, "Male Chauvinism in *Halakha*," *Judaism* (Spring 1975): 231.

3. *Idem*. See Chapter Eight, where I explain why I included R. Perez among those rabbis who uncategorically reject wifebeaters, despite what I quote here from Sigal.

4. Geonic responsa *Sha-arei Ztedek*, part 4, p. 13.

5. For more on Rashba, see Chapter Seven.

At any rate I don't see that the *beit din* can do more than tell him in strong words not to beat her and warn him that if he beats her, *not according to law*, he will have to divorce her and give his wife her *ketubah*.[6]

In Chapter Seven we saw that R. David B. Solomon Ibn Avi Zimra (Radbaz) (1479–1573), strongly objected to the ruling by R. Simhah of Speyers, who allowed civil authorities to force a man to divorce his wife if he beat her. Radbaz reasoned that if a forced divorce were allowed, any children by a possible remarriage would be considered an illegitimate issue (*mamzerim*). We saw that there is a double standard that is accepted by all those who are interested in being halakhic Jews; namely, that it is the woman's problem, not the man's, because adultery only applies to a married woman. Only the man can grant divorce by his "will." This double standard puts the woman at the man's mercy, for if he refuses to divorce her, there is not much she can do.

Morrell, in his summary of Radbaz's responsum, shows the inherent problematics of an "evasive" responsum:

A man accused of wifebeating claimed that he was chastising his wife for improper deeds which he did not want to publicize. Radbaz accepts the right of a husband to chastise his wife, "since she is under his authority," but in theory only. He insists on witnesses to her misdeed. He refuses to accept the husband's word in such a case, and entertains a presumption of unjustified wifebeating. Furthermore, he makes the important qualification that he has no right to beat her for matters involving them personally.[7]

Yet despite Radbaz's unwillingness to accept the husband's word, it is still not justification for a forced divorce.

R. Joseph Caro (1488–1575)

R. Joseph Caro is best known as the author of the influential *Shulhan Arukh*; however, his magnum opus is *Beit Yosef*, a commentary on the *Arba'ah Turim* (the *Tur*) of Jacob ben Asher (c. 1280–1340). The purpose of *Beit Yosef* (published between 1550–1558), as stated in his introduction, was to investigate

---

6. *Responsa* of Rashba, page 93, #102.
7. Morrell, "An Equal or a Ward," p. 198; or *ibn Zimra, Responsa*, # 888/1228.

the origin of every practical law, mention different viewpoints, and establish what the practice should be. Caro arrived at his decisions by following two of the three major figures in Jewish law who preceded him: Isaac ben Jacob Alfasi (Rif) (1013–1103), Maimonides, and Asher ben Yehiel (Rosh) (1250–1327). Although Caro was a Sephardi rabbi, *Beit Yosef* was based on more than just Sephardi sources. In fact, it is possible that besides the obvious contributions of Alfasi and Maimonides, Caro included more Ashkenazi material in this work. The *Tur* itself was written by the son of the Rosh, who came from the Ashkenazi communities of medieval Germany. However, Maimonides' work clearly influenced Caro; so much so, that he wrote his own commentary, *Kesef Mishneh* (1574–75) on Maimonides' *Mishneh Torah.*

It was only in 1555 that Caro completed his *Shulhan Arukh* (A Set Table), which was a digest of *Beit Yosef.* Although the work was intended for scholars and students, Caro eliminated many of the theoretical aspects of the *Tur* and *Beit Yosef* in order to stress behavior and practice rather than theory. It was written in clear Hebrew and was originally published as a short work. Only later were the many commentaries written about this book and published as part of the *Shulhan Arukh.*[8]

Caro's views on wifebeating are not consistent in the several works of his we will look at. These views are further complicated by R. Moses Isserles, the glossator of the *Shulhan Arukh.* Caro's views on wifebeating appear in *Beit Yosef* (his commentary on the *Tur*), and the *Kesef Mishneh* (his commentary on Maimonides' *Mishneh Torah*). Because of Caro's acceptance by future generations of both Sephardi and Ashkenazi Jews, it is unfortunate that his views are inconsistent. His view that wifebeating should not be encouraged on the one hand, and that wifebeating is not a cause for forced divorce, on the other, is why I include Caro in the group of rabbis who take an evasive position.

Our first source is *Kesef Mishneh,* Caro's commentary on Maimonides' *Mishneh Torah.*[9] As we saw in Chapter Seven (above) Maimonides writes that a husband should force—with a stick—the wife who does not do her duties. Caro points to the inconsistency in Maimonides' writing, since in an earlier discussion of the rebellious wife, Maimonides does not force her to do the

---

8. Howard Adelman, "From Zion Shall Go Forth the Law: On the 500th Anniversary of the Birth of Joseph Caro," *Jewish Book Annual* 45 (1987–88): 143–157; and Israel Ta-Shma, "Rabbi Joseph Caro and His Beit Yosef," in *Moreshet Sepharad: The Sephardi Legacy,* ed. Haim Beinart, vol. 2 (Jerusalem: Magnes Press, 1992), pp. 192–206.

9. Nashim, *Hilchot Issut* 21:10.

work if she gives up her rights to be supported. Yet here Maimonides suggests beating her with a stick.

Caro does not see this as inconsistency or contradiction and distinguishes between the two cases. The wife who Maimonides said should be beaten refuses to do her work, yet does not waive financial support. However, in the case of the rebellious wife, she waives support. Unlike some commentators we have seen on this passage, Caro, in *Kesef Mishneh*, seems to agree that the wife's duties are so important that a husband may beat her if she refuses to perform them.

Our next source is *Beit Yosef*, Caro's commentary on the *Tur*. In the *Tur* itself, it is unclear what the opinion of the author, Rabbenu Ya'akov b. Asher (b. 1275), is about punishing one's wife with a beating. The *Tur* does not take a single stand, for it is a code of law that records divergent opinions. R. Ya'akov cites Maimonides, R. Abraham b. David of Posquieres, and his father Asher's opinion, who is against beating the wife.[10]

There are three sources in *Beit Yosef*: Even ha-Ezer 74:7–12; 80:15–16; and 154:3. The first half of *BY* 74 includes the responsum of R. Solomon b. Abraham Aderet (Rashba), which we discussed in Chapter Seven.[11] Caro is astonished that Rashba rules that the rabbinic court cannot force the husband to swear he will stop habitually beating his wife. He prefers instead what R. Jonah b. Abraham of Gerona writes in the *Gate of Repentance* (see Chapter Eight)—that anyone who beats his wife transgresses two negative commandments.

Caro suggests excommunicating the perpetrator so that he not transgress the laws of the Torah: Chastising him is too mild a penalty. To support this position he cites R. Simhah of Speyer (see Chapter Eight) and R. Yeruham b. Meshullam's (Provence, 1290–1350) work, *Sefer Meisharim*. Although Yeruham is talking about the case of *hovel be'ishto*, or causing injury to one's wife (see Chapter Seven), Caro seems to consider this case as being interchangeable with wifebeating. Caro agrees with his predecessors that if the husband is a habitual wifebeater, and bruises her (*hovel*), the court can even cut off his hand.

---

10. *Tur: Even ha-Ezer*, at the end of p. 80.
11. Caro attributes this responsum to Nahmanides, although Golinkin maintains that Caro knew better.

Thus, in BY 74, Caro makes clear that the wife who flees her abusive husband is not a rebellious wife, and that the husband must either honor her more than himself or divorce her and pay her the money from her marriage contract. It appears, from the sources he cites in opposing Rashba's views, that Caro is totally opposed to wifebeating—for any reason.[12]

Caro again refers to wifebeating in BY 80 in a fairly long discussion of Maimonides' statement that a husband can beat the wife who does not perform her required work (see Chapter Seven). Although Caro quotes all of the sources, both those who agree and those who disagree with Maimonides, he does not clearly state his stance with regard to the statement.[13]

It is the third source from Beit Yosef (BY 154) that is most problematic for us and is the reason why I have chosen to discuss Caro in this chapter on "evasion." In BY 154, Caro quotes R. Simhah's responsum (see Chapter Eight) in its entirety, as well as that of Or Zarua[14] and others who favor forcing the husband who beats his wife to give her a divorce—even through recourse to the civil courts. Caro writes at the end of this source: "One cannot rely on the writings of Sefer Aguda and R. Simhah and Or Zarua to force the husband to divorce his wife because none of them rely on the famous decisors [poskim]."

Thus we have a typical attitude of evasion here. On the one hand, Caro clearly does not approve of wifebeating, even in cases where Maimonides sanctions it, yet he also does not view wifebeating as sufficient grounds for a forced divorce. Although he cites authorities, such as R. Simhah, who did

---

12. Caro writes that one can put extreme pressure on the husband to desist from this behavior and says in the name of R. Papa that one can cut off his hand (katz yadah). This reference he gets from R. Yeruham (see above), yet it is not to be found in the Talmud in discussions of wifebeating, since, as we have seen, wifebeating is not discussed in the Talmud. However, in B. Sanhedrian 58b, there is discussion of hitting one's friend attributed to R. Huna (who is often paired with R. Papa), where the expression katz yadah appears.

13. Judith Hauptman in her unpublished article "Traditional Jewish Texts, Wifebeating, and the Patriarchal Construction of Jewish Marriage," (May 1995) writes: "Karo quotes the Maggid Mishneh who states that Rambam is right. Did he do so merely to provide information or to indicate that he agrees with the Maggid Mishneh that the law follows Rambam?" (p. 10).

14. R. Chaim ben Isaac Or Zarua lived in the late thirteenth century. His father, R. Isaac ben Moses of Vienna, composed the famous halakhic commentary to the Talmud, Or Zarua. R. Chaim, too, was called "Or Zarua," after the popular abridgment of the longer work by this name written by his father. He studied under R. Meir of Rothenburg and Rosh, and lived in Germany. His responsa are an important historical source. (Source is capsule biography of Bar-Ilan Responsa Project.)

approve of forced divorce (even by civil authorities), Caro does not feel that they are prominent enough to warrant following them.[15]

Maharitz (1559–1638)

Rabbi Yom Tov ben Moshe Ztahalon (1559–1638) (Maharitz), one of the better-known rabbis of Safed, who visited Italy, Holland, Egypt, and Constantinople, wrote over 600 responsa, which reached many Sefardi communities in Israel and the Diaspora. Two of his responsa deal with wifebeating.

In *responsum* #229, we read about the case of a husband who gambles, drinks, chases after non-Jewish women, and behaves so abominably toward his wife that she runs away to her father's home. The main topic of the responsum has to do with preserving her dowry money and her *ketubah* rights.

Maharitz is very sympathetic toward the woman's plight and would like to help her; however, he is caught in the controversy between Maimonides and Nahmanides (Ramban) on the issue of a forced divorce. Nahmanides opposes Maimonides' liberal interpretation and writes that "one can never force a husband to divorce his wife" (#138). Maharitz compromises and says, if we cannot force him to divorce his wife, we can force him to give her the *ketubah* money—and so at least she will not have to remain destitute.[16] Thus, we have a case of a rabbi who, though he wants to help a battered wife, evades actually freeing her from the abusive marriage.

R. Jacob Reischer (1670–1733)

R. Jacob ben Joseph Reischer was born c. 1670 in Prague, where he studied in his youth. He served in various rabbinical positions in Prague, Ansbach

---

15. Hauptman, in commenting on these sources minimizes the impact of this evasive stand. She writes that, in the *Beit Yosef*, Caro "cites a wide variety of sources, most of which strongly condemn wifebeating in all circumstances. And by disagreeing *only* in regard to forcing a *get*, he suggests again that, in his opinion, beating one's wife is not allowed" (*idem.*) [emphasis added]. I contend that Caro's choice not to follow the "less prominent" authorities is his call and means that he is giving crossed signals—on one hand, he is opposed to wifebeating, on the other, it is not bad enough to warrant a forced divorce—a typical evasive approach.

16. *Bar-Ilan Responsa Project*, Maharitz Responsa #229. It seems that she might have to remain married to him and also have to live with him.

(Bavaria), Worms, and Metz (Germany). His book of responsa, *Shevut Yaakov,* was widely circulated. He died in 1733.

A question concerning a particularly brutal case of wifebeating was brought before him. In his responsum, he wrote that we tend to believe a wife who claims to be beaten, especially when the bruises are in a place where it is difficult for her to inflict them on herself. Yet the verdict is that we will believe her only if she swears, and, if she is not willing to swear before the court that her husband has done this to her, we cannot force him to divorce her. Better yet: if it is possible for the rabbis to be intermediaries between the couple and save the marriage, how wonderful it would be, because there is nothing worthier than peace between a man and his wife.[17]

R. David Pipano *(Bulgaria, 1851–1925)*

Rabbi David Pipano was born in Salonika in 1851, and was educated there. He became known as a rabbi and public speaker *(darshan).* In 1889, he left Salonika and became rabbi and head of the rabbinic court in Sofia, Bulgaria. In 1921, he became chief rabbi of Bulgaria, and served in that capacity until his death in 1925. Many of his writings were lost in the great fire in Sofia in 1915. His responsa include much material on the Bulgarian Jewish community which does not appear in other sources. He was one of the last rabbinic luminaries of Salonika.[18]

In the modern period, guns begin to appear in cases of wifebeating. A wife cries out that her husband has recently threatened her with a gun. He claims it took place when they were joking around. The woman cries out, "Save me from him. I can't live with him anymore. I fear for my life. I don't want anything from him except a divorce." The husband answers that he will change his ways and will stop drinking. He refuses to give her a *get* and asks her father for a lot of money if she wants a *get.*

The response found in Pipano's *Nosei Ha'ephod* is based on a conflict between Rav and Shemuel in Ketubot 77. In the case of a husband who says he will not feed or support his wife, Rav says he has to send her away and give her the *ketubah.* Shmuel says, until they force him to divorce her, they force him to support her. (Then follows a list of the more recent rabbis who

---

17. *Shevut Ya'akov,* part 1, *siman* 113, *piskah* 2–3. The source of biography is from the *Bar-Ilan Responsa Project.*

18. The source is the capsule biography from the *Bar-Ilan Responsa Project.*

follow Rav or Shmuel.) As part of this answer it appears that it is irrelevant whether she has her own money, since if she has to use it, she will have no more money left and she will starve. If they force the husband to divorce her, she can remarry and have someone else support her. The decision rests on whether he can actually support her or not. If they cannot force him to support her, they force him to divorce her, but if they can force him to support her, he follows Shmuel in saying they should not force him to divorce her, but to support her.[19]

The rabbinic solution that upholds the primacy of the halakhic constraints of not forcing a husband to give a *get* to his wife, forces the woman to continue living in harrowing situations such as those described above.

Gabriel Adler Hakohen of Aurbach (1850s)

Adelman uses the responsum by Gabriel Adler Hakohen of Aurbach (1850s) to show that "in Europe the rabbis also became more militant against forcing divorce, protecting what they now articulate as the rights of the husband." This responsum which was published in an Orthodox publication, concerned a wife who fled to her father's house after her husband beat her. She wants a separation, not a divorce, claiming he is repulsive [*mais alai*], but she wants him to continue to support her. The rabbis refer to him as an "anchored husband" and discuss whether they can force her to accept a divorce against her will. They make it clear that the woman cannot "anchor him forever. . . . How could her power be greater than his?" At the end of the responsum he concludes that if she leaves him for at least a year, she must be forced to accept the divorce.[20]

R. Ovadia Joseph (B. Baghdad 1920)

The author of *Yabbia Omer*, R. Ovadia Yoseph was born in Baghdad in 1920. He immigrated to Israel at age four and studied in yeshivot in the Old City of Jerusalem. He was ordained by former Sephardic Chief Rabbi Ben Zion Uzz-

---

19. *Nosei Ha'ephod*, 32, *piskah* 1–2.

20. I would like to thank Howard Adelman, for sharing his unpublished article, "A Disgrace for All Jewish Men."

iel. In 1947, Yossef became chief rabbi and head of the rabbinic court of Cairo. In 1950, he returned to Israel, where he served as rabbi of Tel Aviv, and later as the Sephardic Chief Rabbi of Israel. His political and spiritual influence in modern day Israel is well known. He is known for his total recall of relevant material from rabbinic and post-rabbinic literature and the encyclopedic quality of his responsa. It is particularly relevant that he quotes many of the sources that we have looked at.

Ovadia Joseph discusses whether R. Simhah exaggerated about whether one can force a husband to give a *get* to the wife he beats. Ovadia Joseph follows those (Radbaz, Rambam, Ramban, Rashba) who argue that one cannot beat the husband in order to force him. Even if he is a criminal, we cannot force him; we can only reprove him and warn him that, if he hits her unlawfully, he will have to divorce her and give her the *ketubah*. He quotes a source which says that even if the husband threatens her with a knife we cannot force him to give a *get* or even tell him that he MUST send her away. He also quotes the *Nosei Haephod* and *Mishpat Ztedek*, which say that we can tell him that he *must* send her away, but *not with force.*

His conclusion is that one cannot write in the verdict that the husband *must* divorce his wife. One can only write that the *beit din* (the religious court) *advises* the husband to divorce her. Or, one can write that the *beit din* considers divorcing his wife *the right thing to do. But we can never use language that implies force.* Yabbia Omer's conclusion makes clear that his fellow rabbis respected his decision: "After showing the responsa of Radbaz and *Mishpat Ztedek* to my colleagues in Cairo they corrected their decision and based it on my opinions."[21]

What is the halakhic rationale behind those rabbis who oppose forced divorce? There are two pivotal rabbis whose influence is responsible for this hardened attitude toward divorce. One is the eighteenth century rabbi, the Hatam Sofer, and the other, the twelfth century tosafist Rabbenu Tam.

---

21. *Yabbia Omer*, part 2, Even ha-Ezer, *siman* 10, *piska* 3–6. Note that we have here the deliberate choosing of those rabbis who did not take into consideration the wife's suffering. Had he wanted to, Ovadia Yosef could have referred to the Maharam (Meir of Rotenberg). Clearly he prefers not to. Is this because he is biased in favor of the Sefardi tradition? I have avoided taking sides on this issue. For those who wish to pursue it, see Adelman's and Grossman's articles. I tend to think that the rabbis act according to their individual inclinations, although it is hard to avoid being part of a community. See my discussion of Rabbenu Tam.

R. Moshe Sofer (Schreiber), Hatam Sofer (1763–1839)

In Chapter Eight, I referred to Hatam Sofer, who was rabbi and head of the Pressberg Yeshiva. Hatam Sofer was the spiritual father of Hungarian Orthodoxy in modern times, and his prestige was very great. He was opposed to Maimonides' lenient approach to divorce and held that Maimonides was wrong to allow a divorce decree to stand if there were any question about its having been coerced. Hatam Sofer argued that, not only did the divorce's validity depend upon the husband's consent, but that the consent had to be beyond any doubt. Since there were conflicting rabbinical decisions about whether a given situation justified a forced divorce or not, doubt could always be created by the husband. He could say that, in his case, he prefered the rulings that would define his divorce as a coerced *get*. Thus, Hatam Sofer ruled that any divorce is automatically invalid if there is any doubt about its being a case of coercion.

Hatam Sofer's ruling is still the major opinion followed in rabbinical courts in Israel today, and, since he was completely against a coerced divorce, most authorities continue to comply with his narrow understanding of the *halakha*.

Today when decisions have to be made by rabbis in rabbinical courts, they are often guided by the attitude that it is better for a woman to be in any marriage, no matter how unsuccessful or unhappy, than to be alone. We have traced this metaphoric principle: it begins in Isaiah 4:1, when "seven women shall take hold of one man, saying . . . let us be called by your name—Take away our disgrace"—the disgrace of not having a man. This metaphoric principle takes on halakhic dress when it informs rabbinic decisions.

In one of the Hatam Sofer's responsa on wifebeating, he writes that we do not force a man to divorce his wife, because of the principle of "it is better to live in two (*tan du*) than to dwell alone [*armalu*]."[22] This principle, descriptive of males, is applied to women, not to men and is referred to as "*tov lemeitav*" (lit. best optimum choice). Not only does this principle pressure women into unfortunate marriages, such as with men much older than they or with men who are diagnosed insane after the marriage, but it is part of the mentality of the *dayanim* (judges in rabbinical courts). Knowing this helps us to understand why they are often so unsympathetic to the woman who wants to get out of such a marriage.

---

22. Responsum of Hatam Sofer, part 4 (*Even ha-Ezer* 2), p. 60.

The inability to decide whether to allow forced divorce stems from a general malaise about making changes in *halakha* today. Rabbis claim that this is caused by the fact that there are no great rabbis (*gedolim*) or a Sanhedrin who could make decisions that would be binding on future generations. This leads to much hand-wringing on the part of modern rabbis who convey the sentiment that their hands are tied. According to Ze'ev Falk, the renowned expert on Jewish divorce laws, present-day rabbis generally follow the methods of the Hatam Sofer.

Falk discusses the principle of *"kim li"* (it is acceptable to me), the preference of a decisor who accords with one's own ideas. Despite the fact that forced divorce is allowed in the *gemara* because of the assumption that the husband wants to do what accords with the rabbi's will, if there is a different decision that fits what one wants, the husband can choose what benefits him and not the forced divorce. This principle of *kim li* is what causes the double standard referred to above and causes so many difficulties in the application of monetary laws connected with divorce.[23] Thus the forced *get* only works if the husband goes along with it, and it is clear to him that the forced aspect of this *get* is lawful in the eyes of everyone. However, what generally happens is that the husband, through his lawyer, appeals the verdict and relies on those earlier opinions which support his decision to do what is best for him, not his wife.[24]

Rabbenu Jacob Tam of Ramerupt (1100–1171)

We have shown that the Jewish tradition is not monolithic in its attitude toward forced divorce. There are precedents in the Mishneh that could be interpreted as favoring a forced divorce. Riskin suggests that it was the

---

23. Ze'ev W. Falk, *The Divorce Action by the Wife in Jewish Law*. Institute for Legislative Research and Comparative Law. (Jerusalem: Hebrew University of Jerusalem, Faculty of Law, 1973) [Hebrew].

24. Writing almost twenty years after Falk, She'ar-Yashuv Cohen, Chief Rabbi of Haifa, refers to Hatam Sofer's influence, but cites Herzog (Heichal Yitzchak) and Hazon Ish to imply that the more recent generation of *dayanim* disagree with him. I would like to thank R. She'ar-Yashuv Cohen for sending me a copy of his article, "The Forced *Get* in Our Time," *Tehumim*, 11 (1990): 195–202 [Hebrew]. As I mentioned in Chapter Eight, R. She'ar-Yashuv Cohen backtracked on this, and admitted that a husband can refuse to accept the verdict of a forced *get*. The reality, however, is different, and many rabbis still follow Hatam Sofer and not Herzog.

tosafist Rabbenu Tam, a grandson of Rashi and a giant in talmudic analysis who had a profound effect on the direction of future laws concerning forced divorce. I discussed in Chapter Six the "door" that had been opened by the Talmud and the Geonim which might have granted the wife the right to initiate divorce. This door "was tightly shut by Rabbenu Tam's novel interpretation of the Talmudic passages. He thus single-handedly reversed the direction of the *halakha*, rejecting the position of the Geonim and interpreting the Talmud in a fashion radically different than that of the Spanish authorities, Alfasi and Maimonides."[25]

Riskin wonders if Rabbenu Tam had an extralegal, social, or historical agenda or did he simply interpret the Talmudic text as he understood it? He suggests that the "current of the times often plays an unconscious role" and that the intellectual and religious climate of Rabbenu Tam's time period in Franco-Germany "militated against divorce." He suggests that it would not have looked right for a religious minority like the Jews to be more liberal about divorce matters in a dominant culture that insisted on the permanent nature of marriage. So Rabbenu Tam, in his interpretation of the Talmud, shifted future interpretations against coercing a husband to divorce his wife. Although Riskin sees that this might have worked for the benefit of marital stability among Jews, it did have repercussions for future generations.

Can these interpretations be revised in order to untie the hands of rabbis who claim they are bound by halakhic precedent? We will attempt in the conclusion of this book to suggest some of the halakhic possibilities that can help women out of abusive marriages that threaten their lives.

---

25. Shlomo Riskin, *Women and Jewish Divorce: The Rebellious Wife* (Hoboken, NJ: K'tav Publishing House, 1989), p. 108.

Feminist Halakhic Solutions

Our survey of halakhic literature has shown an inherent lack of symmetry in the status of husbands and wives, particularly as regards divorce. This inherent inequality is a major factor in the ambivalence of *halakha* to wifebeating. Our discussion must end with suggestions for resolving the halakhic problems discussed in this book. However, it is no simple matter to define a halakhic problem. People do not always agree about what constitutes a problem. Even once one arrives at a definition, there might be further questions about the process of change in *halakha* that could legitimately be used to arrive at a solution. Moreover, if and when the need for change and the vehicle for change are generally agreed upon, there is a further question of how the changes are to be implemented and, more importantly, by whom.

One model for change is found in an egalitarian[1] Mishnah (M. Sotah 9:9), which is based on an analogy between the increase in the number of murderers and the increase in the number of adulterers. This Mishnah states that, when the number of murders increased, the ritual of the heifer whose neck is broken [*egla arufa*] when an unclaimed, unidentified body is found, was can-

---

1. See Mayer Gruber, "Marital Fidelity and Intimacy: A View From Hosea 4," in *A Feminist Companion to the Latter Prophets,* ed. Athalya Brenner (Sheffield, UK: Sheffield Academic Press, 1995), p. 177.

celed (Deut. 21:1–9). Similarly, when there were too many adulterers, the ritual of the bitter waters (Numbers 5:11–31) was canceled (see Chapter Two). Clearly this Mishnah reports that changes occurred when circumstances made it necessary to adapt the *halakha*. The prescribed rituals assumed a reality of a rare murder or adultery, and they embodied the approach of the Torah to the exception. But it became futile to try to apply these rituals to a reality of frequent transgressions. To do so would have lessened the social impact of such rituals through incessant repetition, and the rabbis did not want to do that.

One implication of this Mishnah is that, when the assumptions about human behavior underlying a given ritual have changed, and this change is "proven" by the behavior of large numbers of people, then the given ritual is virtually "canceled" by the new facts; that is, the legal implementation of the old assumptions is no longer tenable.

Even though reality has changed dramatically today, serious problems concerning women are not being addressed. We might use the same mechanism and language that the Mishnah uses vis-à-vis today's problems of the status of women in initiating divorce; namely, "when the number of men who refuse to grant divorce increases, when the number of blackmailers increases, then the implementation of the law on which divorce ritual rests—the dependency on the husband's good will—is canceled."[2]

One might argue that the problem of the *agunah* (the anchored/chained woman) and the *mamzer* (illegitimate issue) are "merely" halakhic problems, and, therefore, are not problems for people who do not observe the *halakha*. Thus, in a country where there is separation between religion and state, such as France or the United States, where there is the alternative of civil marriage and divorce, there is not the pressing need to solve these halakhic problems, as there is in Israel.[3]

---

2. I would like to thank Rabbi Michael Graetz for the wording of this suggestion.

3. In May 1996, I was told a story about the female client of a lawyer married to a rabbi. The woman's husband knowingly wrote a halakhically invalid divorce decree with mistakes in it to bypass the New York State *Get* Law, which demands that a Jewish male produce a valid *get* (a Jewish divorce) before granting him a civil divorce. He then was able to extort money from his wife. In the *Jewish Week* of May 10, 1996, there was a story promoting concubines for Jewish religious men so that they do not have to worry about divorcing their wives. Modern Orthodox rabbis responded to this with anger—but this was in the context of a campaign among the ultra-Orthodox to preserve the harmony of marriage and to call a moratorium on all divorces for the coming year. For more on the North American scene see Beverly Horsburgh, "Lifting the Veil of Secrecy: Domestic Violence in the Jewish Community," *Harvard Women's Law Journal* (Spring 1995): 196–271.

In the State of Israel, however, these halakhic problems are inescapable, not only for those members of the Jewish community who call themselves *shomrei mitzvot* (observers of God given commandments), but for the entire community, since there is no separation of church and state.[4] Both women who abide by *halakha* of their own free will, and those who are forced to do so, are doomed to remain in a static situation due to an intransigent approach to their problems by rabbis who seem unwilling to change *halakha*.

Certainly the man who refuses to issue his wife a divorce creates a halakhic problem that needs to be creatively solved, even if the solution involves change in the *halakha*. And, as we have seen above, when there are literally myriads of such men, the need for change is dramatic.

Does the religious establishment today help or hinder a solution? In Israel, it is impossible to properly consider this question without taking into consideration that rabbis are civil servants. Unlike congregational rabbis outside of Israel, who cannot ignore the plight of their congregants, the civil servant rabbi is divorced from the community. He is a bureaucrat who does not have to live with the results of his decision or indecision. He does not have to report back to his constituents, and can even turn his back on them. This is the case even in a system that does not have the aura of "defending the religion" about it.

According to Pinhas Shifman,[5] who advocates civil marriage for all, these civil servant rabbis actually show more sensitivity to the problems of the secular than to their Orthodox constituency, and the latter are hurt more, because they take religion seriously and do not feel free to choose from the alternatives. Thus, even civil solutions will not solve the problem of the religious Jew.

Is it possible to put pressure on the rabbinate from within? We have seen that, where there is a rabbinic will, there is a rabbinic way. Rabbis can solve problems using halakhic methods when they wish to do so. But they do not always wish to do so and one rabbi's solution can be considered anathema by another rabbi—thus creating new problems in the process.

---

4. All-out efforts must be made to solve halakhic efforts for them, according to Pinhas Shifman in *Civil Marriage in Israel: The Case for Reform*, Series #62 (Jerusalem: Jerusalem Institute for Israel Studies Research, 1995).

5. All references to Shifman are from a talk he gave in Hebrew on April 16, 1996 for the Forum at Ben-Gurion University on "Marriage and Divorce in Israel: The Citizen and the Establishment" [sessions were videotaped].

Traditionally, *halakha* is very dependent on the context in which decisions are made. As in the "Rabbi, is the chicken kosher?" paradigm,[6] the answer very often depends on the economic circumstances of the person who asks this question. Morality and compassion enter into the decision. Can the person afford to buy a new chicken for Shabbat if this one is deemed *treif* (unkosher)? If the answer is no, the very same chicken that would be considered *treif* for a rich person will be considered kosher for a poor person. This is an early form of "affirmative action" to help the poor survive in a cruel world, by putting their needs above strict rules. Yet we have seen that the rabbis are not always willing to bend the rules when women are concerned. Why is this so?

Tamar Ross analyzes the writings of Rabbi Abraham Isaac Kook (1865–1935), the first Ashkenazic chief rabbi of modern Israel who played a major role in the rebirth of Jewish life in modern Israel, to show the line that is drawn between valid and invalid methods of halakhic change. She shows that, despite the fact that Kook glorified dynamism and was the "darling of many would-be reformers," he nevertheless expressed several important qualifications regarding the mechanics of the halakhic process of change.[7] She makes clear that "he does not legitimize indiscriminate revision of the *halakha*," and that he "warns against attempts on the part of the individual (or the minority group), that has already reached a level of heightened morality, to impose its standards on the majority in the form of a general prescription, before conditions for implementing formal halakhic change can be obtained." She concludes that "his remarks cannot be taken to encourage the formation of lobby groups to pressure halakhic authorities to change the law carte-blanche. This approach is foreign to the halakhic system. Broad general policies come about by a gradual build-up of individual responsa addressed to individual cases and gaining a cumulative effect."[8]

This book has attempted to show that there *is* a build-up of responsa that has gained a cumulative effect that cries out for change. The question to be addressed now is "from where will my help come?" (Ps. 121:1)

---

6. One of the more important jobs of a local rabbi in small communities, particularly in Europe before World War II, was to make decisions about Kashrut. This is the simplest type of responsum: a question is asked and an answer is given.

7. Tamar Ross, "Can the Demand for Change in the Status of Women Be Halakhically Legitimated?" *Judaism* (Fall 1993): 482.

8. *Ibid.*, p. 485.

Shifman advocates making civil marriage a requirement in Israel for both religious and nonreligious people, since he thinks that the government should not be in the business of deciding who is a rabbi. If everyone gets married civilly, individuals can decide which rabbi, if any, they should go to. While I applaud his suggestion to take the monopoly on marriage away from the chief rabbinate and open the marketplace to competition, I fear that civil marriage will widen the gap between the various religious and secular populations. The religious groups will want to check the genealogy of the secular and will ask hardball questions: Which rabbi married them? What non-Jewish skeletons do they have in the closet? Who is the mother? Who is the grandmother of the mother? Was the divorce kosher? Is the prospective bride or groom a *mamzer*? The "wrong" answers will mean that members of the secular population are not to be considered suitable marriage prospects for the religious population.

ALTERNATIVE APPROACHES

There are alternative approaches to marriage and divorce that have halakhic underpinnings and restore some leverage to the wife. Most of them have been mentioned in the previous chapters during discussions of the responsa literature. I will summarize them and briefly discuss them below before concluding with a proposal for a modern day *takkanah*. Most of the following solutions have been used in the past and continue to be used by rabbis in individual cases, or when the pressure by the public is so great that the rabbis are forced to find solutions.

1. Pre-nuptial agreements: The first approach is to require all couples about to be married that they sign pre-nuptial agreements that would prevent a husband from refusing to issue his wife a divorce in the future and would impose substantial monetary fines on him for each day that he holds up the divorce. This option has finally been offered to Israeli couples after much lobbying on the part of ICAR (The International Coalition for *Agunah* Rights).[9] Another

---

9. The Sephardi Chief Rabbi Eliahu Bakshi-Doron and Rabbi Eliahu Ben-Dahan, the Director of the Israel Rabbinical Court met with representatives of ICAR and worked out the solution which will be offered to couples at the marriage registry. This was reported by Rali Sa'ar, "The Rabbinate Will Encourage Pre-Nuptial Agreements, as a Solution to the Problem of Women Whose Husbands Refuse to Give Them a *Get*," *Ha'Aretz* (18 June 1996) and in "ICAR—A Ray of Hope," *Networking for Women: A Quarterly Publication of the Israel Women's Network* (July 1996): 6.

possibility is *gerushim al t'nai* (a conditional divorce) to be deposited with the rabbinic courts in every case of marriage. This suggestion has antecedents in Geonic times. If the husband does not behave properly, or if he wants to uproot his wife from her home, she can go to the *beit din* and be released from the marriage—possibly losing the money from her *ketubah*, but still free to remarry. The condition is not that the woman will leave the marriage on her own, but that he will have to divorce her.[10]

Another suggestion has been *kiddushin al t'nai* (marriage on condition). In this proposal, the marriage itself is conditional on the granting of divorce, and if one side obstinately refuses the divorce, the marriage is automatically annulled.

2. *Hiyuv get* (obligatory divorce): When the court "obliges" the husband to issue his wife a divorce, it is not considered force, and he cannot go to jail. However, they can order the husband to pay large payments of child support and payment of the *ketubah*, even if his wife works, in an attempt to force him to issue the divorce. He can be excommunicated (put into *herem*), and if he refuses to listen to the court he can be put into jail for not paying his support payments, and so on.

3. *Kfiyat get* (Court forced compulsory divorce): The court forces a recalcitrant husband to issue his wife a divorce when he habitually mistreats her or when he is incurably addicted to drugs, gambling, or alcohol (this follows Rambam's dictum of *meis alai* (he is abhorrent to me)), or when the husband has AIDS, doesn't support her, or is violent. The problem is that with this solution, the wife might lose her rights to the *ketubah*.

4. *Hafka-at Kiddushin*: The fourth is the process of rabbinic annulment of the marriage. Since the rabbis are one of the *deot* (consenting parties, vested with authority) in the contraction of the marriage, if they remove their consent the whole contract is annulled. This can be applied when the husband beats his wife. This was done in the past and there is no reason why it cannot be reintroduced. The Conservative Movement uses this procedure in cases of recalcitrant husbands.

---

10. See Ze'ev Falk, *The Divorce Action by the Wife in Jewish Law* (Jerusalem: Hebrew University of Jerusalem, Faculty of Law, 1973), Chapter Nine [Hebrew].

5. Civil Sanctions: Giving the rabbinical courts the authority to revoke the husband's driver's license, passport, use of credit cards, and access to bank accounts. Since many husbands leave the country without issuing a divorce and leave their wives behind, civil law should have the power to extradite those husbands who are in another country.

6. Vigilante punishment of abusive husbands. Maimonides' suggestion for beating up the husband is alive and well today. If the wife declared that her husband disgusted her and that she could not stand living with him (*meis alai*), Maimonides permitted beating the recalcitrant husband until he "freely" declared he wanted to release her. There are squads of men on patrol in *Mea She'arim* and *B'nei Brak* with beepers who will solve individual problems of battered women whose husbands refuse to issue them a divorce. They are proud of the fact that they "take care of their own" and will beat the husband until he agrees to divorce his wife.[11]

7. Civil disobedience by women: Since a woman must go to the *mikveh* after her menstruation ceases, it is in the husband's interest that she do so, so that the couple can resume sexual relations. In Canada, a group of Orthodox women decided to take collective action against a man who refused to issue his wife a divorce. They all refused to go to the *mikveh* until the husband came forth with the divorce.[12] This group action quickly got their husbands' support, and pressure was put on the husband to issue his wife a divorce so that the community could go back to its normal relationships.

Most of the previous suggestions for change are in keeping with a "reactive" approach to *halakha*. There is a presumption made by *halakha* about the status and function of women. Within this system, women can

---

11. I have no idea how widespread this phenomenon is and doubt whether it is documented anywhere, given the close-mouthedness of the *haredi* (ultra-Orthodox) world. But I have heard it referred to more than once on Mail-Jewish, an Orthodox electronic mail list, and in the Forum on the Family at Ben-Gurion University of the Negev (1995–96). Whenever Orthodox rabbis are willing to talk about domestic violence in the Jewish world, they allude to this unusual manner of problem-solving in the *haredi* world. What we have here is a form of anecdotal evidence.

12. Blu Greenberg (1992), "The Feminist Revolution in Orthodox Judaism," *Lilith* (Summer 1992): 11–17.

react. Rachel Adler points out that "the presumptions select the questions. The categories shape them. Adjudication creates precedents that influence the form and direction of future questions." A "proactive" approach, however, takes into account that these "halakhic rules, categories and precedents were constructed and applied without the participation of women . . . that they are inadequate or inimical to concerns which women themselves might raise if they were legal subjects rather than legal objects."[13]

THE URGENT NEED FOR A *TAKKANAH*

Norma Baumel Joseph, the President of ICAR (The International Coalition for *Agunah* Rights) and a modern Orthodox Jewish scholar and leader, said that "our rabbis have avoided and abandoned (the *agunot*). . . . Many of them have helped individual women. But until there is a global halakhic system for releasing every *agunah*, it is as if they have abandoned all of us."[14]

In a "Prayer for *Agunot*" published by ICAR, God is asked to remove the burden from *agunot*, soften the hearts of their captors, and "Grant wisdom to the Judges of Israel. Teach them to recognize oppression and rule against it. Infuse our rabbis with courage to use their power for good alone." In this prayer, the women are taking a "reactive" approach to the system. However, we have seen that rabbis do not always have courage, nor do they always recognize oppression, and, even when they do, they do not necessarily rule against it by freeing women from life-threatening marriages.

Despite all the legitimate solutions we have seen above, it is still possible in this day and age for a rabbinic court to rule in favor of an adulterous husband who beats his wife. Susan Weiss, an Orthodox attorney, who practices family law in Jerusalem, and teaches women studying to become rabbinical court pleaders [*to-aniot*], wrote that a rabbinic appeal court ruled as follows:

> We accept the husband's appeal. The wife did not prove that the husband beat her or committed adultery. But even had she proven those facts, it is obvious that Jewish law does not obligate a man to divorce

---

13. Rachel Adler, "Feminist Folktales of Justice: Robert Cover as a Resource for the Renewal of *Halakha*," *Conservative Judaism* XLV:3 (1993): 43.

14. "The Weeping Altar," *Networking for Women: A Quarterly Publication of the Israel Women's Network* 7:3 (1994): 2–3.

his wife if he beats her or has relations with other women. Even those who argue that those circumstances warrant compelling a husband to divorce his wife agree that is only after he has been repeatedly warned to correct his ways. Moreover, it is clear that a husband being repulsive to his wife is not grounds for divorce. The divorce must be given of the husband's free will. . . .[15]

Weiss makes clear that there is a moral dilemma because we cannot rely on the rabbinical court system to do justice and that their application of the Jewish law is immoral. She writes: "I cannot accept that there is a higher moral good, unknown to me, inherent in enabling a husband to continue to torment his wife."

We have seen that it is women who are paying the bill and there is a limit to one's faith and patience. It is time to take halakhic means, using a more "proactive" approach, to address the inequities in Jewish law and, in particular, those concerning women's lower status in marriage laws.

What can be done that has not as yet been suggested? I would like to return to the concept of a *takkanah*. Rivkah Haut, an Orthodox activist on behalf of *agunah* rights admits that the rabbis are the problem, "for they have the power to address the issue and they are not acting . . . [they] have not been willing to exercise their halakhic imaginations on behalf of Jewish women. . . . The time has come for the rabbis to make some sort of binding decree—a *takkanah*—to correct this imbalance in Jewish law."[16]

In concluding this book, I would like to argue that there really is no other moral solution that takes into account the needs of our time. The Torah may have tolerated inequity because it had no choice in the past, because, following Eliezer Berkovits's argument, the message would not have gotten across (Chapter Nine). However, today the reverse is true: to tolerate inequity is to hamper the message of the Torah and to promote injustice. A *takkanah*, such as the following, is a start in alleviating the plight of the abused woman. She should not have to bear the double burden of being abused by her husband and being betrayed by Jewish religious law. The larger context of law, which we have seen, includes narrative and metaphor, should determine the

---

15. Susan Weiss, "Unholy on the Face of it," *The Jerusalem Report* (16 May 1996): 54.

16. Sasha Sadan, "The Divorce Trap," *The Jerusalem Post Magazine* (12 March 1993): 10. In Appendix B of this book, there is a detailed historical description and justification for the use of *takkanot*.

construction of particular laws. Legal decisions concerning the status of women must admit the narratives of individual cases of women who have been excluded from the decision-making process until now.[17]

In all societies, women are beaten by their husbands and often choose not to, or are afraid to, leave a bad marriage. It is ironic that the Jewish wife, whose lifestyle incorporates some of the loftiest ethical values the world has ever known, also includes ingrained inequity, which can be used to trap her in a marriage which is dangerous to her and her children. This same lifestyle allows collusion by the system to keep her trapped.[18]

In our day, this should no longer be the case. I therefore propose a *takkanah* to remedy the moral dilemma faced by Jews today. It is a dilemma that has not been faced squarely by either the Conservative or Orthodox movements, because there is a certain degree of interdependence between the two branches of Judaism.[19]

The dilemma has to do with continuing to honor the inequity in marriage, which allows only the husband to grant the decree of divorce to his wife. This inequity has evolved because the structure of rabbinic decisions today are not socially contingent or functionally related to the needs and experiences of women. The mindset of rabbis still functions with social and

---

17. Gordon Tucker, "The Sayings of the Wise are Like Goads: An Appreciation of the Works of Robert Cover," *Conservative Judaism* XLV:3 (1993): 34.

18. Rabbis should be concerned about the fact that blackmail can also create a halakhic defect in the divorce and they should not be involved in helping husbands to extort money from their wives in return for granting a divorce to her. By making the suggestions of extortion and blackmail illegal, rabbis will no longer be aiding and abetting recalcitrant husbands. Sharon Shenhav, a lawyer and head of Na'amat's legal services, relates how she had to excuse herself from a case, since, in the rabbinic court, the rabbis were negotiating the terms of payment for the divorce. "I had to excuse myself from the case . . . blackmail is a criminal act. . . . As a lawyer, under my ethics, I am forbidden to participate in the discussion of a crime. . . . They were very angry at me, the rabbis, because I said my ethics, unlike theirs, forbid me to participate in the discussion of a criminal act. . . . Just recently, I was on a panel with the chief judge of the rabbinical court in Jerusalem . . . and he brought it out in front of the audience. 'Here's a case that if Sharon had told her client to pay the amount of money, she would have received the *get*. . . .'" (Sasha Sadan, "The Divorce Trap," pp. 8–10).

19. As Rachel Adler points out, "People who inhabit a *nomos* together cannot simply 'live and let live' because they are interdependent. Our hermeneutical commitments and their behavioral consequences affect our neighbors' lives as well as our own. This is as true in the Jewish *nomos* as in the secular state" ("Feminist Folktales," p. 44). What an Orthodox rabbi decides has a bearing on Conservative women; when the Reform movement allows patrilineal descent to determine Jewishness, this has consequences for Conservative and Orthodox Jews.

cultural assumptions that exclude women from the decision-making process and accept her dependence on male family members for status and support. It is this inequity that I propose be halakhically amended. I am challenging our rabbis not to abdicate their "responsibility to learn, to hear, to be heard, to re-ratify. . . ."[20]

I believe my proposal is the only halakhic way to keep faith with our traditional texts. I hope that rabbis in one of the above-mentioned religious movements may be inspired by the gauntlet I throw into the arena of halakhic discourse to come up with a halakhic *takkanah* and that the constituency of this rabbi will be willing to follow this ruling. Too often our rabbis are timid and afraid that bold decisions will turn out to be transgressions. They should keep in mind that Harav Kook, in the same passage referred to above, writes "that sometimes the Divine will regarding the future course of *halakha* is conveyed specifically via its transgressors!"[21] The *takkanah*, however, is not a transgression. It is an affirmation of *halakha's* ability to be recreated.[22]

PROPOSAL FOR A *TAKKANAH*

I end this book with a proposed *takkanah*:

> Jewish women of the world have been crying out to their rabbis to help release them from abhorrent marriages. They beg the rabbis to consider recurrent wifebeating as immediate grounds for divorce. The answer has been, "wait." How long can they wait? Their biological clocks are ticking, their reproductive organs are atrophying at an alarming rate—yet they want to bring more children in the world, who will be halakhically recognized. They want to get on with their lives and build new commitments

---

20. Tucker, "The Sayings of the Wise," p. 37.

21. See n. 20 in Tamar Ross's article cited in this chapter.

22. Adler writes, "The purpose of a feminist Jewish hermeneutic is not to reject either text or law but to seek ways of claiming them, and living them out with integrity. It keeps faith with texts by refusing to absolve them of moral responsibility. It honors *halakha* by affirming its inexhaustible capacity to be created anew" ("Feminist Folktales," p. 54). David Golinkin lists many examples of changes, flexibility and development in his pamphlet *Halakha for Our Time: A Conservative Approach to Jewish Law* (issued by the United Synagogue of America, 1991, pp. 21–28). It is strange, however, that he does not use the word *takkanah* to describe "enactments" made by rabbis who changed the *halakha* due to social and economic developments, moral sensitivity, the general benefit of society, and for the sake of peace.

and forget their abusive pasts. Their respect of tradition is being challenged. A *hilul hashem* (disgrace of God's name)[23] is being committed daily as they are forced to stay in marriages that may be dangerous to their health and lives and the health and lives of their children.

We therefore propose that, in keeping with the needs of modern society, and to avoid the continuation of this terrible *hilul hashem* and crime being committed against women, that the husband no longer have the sole power to end the marriage. The concept of *rotzeh ani*, the necessity of the husband issuing the divorce of his own free will, which has been used by the husband to manipulate his wife to give in to his demands, is hereby abrogated. In its stead will come a mutual agreement in which an authorized *beit din* will sit down with the couple and arbitrate terms, which will be mutually agreed upon. If this proves impossible, the *beit din* will grant the divorce decree to the couple, making the woman equal in all matters of personal status.

We hope that this suggestion will lead to others, with the intention that the inequity of Jewish divorce not perpetuate the *hilul hashem*—using God's name for an unjust cause. To paraphrase, "A person who saves a single woman's life, not only saves her entire world, but that of her children and children's children."

---

23. I introduce this concept here, knowing that there are those who feel it is a *hilul hashem* to even talk about wifebeating in the Jewish community. Abraham Twerski writes in the introduction to *The Shame Borne in Silence: Spouse Abuse in the Jewish Community* (Pittsburgh PA: Mirkov Publications, 1996) that there are "those who will say that such subjects should not be aired publicly, and that to do so is a *chilul Hashem*, a disgrace to the sanctity of Judaism, to even imply that Jewish husbands can be wife batterers. I understand that position, but if I must choose between being reprimanded by those who believe that this problem should be concealed or by a wife who has suffered (along with her children) from an abusive husband, and could not receive help because no one believed her, I know where I must make my choice" (p. 3).

Appendix A

Reviving Takkanah in the Halakhic Process
Michael Graetz*

T*akkanah* is a very important tool in the system of *halakha* which, despite its centrality to the viability of the halakhic process, has fallen on disuse. It is, therefore, necessary to reactivate it in our day. One major proponent of this approach is Menahem Elon, who has spelled out the need for *takkanah*, and the expectation—shared by R. Avraham Kook— that it would be a major part of the reconstituted rabbinic judiciary of Israel.[1] Many people are unaware of the continuing use of *takkanah* throughout Jewish history; however, recent collections of *takkanot* attest to their ongoing use as a regular halakhic tool.[2] The most relevant book in

---

* Michael Graetz is the rabbi of the *Masorti* [Conservative] congregation Kehillat Magen Avraham in Omer, Israel (1974–1998). He is a member of the *Va'ad Halakha* of the Rabbinical Assembly of Israel, and Chairperson of the Siddur subcommittee that published *Va'ani Tefillati*, a *siddur* for use in the Masorti Movement in Israel (Jerusalem 1998).

1. See *Ha-Mishpat ha-Ivri*, p. 115 and index; and particularly, "Developments in the Rabbinic Judiciary of Israel," *Dine Israel*, no V (1974): lxxi *ff*.
2. Moshe Aryeh Bloch, *Shaarei Torat ha-Takkanot*; Haim Tikochinsky, *Takkanot ha-geonim*; and Yissrael Szchipinski, *Ha-Takkanot be-Yisrael* (Jerusalem: Mossad Harav Kook, 1993) [all in Hebrew].

recent history is *Takkanot Rabbanei Morocco*, by R. Amar, which is about the regular use of the *takkanah* by Moroccan rabbis to solve difficult halakhic problems up until the 1950s.[3]

The Mishnah fixes the basic tools and principles of *halakha*; thus the place of *takkanah* in the halakhic system is fixed because of its prominent use in the Mishnah. *Takkanot* appear in the Mishnah in almost every area of *halakha*, and this shows its role as a general tool.

EXAMPLES OF *TAKKANOT* IN THE MISHNAH

A *takkanah* that appears in ritual areas is the following:

> *Beforetime* the Lulav [palm branch] was carried seven days in the Temple, but in the provinces one day only. *After the Temple was destroyed*, Rabban Johanan b. Zakkai ordained that [*hitkkin*] in the provinces it should be carried seven days in memory of the Temple . . . (M. Sukkah 3:12).

Here the *takkanah* is used to further the Pharisaic religious agenda.

Takkanah appears in civil laws such as the following:

> [A loan secured by] a *prosbul* [A legal fiction devised to avoid the septennial outlawing of debts] is not canceled [by the Seventh Year]. This is one of the things that Hillel the Elder ordained [*hitkkin*]. When he saw that the people refrained from giving loans one to another and transgressed what is written in the Law—"Beware that there be not a base thought in thine heart . . ." [Deut. 15]—Hillel ordained [*hitkkin*] the *prosbul* (M. Shevi'it 10:3).[4]

The above is the *Prosbul*, a *takkanah* enacted by Hillel the Elder. The Torah law wished to support the poor. Yet, one law states that a loan that has not been repaid is canceled by the Sabbatical Year (Deut. 15:2), and another

---

3. The history and method of their use of *takkanah* has appeared in Israel in two different versions recently: R. Amar, *Takkanot Rabbanei Morocco* (both versions).

4. The Hebrew "*hitkkin*" means to enact a *takkanah*. All quotations from H. Danby, *The Mishnah* (Oxford, UK: Oxford University Press, 1933, 1972) [emphasis added]. Martin Jaffee contends that *takkanah* may be a later development reflected back on the mishnaic material. "The Taqqanah in Tannaitic Literature," *Journal of Jewish Studies* XLI:2 (1990): 204–225. Even so, the *takkanah* is clearly a major category of Jewish law.

verse recognizes that people might act in an evil way by refusing to lend to the poor as the seventh year approached (Deut. 15:9). When Hillel saw that people were transgressing the latter verse, that is, refusing to lend to the poor, he enacted a kind of legal fiction known as *prosbul*, which enabled the lender to collect the loan. In this case the *takkanah* invalidated a particular vehicle for helping the poor, namely annulment of debts, because, as a result of a change in economic reality, that very vehicle was causing a diminishment of support for the poor. The cause of the poor was given priority over the letter of the law, and the only way to so emend the law was by *takkanah*.

Takkanah also appears in connection with issues of personal status, in particular divorce. R. Gamliel enacts a *takkanah* that forbids the practice of a husband going to a *beit din* to annul a divorce he has given to his wife:

> Before time a man used to set up a court [of three] elsewhere . . . but Rabban Gamliel the Elder ordained [*hitkkin*] that they should not do so for the general good [*tikkun olam*] (M. Gittin 4:2).

This is done so that a woman does not remarry on the strength of the canceled *get*. There is some argument among scholars whether this was meant to protect society against the possibility of women not knowing their marital status, or whether it was meant to protect women in particular.[5] In either case, the process of emendation by *takkanah* leads to a more favorable state of affairs for women.

The passages in the Mishnah have in common a process that starts with an old reality, a new situation, that is, a change in reality, which is often expressed in terms such as, "when the sages saw."[6] The next stage is a decreed change (an enactment) in the existing *halakha* that makes the *halakha* viable for the new reality.

Thus, a *takkanah* starts from a premise of a change in reality, the consequence of which is that some "higher principle" or teleological goal of Torah is violated. Some of the purposes that the *takkanah* serves are *tikkun olam* (repairing the world) or *darkei shalom* (promoting peace). Thus the "higher principle" is served by the *takkanah*: an amendment to the law that serves

---

5. See the electronic list, *The Postmodern Jewish Philosophy Network* 3:2 (August 1994).

6. See the following additional passages in the Mishnah: M. Berachot 9:5; M. Shevi'it 10:3; M. Bikurim 3:7; M. Shekalim 7:5–6; M. Yoma 2:2; M. Rosh Hashanah 2:2; M. Rosh Hashanah 4:1; M. Gittin 4:2,3,7; etc.

the "spirit" of the law or what is taken to be the moral purpose of the law. *Takkanah* was carefully used by rabbis throughout history.

TAKKANOT IN MODERN TIMES

In modern times, Elon thought that the Israel rabbinical system should take the lead in restoring this invaluable halakhic tool to its proper place in the halakhic process. It is a rabbinic tool, used when theological beliefs or firmly held ethical principles leave the rabbis no choice but to reject the received halakhic rulings of the majority. By making a *takkanah*, they tacitly admit that those rulings were mistaken; moreover, they appropriate minority views that uphold the principles they wish to normalize.[7]

There are those who claim that *takkanot* have fallen into disuse because most Jews do not obey Jewish law. However, a *takkanah* is a powerful educational tool, and its effect is to engender more respect for the *halakha*. Elon and others have written that the use of *takkanah* has been shelved because many modern rabbis do not want to make changes. If they ignore the tool of *takkanah*, they can claim that "their hands are tied" by the received rulings and can act as if they have no power to make changes.

After the assassination of Prime Minister Yitzchak Rabin, I promulgated a *takkanah* that declared that *halakhot* concerning summary execution should be abolished. There was widespread agreement that this *takkanah* enhanced the reputation of *halakha*.[8]

I have also suggested a *takkanah* regarding women's testimony.[9] Women are disqualified as constitutive witnesses in Jewish Law; that is, they cannot be one of the two witnesses who sign the *ketubah*. Although, the textual arguments to explain this invalidation seem to be flimsy—the Torah uses the word *ish* [man], and not *ishah* [woman], in regard to witnesses—the

---

7. This ending is from my article, "The Right to Medical Treatment in Jewish Law," *Et La-asot 3* (1991): 80–89 [Hebrew].

8. This *takkanah* was widely disseminated throughout the world on electronic mail and had over a hundred signatories, consisting of Conservative, Reform and Orthodox rabbis. See *Responsa of the Va'ad Halakha of the Rabbinical Assembly of Israel*, vol. 7 (Jerusalem: The Masorti Movement, 1997).

9. This appears in Michael Graetz, "*Responsa* Regarding the Ordination of Women as Rabbis," *Responsa of the Va'ad Halakha of the Rabbinical Assembly of Israel*, vol. 5 (Jerusalem: The Masorti Movement, 1994), pp. 17–26 [Hebrew, with English Summary].

halakha does not allow it. Moreover, the social arguments are totally at odds with modern perceptions of women: women no longer have to stay at home; they are out there working as judges, lawyers, doctors, and so on; they sign documents and have legal responsibilities in the "real" world.

The most positive and valid halakhic way to change this and other similar rulings would be by use of *takkanah* in an activist fashion.[10] For example, the principle of the "right to healing and life" for all humans, irrespective of the nation to which they belong or of their religious practice, must be upheld even at the expense of formerly normative opinions.[11] Clearly the *halakhot* concerning wifebeating, the subject of this book, are also an example where the existing rules must be unambiguously changed. The best halakhic instrument on record to achieve that goal was first suggested in the *takkanah* of the thirteenth-century rabbi, Perez b. Elijah of Corbeil. (See Chapter Eight.)

I believe that on these issues we should be guided by the view of Rabbi Abraham Joshua Heschel:

> Judaism is not another word for legalism. . . . The law is the means, not the end. . . . The Torah is guidance to an end through a law. It is both a vision and a law. Man created in the likeness of God is called upon to re-create the world in the likeness of the vision of God.[12]

---

10. Menahem Elon writes about *takkanot*, "As far as the *halakha* is concerned, it is possible and it is desirable to solve difficult questions." He laments the fact that the Israel Chief rabbinate showed promise of using *takkanah* creatively, but since 1950 has promulgated no new enactments ("Developments in the Rabbinic Judiciary of Israel," p. xxvii).

11. For an excellent survey of the whole question, see Shubert Spero, *Morality, Halakha and the Jewish Tradition* (Hoboken, NJ: K'tav Publishing House, 1983). Spero tries to show that there are obligatory moral rules codified in *halakha*, and supererogatory or optional moral rules in Jewish tradition, but these rules are not codified. He makes the distinction based upon what can be enforced by a court and what cannot (for a similar interpretation, see M. Elon, *Ha-Mishpat Ha-Ivri*, p. 171*ff.*). Spero's book is very helpful in analyzing the question, but he, too, does not take account of some of the fundamental questions, such as discrimination against rights of non-Jews or non-observant Jews. Indeed, from this work, one would not even know that such halakhic rules existed!

12. *God in Search of Man* (New York: Harper & Row, 1955), p. 323.

Appendix B
Chronology of Responsa Discussed in This Book

Author	Years	Work/I.D.	Country	View	Chapter
Yehudai Gaon	760s	O.G. Ketubot	Pumpedita	accept	7
Hananya	764	Sh'aarei Ztedek	Pumpedita	accept evade	8 10
Paltoi	842		Pumpedita	reject	7 10
Sar Shalom	848		Sura	accept	7
Tsemach Gaon	884–915		Israel	accept	7
anonymous		Ran on B. Ketubot 63b		accept	7
Shmuel ha-Nagid	936–1056	Ben Mishlei	Moslem Spain	accept	7
Isaac b. Jacob Alfasi	1013–1103	Rif	Algeria/Spain		10
Rabbenu Jacob Tam (grandson of Rashi)	1100–71	Sefer ha-Yashar	Ramerupt	deny	9 10
Abraham b. David of Posquieres	1125–1198	Hasagat ha-Rabad	Provence	deny	10
Maimonides	1135–1204	Mishneh Torah Isshut 21:10	Spain/Egypt	accept	7
Simhah b. Samuel of Speyer	d. 1225–1230	quoted by Mordecai/Caro	Rhine Provences	reject	8
Meir b. Baruch Rotenburg	1220–1293	Maharam	Germany	reject	8

Author	Years	Work/I.D.	Country	View	Chapter
Chaim b. Isaac	late 13th century	Or Zarua	Germany	reject	10
Perez b. Elijah of Corbeil	d. end 13th century	Takkanah	France	reject	8
Moses of Coucy	13th century	Semag (sefer mitzvot gadol)	France	accept	7
Jonah b. Avraham of Gerondi	d. 1263	Sha'arei Teshuva Iggeret Ha-Teshuva	Gerona	reject accept	8 7
Solomon b. Abraham Aderet	1235–1310	Rashba	Barcelona	reject/ accept evade	8 7 10
Mordecai b. Hillel	1240–1298	Mordecai	Germany	reject	7
Menachem b. Solomon Meiri	1249–1306	Hameiri	Provence	reject	6
Jacob b. Asher son of Rosh	d. 1340	The Tur Arba Turim	Germany	evade	10
Shem Tov Even Gaon	d. 1312	Migdal Oz	Spain/Safed	accept	7
Yeruham b. Meshullam	1290–1350	Sefer Meisharim	Provence	reject	10
Nissim Gerondi	1310–1375	Ran	Gerona/Spain	accept	7
Vidal of Tolosa	14th century	Maggid Mishnah	N. Spain	accept	7
Shimon Bar Tzemach Duran	1361–1444	Tashbetz	Algeria	reject	8
Israel of Krems	14th–15th century	glosses on B. Baba Kama 32a	Austria	reject	8
Israel Isserlein	1390–1460	Sefer Trumat Hadeshen	Vienna/ Austria	accept	7
David b. Solomon Ibn Avi Zimra	1479–1573	Radbaz	Spain/Egypt/ Palestine	accept/ evade	7 10
Joseph Caro	1488–1575	Beit Yosef Shulhan Arukh Kesef Mishneh	Spain/Turkey	incon-sistent	10
Moses Isserles	1520–1572	Darkei Moshe Glosses to Shulhan Arukh	Cracow/ Eastern Europe	accept	7

Author	Years	Work/I.D.	Country	View	Chapter
Solomon b. Yehiel Luria of Lublin	1510–1574	*Yam Shel Shlomo,* Maharshal on *Baba Kama*	Lublin, Poland	accept	7
Binyamin Ze'ev b. Mattathias	16th century	*Responsa*	Arta, Turkey	reject	8
Moses b. Joseph Trani	16th century	*Mabit*	Greece/ Turkey/ Safed	reject	8
Shlomo b. Abraham Hacohen	1520–1601	Maharshach	Greece/ Yugoslavia	reject	8
Yom Tov b. Moshe Ztahalon	1559–1638	Maharitz	Safed	evade	10
Jacob b. Joseph Reischer	1670–1733	*Shevut Ya'kov*	Prague (Metz)	evade	10
Eliezer Papu	d. 1824	*Peleh Yoetz*	Yugoslavia/ Bulgaria	reject	8
Moshe Schreiber	1763–1839	Hatam Sofer	Pressburg	evade	8 10
Hayim Palaggi	1788–1869	*Ruach Hayim Hayim Veshalom*	Smyrna, Turkey	reject	8
Avraham Yaakov Paperna	1840–1919	Polemic	Radom, Poland	reject	8
Raphael Aharon b. Shimon	1848–1928	*Umitzur Devash*	Cairo	reject	8
David Pipano	1851–1925	*Nosei Haephod*	Salonika/ Bulgaria	reject evade	8 10
Isaac Herzog	1888–1959	*Heichal Yitzchak*	Ireland/ Israel	reject	8
Moses Feinstein	1895–1986	*Igrot Moshe*	America	reject	8
Eliezer Waldenburg	b. 1917	*Tzitz Eliezer*	Israel	reject	8
Ovadia Yosef	b. 1920	*Yabia Omer*	Baghdad/ Israel	evade	10
She'ar Yashuv Cohen	b. 1927	see article in *Techumim*	Haifa	reject	8

Glossary

Aggadah. lit. narration or telling. That portion of rabbinic literature and tradition that consists of sayings, homiletic interpretations, historical information, legends, anecdotes, stories about biblical or rabbinic figures, ethical teachings, or interpretations of Scripture that teach the principles of Jewish thought and theology. The *aggadah* also includes the reasons for the commandments, but is distinguished from *halakha*, which refers to the legal-ritual material.

Agunah. lit. bound or tied. The term is usually used of a married woman whose husband is missing and presumed dead, but whose death has not been definitively confirmed. A deserted wife, whose husband cannot be located, is also an *agunah*. A woman whose husband refuses to grant her a Jewish divorce, although technically called a *masorvei get* (one who is denied a divorce), is also considered an *agunah*. An *agunah* is not a divorcée nor a widow, and under rabbinic law she cannot remarry, but must remain bound to her husband until his death is confirmed or until he grants her a divorce.

Am-Ha'aretz. lit. people of the land. Ignorant, unlettered person.

Amidah. lit. standing (prayer). The Eighteen Benedictions, which constituted the core of the rabbinic daily prayer service.

Amoraim. The teachers of the Talmud or Gemara (ca. 200–500 C.E.), whose main activity was interpreting the Mishnah and tannaitic traditions.

Apocrypha. The books found in the Septuagint Bible, but not in the canon of the Hebrew Bible. More loosely, this term can refer to pseudo-biblical books composed in the Second Temple period.

Ashkenazi. Jew of German and Eastern European descent (as distinct from Sephardi and Mizrahi).

B.C.E./C.E. Abbreviations for Before the Common Era and Common Era, which are Jewish designations for B.C. and A.D.

Baraita. A tannaitic tradition not included in the Mishnah.

Beit Din. Court of Law that operates under Jewish law.

Beit Hillel. School of Hillel. One of the two major schools of Tannaitic times in the basic development of Jewish law. Its main characteristic is a broad and more lenient interpretation of *halakha* than is that of *Beit Shammai.*

Beit Shammai. School of Shammai took a stricter and more literal interpretation of *halakha* than did the School of Hillel.

Ben. Son of. Used as part of the names of the sages to identify them. For example, R. [rabbi] Issac b. [ben = the son of] Abraham.

Boshet. Shame. One of the five headings under which a person may have to pay damages for an injury caused to another person. If the injured person has been shamed, the person responsible must compensate the victim for the shame.

Canon. The corpus of Holy Scriptures.

Canonization. The process by which the contents of the Holy Scriptures, and specifically each of the sections of the Hebrew Bible, were closed and determined to be authoritative.

Diaspora. Greek for "dispersion," referring to the Jewish population outside of the Land of Israel.

Even Haezer. The third major section of the *Tur* and the *Shulhan Arukh,* treating all aspects of marriage and divorce law.

Exegesis. Interpretation, as in the interpretation of the Bible in the Midrash or of the Mishnah in the Talmud (Gemara).

Exilarch. The political and lay head of the Babylonian Jewish community in the talmudic period. The authority of this official was recognized by the Sassanian Babylonian government.

Ezer Ke-Negdo. Helpmeet. The first woman created for Adam by God so that he would not be alone.

First Temple. The Jerusalem Temple erected by Solomon ca. 961 B.C.E. which was destroyed by the Babylonians in 586 B.C.E.

Galut. lit. Exile. The term is used in three ways: not living in the land of Israel; a condition of oppression and persecution; countries and lands outside of Israel; namely, the *Diaspora.*

Gaon (pl. geonim). Formal title of the heads of the rabbinic academies of Babylonia (Sura and Pumbedita). From the sixth century until the middle of the eleventh century, they were considered to be the highest authorities in matters pertaining to Jewish law.

Gemara. The interpretation of the Mishnah by the amoraim, known also as Talmud although the latter term sometimes designates both the Mishnah and the Gemara together.

Genizah. A storeroom or "burial" room and hiding place of sacred texts (old Hebrew books no longer used for holy purposes). The famous Cairo *genizah,* a lumber room of the Great Synagogue in Cairo, was uncovered in the second half of the nineteenth century. It yielded up a treasure of manuscripts of Second Temple and rabbinic texts.

Get. Jewish bill of divorce.

Haftara. A selection from the Prophets read in the synagogue following the Torah reading on Sabbaths and Festivals. Generally, the *haftara* follows a theme contained in the Torah reading or is connected with the occasion on which it is read.

Hagah. A comment or gloss to a main body of text. Especially referring to the glosses of Isserles on the *Shulhan Arukh.*

Halakha. lit. the way, or going, or the way one should go. Derived from the Hebrew word meaning "walk, go." (1) Body of Jewish law that encompasses both the written Torah and the oral tradition; the Jewish legal system; *hala-*

kha is both the set of normative religious standards and the traditional process for determining those standards. (2) A specific law.

Halitzah. lit. taking off, removing. A childless widow was originally to receive protection and perpetuation of her husband's name through marriage to his surviving brother. The biblical ceremony of *halitzah* was performed by the widow to release her brother-in-law from his obligation to her. In the presence of a Jewish court of five or more, the ceremony is enacted by exchanging prescribed statements and by the widow removing a shoe from the foot of her brother-in-law and spitting on the floor in front of him. Rabbinic law prohibits the surviving brother from marrying his sister-in-law, even if he is willing and single, making *halitzah* a requirement today rather than an option.

Hallah. Special bread, usually braided, served on Sabbaths and festivals.

Haskalah. Enlightenment; a movement to promote modern European culture among Jews during the eighteenth and nineteenth centuries.

Herem. Excommunication; expulsion and/or separation from the Jewish community.

High Holidays. The season which includes Rosh Hashanah and Yom Kippur.

Historiography. The writing of history. This term can also denote the study of how historians often approach their work with preconceptions or ulterior motives that color the manner in which they understand and, hence, write about the past.

Hovel. lit. injuring, wounding. A person who directly injures someone and has to reimburse the victim.

Humash. The five books of Moses; the Pentateuch.

Huppah. The portable canopy under which the bridegroom and bride stand during the wedding service.

Ibn Ezra. Well-known Spanish medieval Jewish exegete (1089–1164).

Kashrut. The laws and Jewish dietary regulations concerning ritually fit ("kosher") food.

Kesef Mishneh. One of the principal commentaries to the Rambam's *Mishneh Torah.* Written by Joseph Caro (1488–1575), the author of the *Shulhan*

Arukh. The major aim of the *Kesef Mishneh* is to identify the talmudic sources underlying the halakhic rulings of the *Mishneh Torah.*

Ketubah. lit. a written document. The Jewish marriage contract given by a husband to his wife on their marriage, stating his obligations towards her during and after their marriage. It includes a lien on the husband's estate payable upon divorce or widowhood.

Kiddush. lit. sanctification. The blessing over a cup of wine.

Kiddushin. lit. consecration; betrothal. The act by which a woman becomes betrothed to a man. The three ways of betrothing a woman are: with money, or something worth money, like a ring; with a document in which the man states that he is betrothing the woman; or through sexual intercourse.

Kinyan. lit. purchase; acquisition. A formal procedure to render an agreement legally binding. After the act of *kinyan* has taken place, the object is legally the property of the buyer. Often the transfer of ownership is by means of a kerchief.

Korban (See *Sacrifice*).

Levirate Marriage (see Hebrew, *Yibbum*).

Maggid Mishneh. One of the principal commentaries on the Rambam's *Mishneh Torah.* Written by Vidal Yom Tom of Tolosa in the fourteenth century. He attempts to resolve difficult passages and often defends the *Mishneh Torah* against the criticisms of R. Abraham ben David of Posquieres (Rabad).

Maharam. Acronym for Morenu Harav (lit., our teacher, the rabbi) Meir, R. Meir of Rotenberg (c. 1220–1293), one of the great tosafists.

Mahzor. The special Jewish prayer book for festivals. Usually this term designates the liturgy for the High Holidays: Rosh Hashanah and Yom Kippur.

Maimonides. Leading authority of the Jewish middle ages in Cairo; legalist, philosopher, commentator; also known as Rambam, an acronym for his name: Rabbi Moses ben Maimon (1138–1204).

Mamzer. A child born from an incestuous or adulterous relationship; that is, a child born from relations between a married woman and a man other than her husband, or between relatives who are forbidden to marry by Torah law. The offspring of a menstruating woman (see *niddah*) is not a *mamzer*, nor is the offspring of an unmarried couple. A *mamzer* may only marry another *mamzer* or a convert to Judaism. The offspring of such a union is a *mamzer*.

Masoretic Text. The traditional, received Hebrew text of the Bible, which has been considered authoritative by Jews from tannaitic times until the present.

Midrash Rabbah. The general name given to a collection of ten midrashic works on the five books of the Pentateuch and on the five scrolls (Song of Songs, Ruth, Lamentations, Ecclesiastes, Esther). These collections achieved their final literary form between the fifth and twelfth centuries C.E. Each book (e.g., Genesis Rabbah, Ruth Rabbah) is an independent composition, and the style and purposes of each can vary considerably.

Midrash. The linguistic root of the term means "search, inquiry, investigate." A genre of rabbinic literature. (1) An interpretation and elaboration of a verse or part of biblical texts and forming a running commentary on particular books of the Bible. (2) The process of interpretation: A rabbinic method of analysis or commentary typically employed in relation to the Bible. Midrash is a process of deriving or uncovering layers of meaning, legal implications, "historical" details, and so on, over and beyond the strictly literal sense of the text. Midrashic works usually take the form of either a sustained homiletic presentation on a certain theme or a line-by-line exegesis of a biblical text. (3) An anthology or collection of such interpretations produced by the rabbis of such interpretations.

Mikvah. Ritual bath; pool of water used for the rite of purification used by married women after menstruating and following childbirth.

Minyan. Quorum (lit. number). Usually a quorum of ten adults, which is needed to constitute a congregation or to perform rituals that are considered holy, such as public prayer, recitation of the mourner's prayer (*kaddish*).

Mishnah. Collection of tannaitic rabbinic legal codes, edited by the sage, R. Judah the Prince (Ha-Nasi), ca. 200 C.E., arranged topically. It forms the basis of the Talmud. This term can also designate a particular paragraph of this code.

Mitzvah (pl. *mitzvot*). A commandment or good deed; an act that a Jew is obligated to do because it is commanded by God in the Torah as interpreted by the rabbis.

Niddah. A menstruating woman; also refers to the laws surrounding menstrual purity and impurity.

Nomos. A universe of meanings, values, and rules embedded in stories.

Onah. The "conjugal dues" a husband owes his wife at specified intervals.

Parasha (See *Sidra, Portion*). Weekly torah reading.

Pen Yosif. lit. not to excess.

Pentateuch. The first five books of the Hebrew Bible, also known as the Five Books of Moses, or the Torah.

Peshat. The plain meaning or contextual sense among the different levels of interpretation.

Pilegesh. Concubine, a woman who cohabits with a man in a common-law marriage, whose children are as legitimate as those of a proper marriage. The *pilegesh* does not have a *ketubah*, which is required to legalize her status.

Posek. A rabbi of stature and authority who makes rabbinic rulings.

Proem. The introduction to a section of exegetical Midrash. The *proem* begins with a seemingly irrelevant quotation from the Prophets or Writings and then works its way back to the verse that it seeks to interpret.

Prosbul. A rabbinic enactment devised by Hillel the Elder that allows loans to be collected after the Sabbatical year.

Qiddushin (See *Kiddushin*).

R. The accepted abbreviation for Rav [rabbi], the Hebrew title designating a learned man or, more commonly, a teacher.

Rabbenu Tam. Rabbi Jacob ben Meir (1096–1171). France. A grandson of Rashi. R. Tam was the most authoritative rabbinical figure of his time throughout France, Germany, and other parts of the Jewish world. Besides his status as a decisor of *halakha*, he was the principal force behind the creation of the system of talmudic analysis known as *tosafot*.

Rabbenu. Our teacher. A title of respect given to a great sage and teacher.

Rabbi (R.). Hebrew for "my master, my teacher," referring to the teachers and judges of the Jews of Palestine in the Roman and Byzantine periods. This term became the designation for the Jewish clergy in the Middle Ages.

Radak. Rabbi David Kimhi (1157–1236); well-known Spanish medieval exegete, specialist in grammar and syntax, author of commentary on the Torah.

Radbaz. Rabbi David ben Solomon ibn Avi Zimra known as Radbaz (b. Spain, 1479; d. Safed, 1573). Best known for the prolific amount of responsa of which more than 10,000 are extant.

Rambam. Rabbi Moses ben Maimon, known also as Maimonides (Spain and Egypt, 1135–1204) was a halakhist and philosopher whose works include the *Guide to the Perplexed* and the *Mishneh Torah*, a comprehensive account of Jewish law.

Rashba. Rabbi Solomon ben Abraham Adret (Spain, 1235–1310) is best known for his tremendous production of responsa, numbering well over 10,000. He dealt with problems of exegesis and philosophy and commented extensively on the Talmud.

Rashi. Rabbi Solomon Yitzhaki (Troyes, France, 1040–1105) was the premier medieval commentator on the Bible and Talmud. His commentaries are accessible to the masses and are virtually synonymous with Bible and Talmud study.

Rav. Hebrew for "master, teacher." Technically this term designates the rabbis of Babylonia who were called Rav, not Rabbi. In the Middle Ages this became the standard Hebrew word for a rabbi.

Redact, Redaction. This verb and noun refer to the act of collecting, selecting, and editing traditions.

Rema. Rabbi Moses ben Israel Isserles (Poland, 1525–1572) one of the leading halakhic authorities for Ashkenazic Jewry (Germany, Eastern Europe, Russia) whose supplementary notes (glosses) to the *Shulhan Arukh*, reflecting Ashkenazi traditions and customs, made it possible for the *Shulkhan Arukh* to become a universally accepted authority.

Responsum (pl. responsa). [*she-aylot u-teshuvot*, lit., questions and answers; sometimes referred to in Hebrew as a *teshuvah* or *shut*). The written answer to an official query directed to a scholar that clarifies a question of Jewish law. Collection of legal opinions written by rabbis in response to questions about actual cases.

Rif. Rabbi Isaac ben Jacob Alfasi (North Africa, 1013–1103) is the author of *Sefer Halakhot*, the most important code of Jewish law prior to the Rambam's

Mishneh Torah. His work was an attempt to summarize and give the final rulings of talmudic discussions. In doing so he tried to preserve the language and structure of the Talmud as much as possible.

Rosh. Rabbi Asher ben Yehiel (France, Germany, and Spain, 1250–1327) was an outstanding halakhic authority and talmudic scholar whose legal decisions were one of the three principal sources upon which the rulings of the *Shulhan Arukh* were based. His schools also produced extensive *tosafot.* He was one of the few rabbis to exercise direct influence in his own lifetime over both Ashkenazi and Sefardi Jewry.

Sacrifice. The offering to God of the produce of the field or the animals of the flock for purposes of commemoration of sacred occasions, expiation of transgressions, or thanking God.

Sanhedrin. The highest court or council of the Jews in the last years of the Second Temple.

Savoraim. The scholars who put the finishing touches on the Babylonian Talmud, adding explanations and legal decisions to the text they received.

Second Commonwealth. The political organization of the Jewish people in the Land of Israel from the return from exile in the sixth century B.C.E. until the final dismantling of the Herodian dynasty in the first century C.E.

Second Temple. The Jerusalem Temple that was in use from 520 B.C.E. until its destruction by the Romans in 70 C.E. This term can also designate the period in which this Temple stood.

Sephardi. Jew of Spanish or Portuguese descent (as distinct from Ashkenazi and Mizrahi).

Septuagint. The Greek translation of the Bible produced in Egypt in the Hellenistic period (See *Apocrypha*).

Setam. Hebrew for "anonymous," referring to those portions of the Tannaitic and Amoraic texts that are not attributed to any specific rabbi.

Shabbat. The Sabbath, the seventh day of the week, a day of rest, surcease from prescribed forms of work.

Shalom Bayit. lit. Peace in the home.

Shema. The Jewish prayer recited morning and night proclaiming acceptance of God's kingdom and His commandments. "Hear O Israel, the Lord our God, the Lord is One." It consists of biblical verses beginning with the word Shema ("hear"), Deut. 6:49, Deut. 11:13–22, and Num. 15:37–41.

Shulhan Arukh. Hebrew for "Prepared or Set Table." Composed by Joseph Caro with additions by Isserles and first published in 1565. This work became the major authority for halakhic practice throughout the Jewish world. It is divided into the same four major divisions as the *Tur* of Jacob ben Asher. It contains concise rulings in all areas of Jewish tradition.

Siddur. The Jewish Sabbath and daily prayer book, from a Hebrew root meaning "to arrange in order," hence, "order of prayers."

Sidra. lit. arrangement. The portion [*parasha*] from the Pentateuch read on Sabbath mornings in the synagogue.

Sotah. A woman suspected by her husband of having been unfaithful (Num. 5:11–31).

Sugyah (pl. *sugyot*). A unit of talmudic discussion that investigates a particular issue or theme, and proceeds logically through a series of questions and answers until it reaches its conclusion.

Synagogue. A Jewish house of worship. In Hellenistic usage, this term can also refer to a Jewish community.

Takkanah. Rabbinic legislation, ordinance, or directive, decreed by a Jewish scholar or a Jewish legislative body that can alter or amend the law and which has the force of law.

Talmud. Code of Jewish law, philosophy and ethics. The central text of rabbinic Judaism, containing the Mishnah (a law book compiled by topic, ca. 220 C.E.) and the Gemara (the Amoraic discussions of the Mishnah) compiled between 200–500 C.E. in both Palestine and Babylon. The two codices are referred to by J (Jerusalem) and B (Babylonia).

Tanakh. The Jewish Bible, consisting of the Torah (Pentateuch), *Nevi'im* (prophets), and *Ketuvim* (writings).

Tannaim. The teachers of the Mishnah, Tosefta, and halakhic midrashim who flourished ca. 20–200 C.E.

Tefillin. Phylacteries. Small black leather boxes containing passages from the Bible which are affixed, by means of black leather straps, to the head and arms during weekday morning prayers.

Teshuva. Repentance; requires acknowledging one's sin, asking forgiveness, resolving not to commit the sin again; and being tested.

Torah Portion (See *Parasha, Sidra*).

Torah. lit. instruction, teaching. (1) The first five books of Moses: Genesis, Exodus, Leviticus, Numbers, and Deuteronomy; the Pentateuch; (2) a hand-written scroll containing the first five books of the Bible, which is read in the synagogue; (3) the oral law; all of Jewish teaching.

Tosafist. The term used to refer to the Jewish sages of the twelfth through fourteenth centuries who studied and explained the Talmud.

Tosafot. Additions to the Talmud added as glosses by the Tosafists. A method of talmudic analysis that developed in the rabbinical academies of France and Germany from the twelfth to the fourteenth century. These schools produced an extensive literature of talmudic commentary, and their method of study spread throughout most parts of the Jewish world. The standard editions of the Talmud have Rashi's commentary on one side of the page and a set of *Tosafot* on the other side.

Tosefta. A collection of tannaitic traditions that were not included in the Mishnah. The *Tosefta* is an early commentary that parallels the organizational structure of the Mishnah.

Tradent. A rabbi who passes on a tradition to others, often his students of the next generation.

Tzitzit. The ritual fringes attached to the *tallit* to remind the wearer of the commandments of God.

Tur. Also known as the *Arba'ah Turim,* "The Four Rows." A major halakhic compendium written by Jacob ben Asher (1270–1340) in Spain. The *Tur* became particularly significant for its organizational structure, which was adopted by almost every subsequent code of Jewish law, most importantly the *Shulhan Arukh.* It is divided into four main sections: *Orah Hayyim* (everyday ritual, prayer, Sabbath and holidays); *Yoreh De'ah* (dietary rules, sexual regulations, laws of conversion, mourning, and various other topics); *Even*

Haezer (laws of marriage and divorce); and *Hoshen Mishpat* (civil and judicial procedure).

Yeshiva (pl. *yeshivot*). Traditional Jewish religious academy or seminary devoted to studying the Talmud, its commentaries, and related rabbinic literature.

Yibbum, Yavam. Levirate marriage. A man whose brother died without children is obliged by the Torah to marry his deceased brother's widow or grant her *halitzah* (see Deut. 25:5–10). As long as neither *yibbum* or *halitzah* has taken place, she is forbidden to marry another person. The deceased husband's brother is called a *yavam* and in most Jewish communities he is required to free his brother's widow of her obligation through *halitzah*.

Yom Kippur. The Day of Atonement; a full day of fasting and prayer for forgiveness of sins.

Zonah. A prostitute; a woman who engages in sexual promiscuity or prostitution (*zenut*).

Bibliography

Abrahams, Israel. *Jewish Life in the Middle Ages*. Philadelphia: Jewish Publication Society, 1896 (reprinted 1961).

"Acquisition." *Encyclopedia Judaica*, vol. 2, pp. 216–221. Jerusalem: Keter, 1971.

Adams, Carol J. *The Sexual Politics of Meat*. New York: Continuum, 1990.

Adelman, Howard. "'A Disgrace for All Jewish Men': Methodological Considerations in the Study of Wife-Beating in Jewish History." Unpublished paper by courtesy of author.

———— "From Zion Shall Go Forth the Law: On the 500th Anniversary of the Birth of Joseph Caro." *Jewish Book Annual* 45 (1987–88): 143–157.

———— "Images of Women in Italian Jewish Literature." *Proceedings of the Tenth World Congress of Jewish Studies*, Division B, vol. 2, Jerusalem: World Union of Jewish Studies, 1990.

———— "The Changing Influences of Islamic and Catholic Law Upon Jewish Approaches to Forced Divorce and Marital Cruelty During the Middle Ages." Unpublished paper presented at the *New England Medieval Conference*, Trinity College, 1995.

———— "Wife-Beating Among Early Modern Italian Jews, 1400–1700." *Proceedings of the Eleventh World Congress of Jewish Studies*, Division B, vol. 1, pp. 135–142. Jerusalem: World Union of Jewish Studies, 1994.

———— "Wife-Beating in Jewish History." *Association for Jewish Studies: Twenty-Fourth Annual Conference*. Unpublished paper delivered in Boston, 1992.

Adler, Rachel. "Feminist Folktales of Justice: Robert Cover as a Resource for the Renewal of Halakhah." *Conservative Judaism* XLV:3 (1993): 43.

Agus, Irving. *Rabbi Meir of Rothenburg.* Philadelphia: Jewish Publication Society, 1947.

Andersen, Francis I., and Freedman, David Noel. *Hosea: A New Translation.* The Anchor Bible. New York: Doubleday, 1980.

Anson, Ofra, and Sagy, Shifra. "Marital Violence: Comparing Women in Violent and Nonviolent Unions." *Human Relations* 48:3 (1995): 285–305.

Ardey, Robert. *The Territorial Imperative.* New York: Athenaeum, 1966.

Assis, Yom Tov. "Crime and Violence among the Jews of Spain (13th–14th centuries)." *Zion Jubilee Volume* 50 (1986): 221-240 [Hebrew].

———— "Sexual Behavior in Medieval Hispano-Jewish Society." In *Jewish History: Essays in Honor of Chimen Abramsky,* ed. Ada Rapoport-Alpert and Steven J. Zipperstein, pp. 25–59. London:1988.

Atwood, Margaret. *The Handmaid's Tale.* Toronto, Canada: McClelland and Stewart, 1985.

Bar-Ilan Responsa Project: The Database for Jewish Studies.

Baron, Salo. *The Jewish Community,* vol. 2. Philadelphia: The Jewish Publication Society, 1942.

Bashan, Eliezer. "The Sages Attitudes to Husband's Violence Towards His Wife." *Giliyon* (Nissan, 1994): 22–26 [Hebrew].

Baskin, Judith. *Jewish Women in Historical Perspective.* Detroit: Wayne State University Press, 1991.

———— "Feminism Within Orthodoxy." *Reconstructionist* (Winter 1991–1992): 29.

Bass, Ellen, and Davis, Laura. *The Courage to Heal: A Guide for Women Survivors of Child Sexual Abuse.* New York: Harper Row, 1988.

Bauer, Carol, and Ritt, Lawrence. "'A Husband Is a Beating Animal': Frances Power Cobbe Confronts the Wife-Abuse Problem in Victorian England." *Journal of Women's Studies* 6 (1983): 99–118.

Bauman, Batya. "Women-identified Women in Male Identified Judaism." In *On Being a Jewish Feminist,* ed. Susannah Heschel. New York: Schocken, 1983.

Beinart, Haim. *Moreshet Sepharad: The Sephardi Legacy.* Two Volumes. Jerusalem: Magnes Press, 1992.

Benjamin, Sophia. "God and Abuse: A Survivor Story." In *Four Centuries of Jewish Women's Spirituality: A Sourcebook,* ed. Ellen M. Umansky, and Dianne Ashton, pp. 326–334. Boston: Beacon Press, 1992.

Berkovits, Eliezer. *Jewish Women in Time and Torah*. Hoboken, NJ: K'tav, 1990.

Berman, Saul. "The Status of Women in Halakhic Judaism." In *The Jewish Woman*, ed. L. Koltun, pp. 114–128. New York: Schocken Books, 1976.

Biale, Rachel. *Women and Jewish Law: An Exploration of Women's Issues in Halakhic Sources*. New York: Schocken Books, 1984.

Bird, Phyllis A. "Male and Female He Created Them." *Harvard Theological Review* 74:2 (1981): 129–159.

———. "'To Play the Harlot': An inquiry Into an Old Testament Metaphor." In *Gender and Difference in Ancient Israel*, ed. Peggy L. Day, pp. 75-94. Minneapolis, MN: Fortress Press, 1989.

Bledstein, Adrien Janis. "The Genesis of Humans: The Garden of Eden Revisited. " *Judaism* 26:2 (1977): 197–198.

Bleich, David. "Halakhah as an Absolute." *Judaism* 29 (1980): 30-37.

———. "Indirect Coercion in Compelling a Get." *Contemporary Halakhic Problems*, vol. 2, pp. 93–100. Hoboken, NJ: K'tav, 1983.

Blumenthal, David. *Facing the Abusing God: A Theology of Protest*. Louisville KY: Presbyterian Publishing House, 1993.

Bograd, M. "Feminist Perspectives on Wife Abuse: An Introduction." In *Feminist Perspectives on Wife Abuse*, ed. K. Yllo, and M. Bograd, pp. 11–26. Newbury Park, CA: Sage, 1988.

Breuer, Mordecai. *Jewish Orthodoxy in the German Reich: 1871–1918*. Jerusalem: Zalman Shazar Center, 1990.

Brichto, H.C. "The Case of the Sotah and a Reconsideration of Biblical 'Law'." *HUCA* 46 (1975): 55–70.

Brod, Harry. *A Mensch Among Men: Explorations in Jewish Masculinity*. Freedom, CA: The Crossing Press, 1988.

Brodbar-Nemzer, J. Y. "Divorce and Group Commitment: The Case of the Jews." *Journal of Marriage and the Family* 48 (1986): 329–340.

———. "Divorce in the Jewish Community: The Impact of Jewish Commitment." *Journal of Jewish Communal Service* 61 (1984): 150–159.

Bullough, Vern L. *The Subordinate Sex*. Urbana, IL: University of Illinois, 1974.

Cantor, Aviva. *Jewish Women/Jewish Men: The Legacy of Patriarchy in Jewish Life*. San Francisco, CA: Harper, 1995.

Carlebach, Julius. "Family Structure and the Position of Jewish Women." In *Revolution and Evolution: 1848 in German Jewish History*, ed. Werner E. Mosse, pp. 156–187. Tubingen, Germany: J.C.B. Mohr (Paul Siebeck), 1981.

"Carmella Lobby Combats Domestic Violence." *Na'amat Woman* (March–April 1995): 24.

Center for the Prevention of Sexual and Domestic Violence. "To Save a Life: Ending Domestic Violence in Jewish Families." 35 minute video tape available from the Center at 936 North 34th St., Suite 200, Seattle, WA 98103.

Cohen, Boaz. "Betrothal in Jewish and Roman Law." *Proceedings of the American Academy for Jewish Research,* no XVIII (1948–1949).

Cohen, Gerson. "The Song of Songs and the Jewish Religious Mentality." In *Studies in the Variety of Rabbinic Cultures.* Philadelphia: Jewish Publication Society, 1991.

Cohen, Shaye J.D and Greenstein, Edward L. *The State of Jewish Studies.* Detroit, MI: Wayne State University Press, 1990.

———— "Purity and Piety: The Separation of Menstruants." In *Daughters of the King: Women and the Synagogue,* ed. Susan Grossman and Rivka Haut, pp. 103–115. Philadelphia: Jewish Publication Society, 1992.

Cohen, She'ar-Yashuv. "The Forced Get in Our Time." *Tehumim* 11 (1990): 195–202 [Hebrew].

Cohen, Steven M., and Hyman, Paula E. *The Jewish Family: Myths and Reality.* New York: Holmes and Meier, 1986.

Cover, Robert. "The Supreme Court, 1982 Term-Foreword: *Nomos* and Narrative." *Harvard Law Review* 97 (1983).

Crumley, Gene. "Hosea." *Judaism* 33 (1984): 345.

Culler, Jonathan D. *On Deconstruction.* Ithaca, NY: Cornell University Press, 1982.

Cwik, Marc S. "Peace in the Home? The Response of Rabbis to Wife Abuse Within American Jewish Congregations—Part 2." *Journal of Psychology and Judaism* 21:1 (1997): 5–81.

———— "Rabbi . . . Your Help Is Needed. " Five-page questionnaire to elicit rabbis knowledge of wife abuse in their communities. Master's Candidate at University of Wisconsin, Madison, 1996 (adviser Professor Inge Bretherton).

Daly, Mary. *Beyond God the Father.* Boston, MA: Beacon Press, 1973.

Danby, Herbert. *The Mishnah.* Oxford, UK: Oxford University Press, 1938.

Darr, Katheryn. "Ezekiel's Justifications of God." *JSOT* 55 (1992): 97–117.

Darrand, Tom Craig, and Shupe, Anson. *Metaphors of Social Control in a Pentecostal Sect.* Lewiston, NY: Edwin Mellen Press, 1983.

Davidson, Terry. "Wifebeating: A Recurring Phenomenon Throughout History." In *Battered Women,* ed. Maria Roy, pp. 2–23. New York: Van Nostrand Reinhold [original] 1977.

Delany, Sheila. "'This Borrowed Language': Body Politic in Judges 19." *Shofar* 11:2 (1993): 97–109.

Dickstein, Leah J. "Spouse Abuse and Other Domestic Violence." *Psychiatric Clinics of North America* 11:4 (1988): 611–627.

Dinnerstein, Dorothy. *The Mermaid and the Minotaur: Sexual Arrangement and Human Malaise.* New York: Harper and Row, 1976.

Dorff, Elliot N. "Family Violence." *Committee on Jewish Law and Standards.* New York: The Rabbinical Assembly. Teshuvah, September 1995.

———— and Rosett, Arthur. *A Living Tree: The Roots and Growth of Jewish Law.* Albany, NY: State University Press of New York, 1988.

———— *Mitzvah Means Commandment.* New York: United Synagogue of America, 1989.

Dresner, Samuel. "Homosexuality and the Order of Creation." *Judaism* 40:3 (Summer 1991): 309–321.

Eidelberg, S. *Jewish Life in Austria in the XVth Century: As Reflected in the Legal Writings of Rabbi Israel Isserlein and His Contemporaries.* Philadelphia: Dropsie College, 1962.

Eilberg-Schwartz, Howard. *The Savage in Judaism: An Anthropology of Israelite Religion and Ancient Judaism.* Bloomington, IN: Indiana University Press, 1990.

Elon, Menahem. "Developments in the Rabbinic Judiciary of Israel." In *Mishpat Ivri.* Three volumes. Jerusalem: Magnes Press, 1973 [Hebrew].

El-Or, Tamar. "The Length of the Slits and the Spread of Luxury: Reconstructing the Subordination of Ultra-Orthodox Jewish Women Through the Patriarchy of Men Scholars." *Sex Roles* 29:9/10 (1993): 585–598.

Epstein, Isidore. *The "Responsa" of Rabbi Solomon Ben Adreth of Barcelona (1235-1310) As a Source of the History of Spain.* London: Kegan Paul, Trench, Trubner, 1925.

———— *The Babylonian Talmud.* London: Soncino Press, 1935.

Esposito, John. *Women in Muslim Family Law.* Syracuse, NY: Syracuse University Press, 1982.

Exum, J. Cheryl. "The Ethics of Biblical Violence Against Women." In *The Bible in Ethics,* ed. John W. Rogerson, et al., pp. 248–271. Sheffield, UK: Sheffield Academic Press, 1995.

"*Eyn Adam dar im nachash be-kefifa achat.*" *Encyclopedia Talmudit.* Jerusalem: Yad Harav Herzog, 1993 [Hebrew].

Falk, Ze'ev. *Jewish Matrimonial Law in the Middle Ages.* London: Oxford University Press, 1966.

———— *The Divorce Action by the Wife in Jewish Law.* Institute for Legislative Research and Comparative Law. Jerusalem: Hebrew University of Jerusalem, Faculty of Law, 1973 [Hebrew].

Finkelstein, Louis. *Jewish Self-Government in the Middle Ages.* New York: Jewish Theological Seminary of America, 1924.

Fisch, Harold. "Hosea: A Poetics of Violence." In *Poetry With a Purpose.* Bloomington, IN: Indiana University Press, 1990.

Forst, Clair, and Macner, Esther. "Domestic Violence." *International Conference on Feminism and Orthodoxy.* New York City: February 1997 (audio tape available A-9).

Freedman, H., and Simon, Maurice, ed. *The Midrash.* Ten Volumes. London: The Soncino Press, 1983.

Freehof, Solomon B. *The Responsa Literature.* Philadelphia: Jewish Publication Society of America, 1959.

Freiman, Avraham. *Seder Kiddushin ve Nissuin.* Jerusalem: Mossad Harav Kook, 1964 [Hebrew].

Friedman, Mordecai A. "Book Review." *JAOS* 100:2 (1980).

———— "Marriage as an Institution: Jewry Under Islam." In *The Jewish Family: Metaphor and Memory,* ed. David Kraemer, pp. 31–45. New York: Oxford University Press, 1989.

———— "The Ethics of Medieval Jewish Marriage." In *Religion in a Religious Age,* ed. S.D. Goitein, pp. 83–102. New York: K'tav, 1973.

Friedman, Theodore. "The Shifting Role of Women, From the Bible to Talmud." *Judaism* 36 (1987): 479–487.

Frishtik, Mordecai. "Physical and Sexual Violence by Husbands as a Reason for Imposing a Divorce in Jewish Law." *The Jewish Law Annual* IX (1991/2): 145–169.

———— "Violence Against Women in Judaism." *Journal of Psychology and Judaism* 14:3 (1990): 131-153.

Frye, Northrop. *The Great Code: The Bible and Literature.* New York: Harcourt Brace Jovanovich, 1982.

Frymer-Kensky, Tikva. *In the Wake of Goddesses.* New York: The Free Press, 1992.

"Gaon." *Encyclopedia Judaica,* vol. 7, pp. 315-324. Jerusalem: Keter, 1971.

Gelles, Richard J. "Abused Wives: Why Do They Stay." *Journal of Marriage and the Family* 38: 2 (1976): 659–68.

———— "Violence in the Family: A Review of Research in the Seventies." *Journal of Marriage and the Family* 42 (1980): 873–885.

Giller, Betsy. "All in the Family: Violence in the Jewish Home." In *Jewish Women in Therapy*, ed. Rachel Josefowitz Siegel, and Ellen Cole, pp. 101–109. New York: Harrington Park Press, 1991.

Ginsberg, H.L. "Hosea, Book of." *Encyclopedia Judaica*, vol. 8, pp. 1010–1025. Jerusalem: Keter, 1971.

——— "Studies in Hosea 1–3." In *Yehezkel Kaufmann Jubilee Volume*, ed. Menahem Haran, pp. 50-69. Jerusalem: Magnes Press, 1960.

Ginzberg, Louis. *The Legends of the Jews*. Philadelphia: Jewish Publication Society, 1909, 1968.

Girondi, Jonah. *Iggeret ha-teshuvah* (Letter of Repentance). Cracow: 1586 and Prague: 1596 [Hebrew].

Gluck, Bob. "Jewish Men and Violence in the Home—Unlikely Companions?" In *A Mensch Among Men: Explorations in Jewish Masculinity*, ed. H. Brod, pp. 162–173. Freedom, CA: Crossing Press, 1988.

Goitein, S.D. *A Mediterranean Society*. Los Angeles: University of California Press, 1978.

Goldberg, Harvey. *Jewish Life in Muslim Libya*. Chicago: University of Chicago Press, 1990.

Goldin, Simha. "The Role and Function of the *Herem* and *Takkana* in the Medieval Ashkenazic Community." *Proceedings of the Eleventh World Congress of Jewish Studies*, Division B, vol. 1, pp. 105–112. Jerusalem: World Union of Jewish Studies, 1994 [Hebrew].

Goldman, Israel M. *The Life and Times of Rabbi David Ibn Avi Zimra*. New York: Jewish Theological Seminary of America, 1970.

Goldner, Virginia, et al. "Love and Violence: Gender Paradoxes in Volatile Attachments." *Family Process* 29:4 (1990): 343–364.

Goldsmith, Ellen. "Violence in the Jewish Family." *Reform Judaism* 4:12 (1983): 20.

Golinkin, David. *Halakhah for Our Time: A Conservative Approach to Jewish Law*. Issued by the United Synagogue of America, 1991.

Gordis, Robert. *The Dynamics of Judaism*. Bloomington, IN: Indiana University Press, 1990.

Gordon, Linda. *Heroes of their Own Lives: The Politics and History of Family Violence, Boston, 1880–1960*. New York: Viking, 1988.

Gordon, Pamela, and Washington, Harold C. "Rape as a Military Metaphor in the Hebrew Bible." In *A Feminist Companion to the Latter Prophets*, ed. Athalya Brenner. Sheffield, UK: Sheffield Academic Press, 1995.

Graetz, Michael. "Responsa Regarding the Ordination of Women as Rabbis." *Responsa of the Va'ad Halakha of the Rabbinical Assembly of Israel*, vol. 5, pp. 17–26. Jerusalem: The Masorti Movement, 1994 [Hebrew, with English Summary].

—— "The Right to Medical Treatment in Jewish Law." *Et La-asot* 3 (1991): 80–89 [Hebrew].

Graetz, Naomi. "God is to Israel as Husband is to Wife." In *A Feminist Companion to the Latter Prophets,* ed. Athalya Brenner, pp.126–145. Sheffield, UK: Sheffield Academic Press, 1995.

—— "Jerusalem the Widow." delivered at *the Western Jewish Studies Association Third Annual Conference* (April 6–8, 1997) at the University of Arizona, Tucson (forthcoming in *Women in Jewish Life and Culture,* a special *Shofar* volume) .

—— "Dinah the Daughter." In *A Feminist Companion to Genesis,* ed. Athalya Brenner, pp. 306–317. Sheffield, UK: Sheffield Academic Press, 1993.

—— "Miriam: Guilty or Not Guilty?" *Judaism* 40:2 (1991): 184–192.

—— "Rejection: A Rabbinic Response to Wife Beating." In *Gender and Judaism: The Transformation of Tradition,* ed. T. M. Rudavsky, pp. 13–24. New York: New York University Press, 1995.

—— "Some Halakhic Aspects of Wife-Beating in the Jewish Tradition." *Proceedings of the Eleventh World Congress of Jewish Studies,* Division B, vol. 1, pp. 143–150. Jerusalem: World Union of Jewish Studies, 1994.

—— "The Haftorah Tradition and the Metaphoric Battering of Hosea's Wife." *Conservative Judaism* XLV:1 (1992): 29–42.

—— *S/He Created Them: Feminist Retellings of Biblical Stories.* Chapel Hill, NC: Professional Press, 1993.

Granot, Naomi. "Review of *Chattel or Person?* by Judith Romney Wegner." *Journal of Jewish Studies* XLII:2 (1991): 274–280.

Greenberg, Blu. "The Feminist Revolution in Orthodox Judaism." *Lilith* 17:3 (Summer 1992): 11–17.

—— "Marriage in the Jewish Tradition." *Journal of Ecumenical Studies* 22:1 (1985): 3–20.

—— *On Women and Judaism.* Philadelphia: Jewish Publication Society, 1982.

Greenberg, Irving. "Confronting Sexual Abuse in Jewish Families: Rabbis Can Help by Speaking Out." *Moment* (April 1990): 49.

Griffin, Susan. *Pornography and Silence.* New York: Harper & Row, 1981.

Grossman, Avraham. "Medieval Rabbinic Views of Wife Beating: (8th–13th Centuries)." *Proceedings of the Tenth World Congress of Jewish Studies,* Division B, vol. 1. Jerusalem: World Union of Jewish Studies, 1990 [Hebrew].

———— "Spanish and Ashkenazi Jewry." In *Moreshet Sepharad: The Sephardi Legacy*, ed. Haim Beinart, vol. 2, pp. 220–239. Jerusalem: Magnes Press, 1992.

———— "Legislation and Responsa Literature." In *Moreshet Sepharad: The Sephardi Legacy*, ed. Haim Beinart, vol. 2, pp. 188–219. Jerusalem: Magnes Press, 1992.

———— "Medieval Rabbinic Views on Wife Beating, 800–1300." *Jewish History* 5 (1991): 53–62.

———— "The Historical Background to the Ordinances on Family Affairs Attributed to Rabbenu Gershom Me'or ha-Golah ('The Light of the Exile')." In *Jewish History: Essays in Honor of Chimen Abramsky*, ed. Ada Rapoport-Alpert and Steven J. Zipperstein, pp. 3–23. London: 1988.

———— "Violence Against Women in Medieval Mediterranean Jewish Society." In *A View Into the Lives of Women in Jewish Societies: Collected Essays*, ed. Yael Azmon, pp. 183–207. Jerusalem: Zalman Shazar Center for Jewish History, 1995.

Grossman, Naomi. "Women Unbound." *Lilith* 18:3 (Summer 1993): 8–12.

Grossman, Susan and Haut, Rivka. *Daughters of the King: Women and the Synagogue*. Philadelphia: Jewish Publication Society, 1992.

Gruber, Mayer I. "The Motherhood of God in Second Isaiah." *Revue Biblique* 3 (1983).

———— "The Mishna as Oral Torah." *The Motherhood of God and Other Studies*. Atlanta, GA: Scholar's Press, 1992.

———— "Marital Fidelity and Intimacy: A View from Hosea 4." In *A Feminist Companion to the Latter Prophets*, ed. Athalya Brenner, pp.169–179. Sheffield, UK: Sheffield Academic Press, 1995.

Guedmann, M. *Geschichte des Erziehungswesens und der Cultur der abendlandischen Juden wahrend des Mittelalters*. Translated into Hebrew. Warsaw: Ahiasaf, 1877 (Reprinted in Jerusalem: 1972).

Guterman, Neil B. "Confronting the Unknowns in Jewish Family Violence." *Journal of Jewish Communal Service* 70:1 (Fall 1993): 26–33.

Haas, Peter J. "The Modern Study of Responsa." *Approaches to Judaism in Medieval Times*, ed. David R. Blumenthal, vol. 2, pp. 35–71. Chico, CA: Scholars Press, 1985.

Haddad, Yvonne Y. and Findly, Ellison B. *Women, Religion and Social Change*. Albany, NY: SUNY Press, 1985.

"Halakha." *Encyclopedia Judaica*, vol. 6. Jerusalem: Keter, 1971.

Halbertal, Moshe, and Margalit, Avishai. *Idolatry.* Trans. Naomi Goldblum. Cambridge, MA: Harvard University Press, 1992.

Hauptman, Judith. "Traditional Jewish Texts, Wife-Beating, and the Patriarchal Construction of Jewish Marriage." Unpublished paper by courtesy of author.

Heilbrun, Carolyn G. *Writing a Woman's Life.* New York: Ballantine Books, 1988.

Helm, Vietta. "New Domestic Violence Wheel." An electronic mail communication dated Tuesday, 2 July 1996, from fivers@athens.net (a moderated list for professionals and interested scholars in domestic violence).

Herman, Judith Lewis with Hirschman, Lisa. *Father-Daughter Incest.* Cambridge, MA: Harvard University Press, 1981.

—— *Trauma and Recovery: The Aftermath of Violence From Domestic Abuse to Political Terror.* New York: Basic Books, 1992.

Hertz, J. H. *The Pentateuch and Haftorahs.* 2nd ed. London: Soncino Press, 1936, 1962, 1971.

Heschel, Abraham Joshua. *God in Search of Man.* New York: Harper & Row, 1955.

—— *The Prophets.* Philadelphia: Jewish Publication Society, 1962.

Heschel, Susannah. *On Being a Jewish Feminist: A Reader.* New York: Schocken, 1983.

—— "Anti-Judaism in Christian Feminist Theology." *Tikkun* 5:3 (1990): 25-28, 95-97.

—— "Configurations of Patriarch, Judaism, and Nazism in German Feminist Thought." In *Gender and Judaism,* ed. T.M. Rudavsky, pp.135–154. New York: New York University Press, 1995.

Hirsch, Samson Raphael. *Judaism Eternal,* vol. 2. London: Soncino Press, 1956.

Holtz, Barry W. *Back to the Sources.* New York: Summit, 1984.

Horsburgh, Beverly. "Lifting the Veil of Secrecy: Domestic Violence in the Jewish Community." *Harvard Women's Law Journal* 18 (Spring 1995): 171–217.

"Hovel" [damages], *Encyclopedia Talmudit,* vol. 12, Jerusalem: Yad Harav Herzog, 1993 [Hebrew].

Hurwitz, S. *The Responsa of Solomon Luria (Maharshal).* New York: Bloch Publishing, 1938.

Hyman, Paula. "The Jewish Family: Looking for a Usable Past." In *On Being a Jewish Feminist,* ed. Susannah Heschel, pp. 19–26. New York: Schocken, 1983.

—————— "The Modern Jewish Family: Image and Reality." In *The Jewish Family: Metaphor and Memory*, ed. David Kraemer, pp. 179–193. New York: Oxford University Press, 1989.

—————— *The Emancipation of the Jews of Alsace*. New Haven, CT: Yale University Press, 1991.

Ibn Zabara, Joseph ben Meir. *Sepher Shaashuim: A Book of Medieval Lore*, ed. Israel Davidson. New York: Jewish Theological Seminary, 1914.

"ICAR—A Ray of Hope." *Networking for Women: A Quarterly Publication of the Israel Women's Network* (July 1996): 6.

Jacobs, Janet L. "Gender and Power in New Religious Movements: A Feminist Discourse on the Scientific Study of Religion." *Religion* 21 (1991): 345–355.

—————— "The Economy of Love in Religious Commitment: The Deconversion of Women From Nontraditional Religious Movements." *Journal for the Scientific Study of Religion* 23:2 (1984): 155–171.

Jacobs, Joseph. "Triennial Cycle." *The Jewish Encyclopedia*, vol. 12, pp. 254–257. New York: Funk and Wagnalls, 1916.

Jacobs, Lynn, and Dimarsky, Sherry Berliner. "Jewish Domestic Abuse: Realities and Responses." *Journal of Jewish Communal Service* 68:2 (1991–1992): 94–113.

Jaffee, Martin S. "The Taqqanah in Tannaitic Literature." *Journal of Jewish Studies* XLI:2 (Autumn 1990): 204–225.

Jastrow, Marcus. *A Dictionary of the Targumim, the Talmud Bavli and Yerushalmi, and the Midrashic Literature*. Berlin: Verlag Choreb, 1926.

Joseph, Norma Baumel. "Mehitzah: Halakhic Decisions and Political Consequences." In *Daughters of the King: Women and the Synagogue*, ed. Susan Grossman and Rivka Haut. Philadelphia: Jewish Publication Society, 1992.

Kanarfogel, Ephraim. "Preservation, Creativity, and Courage: The Life and Works of R. Meir of Rotenberg." *Jewish Book Annual* 50 (1992): 249–259.

Kaplan, Marion. "A Comment on Family Structure and the Position of Jewish Women." In *Revolution and Evolution: 1848 in German Jewish History*, ed. Werner E. Mosse, pp. 189–203. Tubingen, Germany: J.C.B. Mohr (Paul Siebeck), 1981.

Karp, Judith. *Committee Report on Family Violence Between Couples*. Jerusalem: Ministry of Justice, 25 October 1989 [Hebrew].

Klein, Isaac, trans. *The Code of Maimonides*. Yale Judaica Series, vol. 19. New Haven, CT: Yale University Press, 1972.

Koltun, Elizabeth. *The Jewish Woman: New Perspectives.* New York: Schocken, 1976.

Kramer, C. "An Historical Perspective on Domestic Violence." *Jewish Social Work Forum* 26 (1990): 51–56.

Kutz, Ilan. "Behind the Pillar of Salt." *The Jerusalem Report* (October 31, 1996): 46.

Lakoff, George, and Turner, Mark. *More than Cool Reason: A Field Guide to Poetic Metaphor.* Chicago: University of Chicago Press, 1989.

Lamdan, Ruth. *A Separate People: Jewish Women in Palestine, Syria and Egypt in the 16th Century.* Tel Aviv: Tel-Aviv University and Bitan, 1996 [Hebrew].

Laytner, Anson. *Arguing With God: A Jewish Tradition.* Northvale, NJ: Jason Aronson Inc., 1990.

Leith, Mary Joan Winn. "Verse and Reverse: The Transformation of the Woman, Israel, in Hosea 1-3." In *Gender and Difference in Ancient Israel,* ed. Peggy L. Day, pp. 95–108. Minneapolis, MN: Fortress Press, 1989.

Lesko, Barbara S. *Women's Earliest Records From Ancient Egypt and Western Asia.* Atlanta, GA, Scholars Press, 1989.

Levenson, Alan T. "An Adventure in Otherness: Nahida Remy-Ruth Lazarus (1849–1928)." In *Gender and Judaism,* ed. T.M. Rudavsky, pp. 99–111. New York: New York University Press, 1995.

Levin, S. "A Battered People Syndrome?" *Judaism* 26:2 (1977): 217–221.

Levine, Lee. *The Status of the Sages in the Land of Israel in the Talmudic Era.* Jerusalem: Yad Ben Zvi, 1986 [Hebrew].

Lieberman, Saul. *Tosefta ki-Peshutah: A Comprehensive Commentary on the Tosefta.* New York: JTSA, 1988.

Lowenstein, Sharon R. "Confronting Sexual Abuse in Jewish Families." *Moment* (April 1990): 48–53.

Mann, Jacob. *The Bible as Read and Preached in the Old Synagogue.* Cincinatti OH: Hebrew Union Congregations of America, 1940.

Marcus, Ivan. "Jewish Learning in the Middle Ages." *The Melton Journal* (Autumn 1992): 22, 24.

Martin, Del. *Battered Wives.* New York: Pocket Books, 1983.

Mayer, Ann Elizabeth. *Islam and Human Rights.* Boulder, CO: Westview Press, 1991.

McFague, Sallie. *Metaphorical Theology.* Philadelphia: Fortress, 1982.

Meiselman, Moshe. *Jewish Woman in Jewish Law.* New York: K'tav, 1978.

Mernissi, Fatima. *The Veil and the Male Elite.* UK: Addison-Wesley, 1991.

Meyers, Carol. *Discovering Eve: Ancient Israelite Women in Context*. New York: Oxford University Press, 1990.

Millett, Kate. *Sexual Politics*. London: Sphere Books, 1971.

Moehling, Kathryn. "Battered Women and Abusive Partners." *Journal of Psycho-Social Nursing* 26:9 (1988): 9–17.

Moi, Toril. "Kate Millett." *Sexual Textual Politics*. London: Methuen, 1985.

Momeyer, Richard. "Death Mystiques: Denial, Acceptance, Rebellion." *Mosaic* 15:1 (1982): 1–12.

Moran, Richard. "Seeing and Believing: Metaphor, Image, and Force." *Critical Inquiry* 16:1 (1989): 87–112.

Morrell, Samuel. "An Equal or a Ward: How Independent Is a Married Woman According to Rabbinic Law?" *Jewish Social Studies* 44 (1982): 189–210.

Morris, Desmond. *The Naked Ape*. New York: McGraw-Hill, 1967.

Morris, Nathan. *A History of Jewish Education*, vol. 2. Tel-Aviv: Amanut, 1964 [Hebrew].

Nadelhaft, Ruth. "Domestic Violence in Literature: A Preliminary Study." *Mosaic* 17:2 (1984): 242–259.

National Clearinghouse on Domestic Violence. *Wife Abuse in the Medical Setting: An Introduction For Health Personnel*. Domestic Violence Monograph Series, no. 7 (April 1981).

Newsome, Carol A., and Ringe, Sharon H. *The Women's Bible Commentary*. Louisville, KY: Westminster, 1992.

"Niddah." *Encyclopedia Judaica*. Jerusalem: Keter, 1971.

Niditch, Susan. "The Sodomite Theme in Judges 19-20: Family, Community, and Social Disintegration." *Catholic Biblical Quarterly* 44:3 (1982): 365-378.

———— *War in the Hebrew Bible*. New York: Oxford, 1993.

Novack, David. "For This Question, A Responsum." *Sh'ma* 21:404 (1990): 29–30.

———— *Law and Theology in Judaism*. New York: K'tav, 1974.

———— *The Image of the Non-Jew in Judaism*. New York: Edwin Mellon, 1983.

Nye, Andrea. *Words of Power: A Feminist Reading of the History of Logic*. London: Routledge, 1990.

Ochshorn, Judith. *The Female Experience and the Nature of the Divine*. Bloomington, IN: Indiana University Press, 1981.

Oliver, Anne Marie and Paul Steinberg. "Pornography as Political Weapon." *The Jerusalem Report* (May 2, 1991): 33.

Oppenheimer, Aharon. *The 'Am-Ha-aretz*. Leiden: E.J. Brill, 1977.

Orenstein, Debra with Jay Stein. "Domestic Violence and Jewish Responsibility." *Women's League Outlook* (Fall 1995): 23–24.

——— "How Jewish Law Views Wife Beating." *Lilith* 20 (1988): 9.

Ovadia, Debbie. *Hotline for Battered Women.* Jerusalem: National Security Institute, 1991 [Hebrew].

Paperna, Avraham Yakov. *Complete Works.* Vilna: 1867 [Hebrew].

Pardes, Ilana. *Countertraditions in the Bible.* Cambridge, MA: Harvard University Press, 1992.

Paul, Shalom. *Studies in the Book of the Covenant in The Light of Biblical and Cuneiform Law.* Leiden: Brill, 1970.

Plaskow, Judith. "Blaming the Jews for the Birth of Patriarchy." In *Nice Jewish Girls: A Lesbian Anthology,* ed. Evelyn Beck, pp. 250–254. Watertown, MA: Persephone Press, 1982.

——— "Halakha as a Feminist Issue." *Melton Journal* 22 (Fall 1987): 3–5.

——— "The Year of the Aguna." *Tikkun* 8:5 (1993): 52–53; 86–87

——— *Standing Again at Sinai: Judaism From a Feminist Perspective.* San Francisco: Harper and Row, 1990.

Plaut, Gunter. *The Torah: A Modern Commentary.* New York: Union of American Hebrew Congregations, 1981.

Prescott, S., and Letko, C. "Battered Women: A Social Psychological Perspective." In *Battered Women: A Psychosocial Study of Domestic Violence,* ed. M. Roy, pp. 72–96. New York: Van Nostrand Reinhold, 1977.

Rabinowitz, Louis, I. "Haftarah." *Encyclopedia Judaica,* vol. 6, pp. 1342–1345. Jerusalem: Keter, 1971.

Ragen, Naomi. *Jephte's Daughter.* New York: Warner Books, 1989.

Rakover, Nahum. "Forced Sexual Relations Between a Husband and Wife." *Hebrew Law Annual* 6–7 (1979–80): 295–317 [Hebrew].

Rank, Otto. *The Incest Theme in Language and Literature.* Baltimore: Johns Hopkins Press, 1975.

Remy, Nahida. *The Jewish Woman.* Fourth Edition. New York: Bloch Publishing Company, 1923.

"Responsa." *Encyclopedia Judaica,* vol. 14. Jerusalem: Keter, 1971.

Riskin, Shlomo. *Women and Jewish Divorce: The Rebellious Wife.* Hoboken, NJ: K'tav, 1989.

——— "The Song of Hol Hamo'ed. " *The Jerusalem Post* (April 13, 1990).

Rogers, K.M. *The Troublesome Helpmate: A History of Misogyny in Literature.* Seattle, WA: University of Washington Press, 1966.

Rosenstock, Bruce. "Inner-Biblical Exegesis in the Book of the Covenant." *Conservative Judaism* (Spring 1992).

Ross, Tamar. "Can the Demand for Change in the Status of Women be Halakhically Legitimated?" *Judaism* (Fall 1993).

Roy, Maria. *Battered Women*. New York: Van Nostrand Reinhold, 1977.

Russ, Ian, et al. *Shalom Bayit: A Jewish Response to Child Abuse and Domestic Violence*. Los Angeles: Jewish Family Service of Los Angeles, Family Violence Project, 1993.

Sadan, Sasha. "The Divorce Trap." *The Jerusalem Post Magazine* (March 12, 1993): 10.

Sales, Jay David. "Kol Nidre 1992." Sermon given at Bnai Abraham Synagogue in Easton, PA.

Scarf, Mimi. "Marriages Made in Heaven? Battered Jewish Wives." In *On Being a Jewish Feminist: A Reader,* ed. Susannah Heschel, pp. 51–64. New York: Schocken Books, 1983.

———— *Battered Jewish Wives: Case Studies in the Response to Rage*. Lewiston, Queenston: The Edwin Mellen Press, 1988.

Schaefer, Peter. "Research Into Rabbinic Literature: An Attempt to Define the Status Quaestionis." *Journal of Jewish Studies* 37:2 (1986): 139–152.

Schaer, Robin Beth. "Israeli Feminists Dramatize Violence Against Women." *Lilith* 19:1 (1994): 5.

Schneider, Susan Weidman. *Jewish and Female: Choices and Changes in our Lives Today*. New York: Simon and Schuster, 1984.

Schwartz, Sharon. "Women and Depression: A Durkheimian Perspective." *Social Science Medicine* 32:2 (1991): 127–140.

Schwarzbaum, Haim. *Jewish Folklore Between East and West: Collected Papers*. Beer-Sheva: Ben-Gurion University of the Negev Press, 1989.

Scolnic, Benjamin. "Bible Battering." *Conservative Judaism* XLV:2 (1992): 43–52.

Segal, Dina, et al. *Special Project for Weaning Families From Violence*. Jerusalem: National Security Institute, 1989 [Hebrew].

Seidler-Feller, Chaim. "Female Rabbis, Male Fears." *Judaism* 33 (1984): 79–84.

Selvidge, Marla. "Mark 5:25–34 and Leviticus 15:19-20." *Journal of Biblical Literature* 103:4 (1984).

Setel, T. Drorah. "Feminist Insights and the Question of Method." In *Feminist Perspectives of Biblical Scholarship*, ed. Adela Yarbro Collins. Chico, CA: Scholars Press, 1985.

———— "Prophets and Pornography: Female Sexual Imagery in Hosea." In *Feminist Interpretation of the Bible,* ed. Letty Russell. Philadelphia: Westminster, 1985.

Shalhoub-Kevorkian, Nadera. "Wife Abuse: A Method of Social Control." *Israel Social Science Research* 12:1 (1997): 59–72.

Shalom Bayit, a newsletter, a publication of The Board of Jewish Education of Greater Washington, 11710 Hunters Lane, Rockville, MD 20852. (Phone 301-984-4455, FAX: 301-230-0267).

Sharshevski, Ben Zion. "The Husband's Obligations to His Wife." *Family Law.* Jerusalem: Rubin Mass, 1967 [Hebrew].

"She'elot u-Teshubot." *Jewish Encyclopedia.* New York, Funk and Wagnalls, 1906.

Shechter, Susan. *Women and Male Violence.* Boston, MA: South End Press, 1982.

Shenhar, Aliza. *Family Confrontation and Conflict in Jewish Folktales.* Jerusalem: Hebrew University Doctoral Dissertation, 1974.

Shields, Mary E. "Circumcision of the Prostitute." *Biblical Interpretation* 3:1 (1995).

Shifman, Pinhas. *Civil Marriage in Israel: The Case for Reform.* Jerusalem: Institute for Israel Studies Research Series #62, 1995.

Shluker, Zelda. "A Silent Plague." *Hadassah* 69:6 (1988): 30–31.

Shokeid, Moshe. "The Regulation of Aggression in Daily Life: Aggressive Relationships Among Moroccan Immigrants in Israel." *Ethnology* 21:3 (1982): 271–281.

Shrock, A.T. *Rabbi Jonah ben Abraham of Gerona.* London: Edward Goldston, 1948.

Sigal, Philip. "Elements of Male Chauvinism in Classical *Halakhah.*" *Judaism* 24:2 (1975): 226–244.

———— "Responsum on the Status of Women." *Proceedings of the Committee on Jewish Law and Standards/1980–1985,* pp. 269–297. New York: Rabbinical Assembly, 1988.

Simons, Jon. "A Miscarriage of Justice." *The Jerusalem Post* (4 November 1994).

Skolnik, Gerald C. "Domestic Violence Against the Backdrop of Jewish Tradition." Speech delivered at a conference in Westchester, NY on Jewish Domestic Violence in April, 1993.

Sliw, Regina. "With an Outstretched Arm: A Historical Analysis of Violence Against Women Within the Jewish World." *Le'Ela* 37 (1994): 17–21.

Spero, Shubert. *Morality, Halakha and the Jewish Tradition.* New York: K'tav Publishing House, 1983.

Spiegel, Marcia Cohn. "Spirituality for Survival: Jewish Women Recovering From Abuse." *Journal of Feminist Studies in Religion* 12:2 (Fall 1996): 121–137.

Spitzer, Julie Ringold. *When Love is Not Enough: Spousal Abuse in Rabbinic and Contemporary Judaism.* New York: National Federation of Temple Sisterhoods, 1985, 1991,1995.

———— "Spousal Abuse in Rabbinic and Contemporary Judaism." (Unpublished Thesis in partial fulfillment of the requirements for Ordination at Hebrew Union College-Jewish Institute of Religion, 1985).

Stansell, Christine. "The Harm at Home." *Tikkun* 3:3 (1988): 89–91.

Stark, Evan, et al. "Medicine and Patriarchal Violence: The Social Construction of a 'Private' Event." *International Journal of Health Services* 9:3 (1979): 461–93.

Straus, Murray A. "Sexual Inequality, Cultural Norms and Wifebeating." *Victimology* 1 (1976): 54–76.

———— and Gelles, Richard J. *Physical Violence in American Families.* New Brunswick, NJ: Transaction, 1990.

———— "A Sociological Perspective on the Prevention and Treatment of Wifebeating." In *Battered Women: A Psychosociological Study of Domestic Violence,* ed. M. Roy, pp. 194–239. New York: Van Nostrand Reinhold, 1977.

———— "Wife Beating: How Common and Why?" *Victimology* 2 (1977): 443–458.

———— and Gelles, Richard J. "Societal Change and Change in Family Violence from 1975 to 1985 as Revealed by Two National Surveys." *Journal of Marriage and the Family* 48 (1986): 465–479.

———— et al. *Behind Closed Doors: Violence in the American Family.* Garden City, NY: Anchor/Doubleday, 1980.

Swirski, Barbara. "Jews Don't Batter Their Wives: Another Myth Bites the Dust." In *Calling the Equality Bluff: Women in Israel,* ed. Barbara Swirski and Marilyn P. Safir, pp. 319–327. New York: Pergamon Press, 1991.

Taitz, Emily. *The Jews of Medieval France: The Community of Champagne.* Westport, CO: Greenwood Press, 1994.

Tanakh: A New Translation of the Holy Scriptures. Philadelphia: Jewish Publication Society, 1985.

Ta-Shma, Israel M. "Rabbi Joseph Caro and His Beit Yosef: Between Spain and Germany." In *Moreshet Sepharad: The Sephardi Legacy,* ed. Haim Beinart, vol. 2, pp. 192–206. Jerusalem: Magnes Press, 1992.

The Quran: Translation and Commentary by Rev. E.M. Wherry, comprising Sale's Translation, vol. 2. London: 1896 (1975).

"The Weeping Altar." *Networking for Women: A Quarterly Publication of the Israel Women's Network* 7:3 (1994): 2–3.

Thistlethwaite, Susan Brooks. "Every Two Minutes: Battered Women and Feminist Interpretation." In *Feminist Interpretation of the Bible*, ed. Letty Russell. Philadelphia: Westminster, 1985.

Tikochinsky, Haim. *The Enactments (Takkanot) of the Gaonim.* Jerusalem, Tel-Aviv: Sura Press, 1960 [Hebrew].

Tomchin, Susan. "He Seemed Like Prince Charming: JWI Confronts Domestic Abuse in the Jewish Community." *JCN Women* (April 1997). An online publication (www.jcn18.com/scripts/jcn18/paper/Article.asp?ArticleID=530).

Trible, Phyllis. "Depatriarchalizing in Biblical Interpretation." *Journal of the American Academy of Religion* (March 1973): 30-48.

—— "Depatriarchalizing in Biblical Interpretation." In *The Jewish Woman: New Perspectives*, ed. Elizabeth Koltun, pp. 217-240. New York: Schocken Press, 1976.

—— *God and the Rhetoric of Sexuality.* Philadelphia: Fortress Press, 1978.

—— *Texts of Terror: Literary Feminist Readings of Biblical Narratives.* Philadelphia: Fortress Press, 1984.

"Triennial Cycle of Readings." *Jewish Encyclopedia*, vol. 12. New York: Funk and Wagnalls, 1906.

Tucker, Gordon. "The Sayings of the Wise are Like Goads: An Appreciation of the Works of Robert Cover." *Conservative Judaism* XLV:3 (1993).

Twerski, Abraham. *The Shame Born of Silence: Spouse Abuse in the Jewish Community.* Pittsburgh, PA: Mirkov Publications, 1996.

Twersky, Isidore. *Rabad of Posquieres: A Twelfth-Century Talmudist.* Cambridge, MA: Harvard University Press, 1962.

United Synagogue of Conservative Judaism. *Judaism and Domestic Violence.* (United Synagogue Resolution Implementation Packet). New York: United Synagogue of Conservative Judaism, Commission on Social Action and Public Policy, February 1995.

van Dijk-Hemmes, Fokkelien. "Sarai's Exile." In *A Feminist Companion to Genesis*, ed. Athalyah Brenner, pp. 222–250. Sheffield, UK: Sheffield Press, 1993.

—— "The Imagination of Power and the Power of Imagination: An Intertextual Analysis of Two Biblical Love Songs: The Song of Songs and Hosea 2." *Journal for the Study of the Old Testament* 44 (1990): 75–88.

——— "The Metaphorization of Woman in Prophetic Speech: An Analysis of Ezekiel XXIII." *Vetus Testamentum* XLIII:2 (1993): 162–170.

Wadud-Muhsin, Amina. *Qur'an and Women*. Kuala Lumpur: Fajar Bakti, 1994.

Walker, Lenore. "Jewish Battered Women: Shalom Bayit or a Shonde?" In eds. Rachel Josefowitz Siegel, and Ellen Cole, *Celebrating the Lives of Jewish Women: Patterns in a Feminist Sampler*. Binghamton, NY: The Harrington Park Press, 1997.

——— "The Battered Woman Syndrome." In *Family Abuse and Its Consequences: New Directions in Research*, ed. G. T. Hotaling, et al, pp. 139–148. Newbury Park, CA: Sage, 1998.

——— *The Battered Woman Syndrome*. New York: Springer, 1984.

——— *The Battered Woman*. New York: Harper and Row, 1979.

Weems, Renita J. "Gomer: Victim of Violence or Victim of Metaphor?" *Semeia* 47 (1989): 87–104.

——— *Battered Love: Marriage, Sex and Violence in the Hebrew Prophets*. Minneapolis, MN: Fortress Press, 1995.

Wegner, Judith Romney. "The Status of Women in Jewish and Islamic Marriage and Divorce Law." *Harvard Women's Law Journal* 5 (1982): 1–33.

——— *Chattel or Person? The Status of Women in the Mishnah*. New York: Oxford University Press, 1988.

Weisman, Avery. *On Dying and Denying: A Psychiatric Study of Terminality*. New York: Behavioral Publications, 1972.

Weiss, Susan. "Unholy on the Face of It." *The Jerusalem Report* (16 May 1996): 54.

Wheelwright, Philip. *Metaphor and Reality*. Bloomington, IN: Indiana University Press, 1962.

Winkler, Gershon. "Battered Women: Jews Not Immune to the Problem." *B'nai Brith Messenger*, Los Angeles (30 September 1983).

Winn Leith, Mary Joan. "Verse and Reverse: The Transformation of the Woman, Israel, in Hosea 1-3." In *Gender and Difference in Ancient Israel*, ed. Peggy L. Day, pp. 1–11. Minneapolis, MN: Fortress Press, 1989.

Yee, Gail A. "Hosea." In *The Women's Bible Commentary*, eds. C.A. Newsom and S.H. Ringe, pp. 195–202. Louisville, KY: Westminster, 1992.

Yllo, Kersti and Bograd, Michele. *Feminist Perspectives on Wife Abuse*. Newbury Park, CA: Sage, 1988.

Zimmels, H.J. *Ashkenazim and Sephardim: Their Relations, Differences, and Problems as Reflected in the Rabbinical Responsa*. London: Oxford University Press, 1958.

Index

ABOUT THE AUTHOR

Naomi Graetz, born in 1943 in New York City, is a Jewish feminist who is grounded both in Jewish tradition and feminist thought. She teaches English reading skills at Ben-Gurion University of the Negev and lectures widely on Women in the Bible and Midrash. She is the author of *S/He Created Them: Feminist Retellings of Biblical Stories*, and her scholarly articles and *midrashim* have appeared in numerous journals and edited books. Naomi Graetz has lectured for many years to the volunteers of Maslan, which operates a shelter for battered women in Beersheba. She is author of *The Rabbi's Wife Plays at Murder*, a mystery novel which incorporates some of the themes of domestic violence discussed in the present book.